Concerto for the Left Hand ⤸

Corporealities: Discourses of Disability
David T. Mitchell and Sharon L. Snyder, editors

Concerto for the Left Hand

Disability and the Defamiliar Body

Michael Davidson ⮑

The University of Michigan Press

Ann Arbor

Copyright © by the University of Michigan 2008
All rights reserved
Published in the United States of America by
The University of Michigan Press
Manufactured in the United States of America
♾ Printed on acid-free paper

2011   2010   2009   2008   4   3   2   1

A CIP catalog record for this book is available from the British Library.

Library of Congress Cataloging-in-Publication Data

Davidson, Michael, 1944–
     Concerto for the left hand : disability and the defamiliar body /
Michael Davidson.
          p.   cm. — (Corporealities: discourses of disability)
     Includes bibliographical references and index.
     ISBN-13: 978-0-472-07033-6 (cloth : alk. paper)
     ISBN-10: 0-472-07033-9 (cloth : alk. paper)
     ISBN-13: 978-0-472-05033-8 (pbk. : alk. paper)
     ISBN-10: 0-472-05033-8 (pbk. : alk. paper)
     1. People with disabilities.   I. Title.

HV1552.D38   2008
362.4—dc22   2007039147

To Rosemarie Garland Thomson

Acknowledgments

An important theme in this book is the role of community in developing a disability consciousness. Many members of the Disability and Deaf communities have helped me locate disability, both in my own work and in the cultural forms that I study in these pages. No one has been more instrumental in this regard than Rosemarie Garland Thomson, to whom the book is dedicated. She first introduced me to disability studies and enabled much of my participation in the field. As many disability scholars will testify, Rosemarie has been instrumental in weaving the various strands of critical gender studies, cultural studies, critical race theory, and disability studies into a coherent field of inquiry whose legacy can be seen in emergent interdisciplinary programs throughout the United States and in an increased consciousness about disability rights in general.

I also want to extend my thanks to Carol Padden, whose advice on matters of deafness and Deaf culture have been of enormous help on a personal and institutional level. Her support as a friend and colleague has helped me see how disability and academic life are not mutually exclusive terms but can be (f)used to make the university a more inclusive space for students and faculty alike.

Other friends in disability studies have contributed generous research and editorial help to parts of this book. For this aid I am especially grateful to Dirksen Bauman, Michael Bérubé, Brenda Brueggemann, Lisa Cartwright, James Charlton, Peter Cook, Lennard Davis, Terry Galloway, Joseph Grigely, Mark Jeffries, Georgina Kleege, Ryan Knighton, Chris Krentz, Cathy Kudlick, Simi Linton, Paul Longmore, Robert McRuer, David Mitchell, Carrie Sandahl, Susan Schweik, David Serlin, Tobin Siebers, Martha Stoddard-Holmes, and Aaron Williamson. I am also grateful to friends and colleagues who advised me on specific issues, especially Darwin Berg, Bob Cancel, Jim Clifford, Norma Cole, Ann DuCille, Ben Friedlander, Bob Gluck, Judith Halberstam, Lyn Hejinian, Aleck Karis, Susan Kirkpatrick, Bob Grenier, Peggy Lott, Lisa Lowe, Peter Middleton, Donald Moore, David Perlmutter, Michael Palmer, Joseph Roach, Nayan Shah, and Winnie Woodhull. It is difficult to know how much of this book was formed through conversations with my students at UCSD, but I want especially to acknowledge the contributions of Neel Ahuja, Scott Boehm, Jessica Cole, Jesse Dubler, Corrine Fitzpatrick, Jim Hartnett, Jenna Lahmann, Bill Mohr, and Liberty Smith.

Versions of these chapters were presented in several public venues, and I would like to acknowledge the help of these forums in generating various aspects of this book: The Academic Senate Distinguished Lecture Series at the University of California, San Diego for nominating me as its 2002–3 Faculty Research Lecturer, for which I presented a version of Chapter 7, "Universal Design"; Tim Powell, for his ASA panel, "Beyond the Binary"; Nicole Markotic for her role in coordinating a conference on disability studies at the University of Calgary; Dirksen Bauman, for inviting me to participate in Gallaudet University's "Revolutions in Sign Language Studies" conference; Henry Abelove and the Wesleyan University Humanities Center; Steve McCaffery of the Poetics program at SUNY Buffalo; Tobin Siebers and the Global Ethnic Studies Seminar at the University of Michigan; the Center for Lesbian and Gay Studies at CUNY for their program on "Claiming Disability: New Work at the Intersection of LGTBQ and Disability Studies"; Kathleen Woodward and Chandan Reddy and the Center for Humanities at the University of Washington, Eniko Bolobas and the faculty at the Pázmány Péter Catholic University, Piliscsaba, Hungary; Abigail Lang of Université de Paris, VII; Katherine Sherwood, Beth Dungan, and Georgina Kleege for their conference at the University of California, Berkeley Art Museum "Blind at the Museum"; Burt Hatlen and the National Poetry Foundation and the 1960s conference at the University of Maine, Orono.

Several versions of these chapters first appeared as journal articles. One section of the introduction appeared in *PMLA* as part of its publication of the proceedings of the MLA sponsored conference, "Disability Studies and the University" at Emory University in 2004; Chapter 1 appeared in *Beyond the Binary: Reconstructing Cultural Identity in a Multicultural Context* (Rutgers U Press); Chapter 2 appeared in a special issue of

GLQ, "Desiring Disability: Queer Theory Meets Disability Studies," edited by Robert McRuer and Abby L. Wilkerson; a version of Chapter 3 appeared in *Disability Studies: Enabling the Humanities*, edited by Sharon L. Snyder, Brenda Jo Brueggemann, and Rosemarie Garland Thomson; (Modern Language Association); chapter 5 appeared in *Sagetrieb;* a condensed version of Chapter 7 appeared in *The Disability Studies Reader*, 2nd ed., edited by Lennard Davis (Routledge). Thanks are extended to the editors of these journals and presses for allowing me to reprint versions of these essays.

I would like to acknowledge the help of Rozenn Quéré and Evgen Bavcar for granting me permission to print Bavcar's photographs and to Benjamin Friedlander and the estate of Larry Eigner for allowing me to reproduce Eigner's typescripts. Permission to reprint versions of Ernest Fenellosa's Chinese ideograms is granted by City Lights Books.

The University of Michigan Press has been extraordinarily supportive of this project. I want to thank David Mitchell and Sharon Snyder, editors of the Corporealities series in which this book appears. I also want to thank LeAnn Fields, senior editor of the press, who has been a stalwart throughout the entire period, and to her editorial assistant, Anna Szymanski, and Marcia LaBrenz, who have shepherded the book through its various copyediting and proofing stages.

Finally, I want to thank Lori Chamberlain and our children, Ryder and Sophie. They are the enablers.

Contents

Prelude

The Pool

What a curse, mobility!
—WINNIE IN SAMUEL BECKETT'S *Happy Days*

At the community pool where I swim every day you can see Disability Nation in broad relief. Today, lanes 1 and 2 are given over to the special ed kids from the nearby middle school. They include at least one child with cerebral palsy, another who is probably autistic, others developmentally and neurologically impaired. In lane 3 Helen, who walks with braces and double canes, shares the lane with Denise, who is doing aqua exercise and whose floppy hat indicates that she is back on her chemotherapy regime. I'm sharing lane 4 with a young man I've never seen before, but when he gets out I notice that he walks with a cane, limping noticeably. The two triathaletes doing sprints in lane 5 have bodies that are nontraditional by any standard. One of them, Bev, a national masters freestyle record holder, is deaf and is a fabulous lip-reader. George and his wife Faye are in lane 6, although Faye has just had hip surgery and is taking it easy. Prostheses litter the pool deck. Fins, goggles, and floats are piled at the ends of the lanes. Helen's two canes and braces are at the pool's edge; glasses cases are on the table along with George's hearing aid. I'm wearing a brightly colored earplug in my one "good" ear to protect what little hearing I have left. We're all working out, floating, diving, doing laps in our lumpy, bony, bald, flabby, hard of hearing, sight-impaired, gimpy bodies. No one is disabled. Everyone is disabled.

A swimming pool is a good place to begin thinking about the complex nature of disability—and perhaps, as Samuel Beckett's Winnie, buried up to her waist in sand, exclaims, the "curse" of compulsory mobility. For one thing, it's a place where bodies are on display, for better or worse. And swimming is easy on joints and cartilage, ideal exercise for persons recovering from injuries or who want to regain muscle tone after an operation. Most of the persons mentioned above probably do not think of themselves as Disabled, capital *D,* yet their wheelchair-adapted school buses, medications, handicap parking stickers, walkers, canes, and glasses are components of a vast medical-industrial complex that often defines the meaning of bodies and the limits of care. If they do not identify with the disability rights movement, they nevertheless are consumers of disability-related products and services. And because many of them qualify for support under the provisions of the Americans with Disabilities Act, they—we—live in its shade. One might say, then, that although each swimmer enjoys a degree of independence and agency at the public pool, each is dependent on material products, social agencies, and public policies that mediate between bodies and meanings that bodies assume. Hence one of the conundrums of disability studies is that it concerns an identity category often unrecognized as such by those who fall under its terms, thereby allowing others to define the category for them. The international disability rights movement, under the banner "Nothing about us without us," has worked to reclaim and define disability as a social category that applies to everyone in the public pool.

The pool offers a Whitmanian metaphor for social inclusion and independent living, yet when that metaphor is subjected to the lived experiences and attitudes of individual swimmers, it begins to dissolve as a term for inclusion. Each of my examples poses a unique variation not only on the theme of disability but on the liberal ideal of social equality and access. The question remains, can this ideal stand the test of differently abled bodies? Can a model of independent living coincide with what Alasdair MacIntyre calls the "virtues of acknowledged dependence" that implicate everyone? (133). When the poet of *Leaves of Grass* invokes his desire for twenty-eight male bathers in section 11 of "Song of Myself," he does so by imagining himself as a wealthy woman, peering at the young men through a curtain of her large house. Adapting this metaphoric vantage to disability, we might say that to "come out" as disabled may involve recognizing forms of dependency and contingency that challenge our ingrained dependence on independence. We become the twenty-ninth bather by becoming someone else.

This mediated relationship to the social contract through disability has been the subject of discussion recently by philosophers and cultural critics who have redefined ethics for a wider, more diverse constituency. Alasdair MacIntyre, Martha Nussbaum, Michael Berubé, Eva Kittay, Anita Silver, and others have pointed out that ideas of justice based on a social contract seldom take disability into account. We may assent to Locke's belief in the "free, equal, and independent" individual who benefits from social intercourse, but we do so by avoiding the contingent nature of social relations. As Nussbaum points out, liberal theories of justice from Rousseau and Hume to Rawls imagine individuals departing the state of nature to contract with each other for mutual advantage. Such contractarian thinking presumes an equal status of all members and does not take into account asymmetrical, unequal levels of access posed, for example, by poverty or mental illness, or, indeed, by our connections to an animal nature. Where Rawls does acknowledge such disproportionate access, his account "must handle severe mental impairments and related disabilities as an afterthought, after the basic institutions of society are already designed" (Nussbaum 98). By imagining a two-stage approach to social justice, the first, foundational stage created by those with adequate means, and the second, created to aid those less free and independent, the idea of a universal theory of justice begins to fray. Although persons with impairments may benefit from the institutions a rational society designs, they "are not among those for whom and in reciprocity with whom society's basic institutions are structured" (98). This disjunctive relationships between a social ideal of inclusion and the absence of disabled persons in the framing of that ideal limits Rawls's Kantian model of justice.[1]

Although *Concerto for the Left Hand* is largely about cultural forms and disability, it begins and ends with issues of social justice to emphasize what is ultimately at stake in the enjoyment of those forms. Whether we are discussing the meaning of Tiny Tim's limp or Ahab's missing leg, or the works of disabled artists, the question of what bodies mean for a social covenant is paramount. Noting how much Rawls's definition of justice relies on ideas of social normalcy, Nussbaum poses what she calls, following Amartya Sen, a "capabilities approach" that recognizes the inherent rights of all persons, regardless of income or property. These capabilities or "core social entitlements" include access to health, bodily integrity, ability to use one's senses and emotions, practical reason, affiliation, play, and control over one's environment, among others (76–78). Although this open-ended catalog of capabilities may not resemble rights as conventionally understood (it would be hard to imagine Hegel or Kant including "play"or "health" as an inalienable right), its stress on a political conception of the individual as dependent and vulnerable challenges a liberal model of social justice. For Nussbaum a rational society, based on shared rights, must imagine forms of mutuality that take into consideration impairment and disability, unequal economic status, or species membership—human relationships to animals. Nussbaum's emphasis on cognitive and physical disabilities is important because it recognizes that although severely disabled individuals are citizens, they require "atypical social arrangements, including varieties of care, if they are to live fully integrated and productive lives" (99). As my chapter 7 suggests, universal design is an admirable goal in architecture and city planning, but it cannot easily translate to underdeveloped nations that cannot afford repairs to existing infrastructure. If Rawls hopes to create a universal theory of justice, he must account for unequal distribution of property, goods, and services.

How might a disability aesthetics intervene in such unequal distribution—not only of goods and services but of ideas and images—to imagine alternative access to the public pool? Or to invoke my title, how might a consideration of works written for a one-armed pianist resituate both music and disabled performer? Unfortunately, the most convenient terms for such consideration stress the *modification* of a norm, *adapted* to special needs, affording *compensation* for a *handicap*. What those modifications and adaptations do to the structure and, indeed, the meaning of art is seldom confronted. Throughout this book I adapt the Russian formalist idea that works of art defamiliarize routinized patterns of thought and usage to speak of the ways that disability challenges ingrained attitudes about embodiment. Rosemarie Garland Thomson notes that identity categories like "able-bodied" and "disabled" are "produced by way of legal, medical, political, cultural, and literary narratives that comprise an exclusionary discourse" (*Extraordinary Bodies* 6). As she says, the task of a critical disability studies is to problematize such categories and in the process expose the cultural logic of their production. But a critical disability perspective also attends to the impact of disability on the life course itself, the ways that physical or cognitive impairment affects everyday life practices. The presumably healthy individual who becomes paralyzed from a spinal cord injury or who undergoes chemotherapy understands how unstable terms like *healthy* and *normal* are (and how inert the body becomes within medical care). Such life-changing experiences demand a narrative that does not reduce the entire life course to the disability, one that provides a redemptive meaning for those who have *not* undergone such trauma and by the grace of some higher power (or better insurance policy) have been spared distress. A good deal of self-help literature has been written to explain how to "endure" or "triumph over" such adversity, and figures who do—Helen Keller, Christopher Reeve, Steven Hawking—are celebrated as exemplars. This ideology of ableism works in part to shore up a fragile sense of embodiment, on the one hand, and to erase the work of those who have lived with a disability all their lives or who have struggled for changes in public policy and social attitudes. Ableism also helps to reinforce a Manichaean binary that divides the world into lives worth living and those that are not, a division that has provoked an extremely shrill debate recently over physician-assisted suicide. A critical disability aesthetics defamiliarizes such entrenched binaries to offer not simply a more humanized perspective on suffering but a way of translating the materiality of the artwork, both as form and practice, into the materiality of the different body.

Lennard Davis points out that ideas of physical and cognitive normalcy are a relatively recent invention, coinciding with the rise in statistics, comparative anatomy, and racial science (see *Enforcing Normalcy* 23–49). I would add that these technologies parallel the emergence of modernist art, which, at the moment the body was being regularized and quantified, shattered ideas of sculptural integrity, single-point perspective, narrative coherence, and tonal harmony. The aesthetic values of modernism that art historians and literary scholars use to explain these changes are seen differently through a disability optic. The ocularcentrism of modernist painting is "seen" differently if we imagine it through an artist who is sight-impaired, such as the late Monet. The values of orality, rhythm, and voice in poetry "sound" differently when viewed through the works of deaf poets who use sign language. The rigorous formal athleticism of modern dance receives new meaning when accomplished through the body of a dancer with one leg such as Homer Avila. Feminists have long argued that considerations of gender and power lie behind genre and canonicity, an observation that applies as well to works whose apprehension demands precisely what Kant said acts of aesthetic appreciation do: imagine that others are similarly moved. If we imagine that those "others" (whom Kant never specified) are moved through identification with a disabled body, then the apprehension of beauty in works of art means something rather different from disinterested appreciation. Returning the body to the aesthetic, then, becomes one of this book's primary concerns. Returning the aesthetic to issues of bodily impairment becomes its second priority.

In *Concerto for the Left Hand* I present various frames through which disability and cultural production exchange terms, methods, and interpretations. In my introduction I define some of the key issues raised within disability studies as it moves into its second (or even third) stage of development. Among the most salient of these is the question of visibility and the various ways that disability is performed, both on the social stage of everyday life but also in artworks that utilize performance as a venue for bringing disability to the foreground. The problem of sight is also one of *site*, the spaces in which disability is defined and the multiple locations in which it occurs—from the interior of the body exposed through neonatal screening to the clinic and asylum where the medicalized body is diagnosed and rehabilitated to the art venues in which disability is displayed. By emphasizing disability as a series of locations rather than a condition or medical diagnosis, I hope to complicate its presumed location in the body and, at the same time, question social constructionist views of disability as discursively produced.

As a test case for studying the intersection of disability and cultural studies, I look in chapter 1 at the case of hemophilia during the AIDS pandemic of the 1980s. This was a time when a blood-born disease was spread as much by discourses about sexuality and deviance as by a virus. I study two homosocial communities, gay men and hemophilic males, who became infected with HIV through pooled blood products in the early 1980s. I am interested in the ways that a chronic disease, carried in the blood, becomes a syndrome carried by homophobia and racial anxiety, a "disease of signification," as Paula Treichler calls it. In order to understand the discursive meaning of the disease, I survey the long cultural history of the bleeder and the threat that such figures present to U.S. national narratives from the early days of the Republic. My example of a modern text that brings these various strands together is William Faulkner's *Absalom, Absalom!*, a novel that frames blood culture through the triangulated relations between sex, race and the Caribbean as they overlap in the rural South following Reconstruction. By studying narratives about fears of racial amalgamation, I notice the degree to which national identity is linked to fears of shared blood and bodily fluids.

The relationship between disabled and queer bodies forms the basis of chapter 2, which looks at representations of disability in film noir of the late 1940s and 1950s. In films such as *Double Indemnity* or *The Lady from Shanghai* or *Walk on the Wild Side*, a figure with a disability often displaces the representation of homosexual or lesbian relationships that must be contained or monitored. My concern here is not only to understand disability as a prosthesis for the film's narrative of sexual normalcy but to show the historical specificity of this prosthetic function in relation to cold war anxieties about bodies in general. At the same time, I want to survey the limits of feminist film theory's psychoanalytic treatment of film noir through its study of the male gaze. I see the emphasis on psychoanalytic models of castration anxiety among male viewers as drawing on disability as "lack" or "absence" that links woman as object with impairment as bodily limit.

In chapters 3 and 4, I focus on deaf poets and the challenge that American Sign Language (ASL) poses for traditional theories of poetics. In the first of these chapters, I diagnose the "scandal of speech" when it appears in the work of poets for whom the use of vocalization or English translation is often considered a violation of culturally Deaf positions. The tendency among many ASL poets to repudiate English translation as a residual sign of hegemonic oralism is modified in the work of of Peter Cook and Kenny Lerner (the Flying Words Project), the British performance artist Aaron Williamson, and Joseph Grigely, an artist and critical theorist. In their work, the eruption of speech into works that deal critically with the position of the Deaf person in hearing society appears not as a concession to that culture but as a critique of its assumption about the authority of orality.

In chapter 4 I continue this investigation of signed poetry, this time by looking at the ways it resites the ocular character of much modernist literature. As in chapter 3, I am interested in the ways that ASL poetry utilizes its site-specific character and visual features to "signify" (in the sense used by Henry Louis Gates) *on* sight but also upon the spaces and places in which deaf persons have formed communities. In the Flying Words Project's whimsical variations on Ezra Pound's use of Ernest Fenollosa's essay on the Chinese written character I see a paradigm for ways that deaf poets intervene into ocularcentric features of modernist poetry. Then through readings of poems by Clayton Valli and Patrick Graybill, I look at the ways that ASL poets use manual signing to represent and "contain" voice and, at the same time, foreground the bicultural nature of many deaf families.

My focus on poetry and poetics continues in chapter 5 with a study of Larry Eigner, a poet who contracted cerebral palsy at birth and who lived with severe mobility impairment throughout a long and productive literary life. My title, "Missing Larry," refers to Eigner's absence from critical accounts of the New American Poetry, despite his importance for the generation that includes Allen Ginsberg, Robert Duncan, and Robert Creeley. The title also refers to the avoidance of cerebral palsy in treatments of his work, thus replicating a new critical tendency to read his work as if his precise observations of his surroundings are not connected to his physical condition. Because Eigner himself seldom mentioned his disability during his lifetime, he poses a test case for thinking about impairment when it is not represented. At the end the chapter, I focus on an unpublished sequence of poems dealing with the Nazi Holocaust that integrate Eigner's position as disabled with his cultural identity as a Jew.

In chapter 6 I continue my exploration of ocularcentrism, this time to investigate the work of blind photographers such as Alice Wingwall, Evgen Bavcar, and Derek Jarman. Their work asks us to question our assumptions about the function of museums and other sites of display when we place the work of sight-impaired artists in them. This question has been the focus of a number of recent exhibitions and symposia dealing with the implications of accommodating blind viewers in museums, but it is a topic that immediately is raised when we consider artists who work in that most visual of media. In the work of Slovenian photographer Evgen Bavcar, oneiric, brightly lit images engage philosophical issues around sightedness and memory, ocular distance and personal signature. In Derek Jarman's last film, *Blue,* the artist creates a work that consists entirely of a blue screen with a voice-over, a gesture that places the viewer in the director's position as someone who lost his sight due to complications of AIDS. By refusing to provide images of AIDS but rather the blank space that AIDS creates, Jarman implicitly criticizes attempts during the 1980s by photographers and journalists to represent the pandemic via images of emaciated, wasting gay bodies. By *not* providing an image, curiously, he imagines alternative—even restorative—lessons to be learned by non-sightedness.

Chapter 7 studies, as its subtitle suggests, the work of disability in a global context. Disability studies has largely been developed in first world countries and academic venues, while the preponderance of disabled persons live in the underdeveloped "majority world" and where access to adequate health care, clean water, and medicine is inadequate or nonexistent. Economic globalization has proposed numerous solutions to this problem, but many of them are founded on restrictive, neoliberal policies for development. Structural adjustment and debt relief proposed by the World Bank or the International Monetary Fund often curtail public sector aid, education, and medical assistance that such relief was designed to address. One function of this chapter is to ask what a disability studies perspective might bring to the debates about global economics. Another issue the chapter raises is what happens to disability studies if we look at the subject globally. To what extent are methods and issues surrounding disability raised in developed countries applicable to cultures with different attitudes toward medicine, religion, health, and the body? To deal with some of these questions, I look at the films of Senegalese film director Diop Mambety and theater for development "edutainment" projects in Africa concerning AIDS education—to show the ways that the invisible form of globalization is being represented in specific sites and spaces.

My final chapter extends this concern with transnational disability by looking at one of the chief narrative tropes through which globalization is being seen: the international trade in body parts. In a number of recent films and novels, the specter of the body as a commodity sold on the black market by unscrupulous dealers and doctors has become the cultural dominant of a globalized economy. Stephen Frears's film *Dirty Pretty Things,* Manjula Padmanabhan's play *Harvest,* and the novels *Never Let Me Go,* by Kazuo Ishiguro, and *Almanac of the Dead,* by Leslie Marmon Silko, are among numerous recent works in which the illegal trade in organs is a primary issue. Although this narrative has not been seen as involving disability, it joins with a larger medical ethical debate about bodily integrity and vulnerability in the long shadows cast by in vitro fertilization, physician-assisted suicide, and genetic engineering. So dominant has the organ sale narrative become in recent fiction that it often serves as a cultural sign of globalization itself, much as hysteria, neurasthenia, or tuberculosis served to mark the effects of industrialized society in the nineteenth century. Moreover, the organ sale narrative links disability with sexuality insofar as it revises a nineteenth-century focus, exemplified in Baudelaire and Marx, on the prostitute as the epitome of the body as commodity form. In these twentieth- and twenty-first-century narratives, the commodity is less the prostitute's body than the body as a series of replaceable parts whose commercialization epitomizes unequal economic relations between donor (seller) and recipient (purchaser).

One theme that knits many of these chapters together is embodied in the brief quote from Samuel Beckett's *Happy Days* that serves as my epigraph. The main character of the play, Winnie, is buried up to her waist in sand, and she spends her day sorting through objects in her purse, hoping—sometimes desperately—that someone is watching her. At one point she turns to watch her husband, Willie, attempt to crawl backward into his cave. Seeing his difficulty, Winnie tries to help: "The hands and knees, love, try the hands and knees. *(Pause.)* The knees! The knees! *(Pause).* What a curse, mobility!" For the able-bodied world, mobility is the default, the position from which agency proceeds. By looking at the world from her disabled perspective, however, Winnie denaturalizes the Darwinian evolutionary imperative and substitutes interdependence as liberatory possibility. However insufficient, Winnie's "strange feeling that someone is looking at me" allows her to see beyond a condition of limited mobility. Winnie is one of many characters in Beckett's novels and plays who are, in some way, disabled. All of the characters in *Endgame* are disabled—Hamm is blind and lacks the use of his legs; Clov is crippled; Nagg and Nell have lost their limbs in an accident. They join dozens of others— Molloy, Malone, Vladimir, Estragon, and Lucky in *Waiting for Godot*, A & B in *Rough for Theater*—who are variously blind, deaf, crippled, bedridden, and while it would be easy to see their impairments as metaphors for alienation and solitude in the modern world—Heidegger's being-toward-death—we might see their codependence as a means of survival, the social contract reduced to its most naked form: two persons who sustain life by telling stories to each other. In a world where dependence implies a hated subservience, in Beckett's work it resembles the human condition itself stripped of its humanist trappings. That Beckett chose to represent his human comedy by disabled figures who stay alive by telling stories offers a parable about the work—the practice—of disability in making normal life strange.

Introduction

Concerto for the Left Hand

Disability Aesthetics ∽

In its short existence as an academic discipline, disability studies has devoted significant attention to the representation of disabled persons in the visual arts, literature, theater, and public life. Disability scholars have studied the ways that cultural forms depend on a putatively normal body to reinforce regimes of national, racial, and sexual normalcy while using the person with a cognitive or physical impairment as a metaphor for the queer, subaltern, or marginal. A common recent criticism among disability scholars is that metaphoric treatments of impairment seldom confront the material conditions of actual disabled persons, permitting dominant social norms to be written on the body of a person who is politely asked to step offstage once the metaphoric exchange is made.[1] Disabled artists and activists have attempted to reverse this pattern, turning their cameo appearances in such theaters back upon the audience, refusing the crippling gaze of an ableist society and reassigning the meanings of disability in their own terms. As Carrie Sandahl says, people with disabilities are "not only staring back, but also talking back, insisting that 'this body has a mouth'"("Ahhhh Freak Out!" 13). This book studies the forms in which this body speaks and the constituencies it enlists in the process.

By framing disability in the arts exclusively in terms of social stigma, on the one hand, and advocacy, on the other, we may limit disability aesthetics largely to thematic matters, leaving formal questions untheorized. How might the aesthetic itself be a frame for engaging disability at levels beyond the mimetic? How might the introduction of the disabled body into aesthetic discourse complicate the latter's criteria of disinterestedness and artisinal closure?[2] Consider Ravel's D major *Concerto for the Left Hand.* Commissioned in 1930 by the pianist Paul Wittgenstein, who lost his right arm during World War I, the Ravel concerto is perhaps the best-known work in a surprisingly large repertoire of works for the left hand. Brahms, Saint-Saëns, Strauss, Janáček, Prokofiev, Scriabin, and Bartók all wrote significant compositions in this vein, often to showcase or strengthen a hand that commonly accompanies more difficult material in the right. It is less often recognized that many of these works were commissioned by pianists who, through repetitive stress disorders, arthritis, or injury, lost the use of one hand. Pianists such as Geza Zichy, Paul Wittgenstein, Leon Fleisher, and Gary Graffman are among the best known of these disabled artists, but most pianists at some point in their career temporarily lose the functioning of one or another hand. In the case of Wittgenstein, at least forty compositions were written at his request, and despite his cool response to the Ravel concerto, it became one of the composer's most popular works.[3]

The one-hand piano repertoire offers us an interesting site for considering the status of disability in the arts. On one level these compositions might seem to propose a kind of aesthetic prosthesis, akin to that which David Mitchell and Sharon Snyder see operative in narrative works in which the presence of a one-legged Ahab or a hunchbacked Richard III serves as a "crutch" in the representation of normalcy. Adapted to music, this prosthetic interpretation could explain the technical difficulty of one-hand playing as a compensatory response for the missing hand, one that requires the pianist to imitate the full pianistic range, coloration, and dynamics of the nineteenth-century virtuoso style. If we treat Ravel's concerto as an able-bodied response to Wittgenstein's impairment, then the latter's performance becomes a triumph over adversity that has rightly been the subject of much disability studies critique.

We might, on the other hand, read this concerto from a different angle, understanding that by enabling Wittgenstein, Ravel disables Ravel, imposing formal demands upon composition that he might not have imagined had he not had to think through limits imposed by writing for one hand. Indeed, the *Concerto for the Left Hand* is a considerably leaner, less bombastic work than most of Ravel's orchestral music. In this regard, Ravel's concerto could be linked to the work of artists whose disability, far from limiting possibilities of design or performance, liberates and changes the terms for composition. One thinks of the late works of Goya, Milton, Beethoven, Nerval, Schumann, Monet, de Kooning, Close, and others, composed when the artists were becoming physically or cognitively impaired. I do not mean to substitute for a politically self-conscious disability arts a canon of well-known artists who happened to be disabled, but to broaden the focus of cultural production to include the larger implications of corporeality in the arts.

By bringing such matters to bear on disability I want to foreground the extent to which the aesthetic, from Baumgarten and Kant to recent performance art, is a matter of the body and of epistemological claims created by incorporating its limits into composition.[4] Terry Eagleton points out that "aesthetics is born as a discourse of the body," an attempt to measure "the whole region of human perception and sensation, in contrast to the more rarefied domain of conceptual thought" (13). Tobin Siebers notes that the term *aesthetics* is based on the Greek word for perception and that "[there] is no perception in the absence of the body" (*Body Aesthetic* 1). In some cases, as in Wincklemann, the physical body becomes the site of human perfection, an ideal that found its dystopic end in National Socialism's vaunting of the ideal Aryan body.[5] In other cases, as in Kant, the body is most conspicuous by its absence, as though aesthetics formed a *cordon sanitaire* against the encroachments of gross sensation and desire. To some extent Kant's privileging of disinterested observation is the cornerstone for modernist theories of impersonality and objectivism by which the aesthetic provides an alternative to passional states as well as instrumental reason. Yet disinterestedness in Kant can only be validated when it appears to elicit a reciprocal response in others: "A judgment of taste determines its object in respect of our liking . . . but makes a claim to *everyone's* assent, as if it were an objective judgment" (16). Here, the specter of social consensus haunts the aesthetic—as though to say, "My appreciation of that which exceeds my body depends on other bodies for confirmation. The body I escape in my endistanced appreciation is reconstituted in my feeling that others must feel the same way." It is this spectral body of the other that disability brings to the fore, reminding us of the contingent, interdependent nature of bodies and their situated relationship to physical ideals. Disability aesthetics foregrounds the extent to which the body becomes thinkable when its totality can no longer be taken for granted, when the social meanings attached to sensory and cognitive values cannot be assumed.

In chapters that follow I trace some of the implications of this claim by looking at a variety of cultural arenas—poetics, narrative, film and film theory, performance, and photography—through a disability optic. In this introduction I want to focus on three interrelated issues that govern my concerns in this book: thinking through the body (embodied knowledge), performing visibility (ocularcentrism and disability), siting disability (the spaces of disability). My attempt in each case is to show how the phenomenological world invoked by these forms depends less on the objects represented than on the knowledge that such phenomena produce and verify. As such, considerations of disability deconstruct or "crip" discourses of compulsory able-bodiedness that underwrite epistemological claims. Crip theory, like queer theory, promises an oppositional critique of bodily normalcy by working within the very terms of opprobrium and stigma to which disabled persons and queers have been subject (see McRuer, *Crip Theory*). What would it mean for the humanities to think through the body and reimagine curricula not around the "history of ideas" but through an armless Venus de Milo, a crippled Oedipus, or a madwoman in the attic? The field of poetics is dominated by tropes of the ear and page—voice, orality, meter, line, consonance—that are complicated in the case of deaf poets whose manual signing challenges the presumed link between text and voice. The same could be said of much modernist art whose ocularcentrism is made problematic by blind photographers such as John Dugdale, Alice Wingwall, or Evgen Bavcar, who create images as much inspired by sound and memory as by visual objects. As I say in chapter 2, disability also complicates feminist film theory's treatment of filmic gaze predicated on an able-bodied male viewer whose castration anxiety is finessed by the director's specular control over the female protagonist. Laura Mulvey's influential essay avoids the alliance between the objectified woman and a disabled male, the latter of whose loss of limb or eyesight is a necessary adjunct to masculine specular pleasure. In each case, aesthetic discourse is underwritten by bodies whose imperfections become the limping meters, fatal flaws, castration complexes, and nervous disorders by which literature is known. The images that often epitomize bodily perfection and that adorn brochures for humanities programs and colloquia often feature Leonardo's Vitruvian Man, who has, after all, four arms and four legs.

The estrangement posed by disability is a corporeal and sensory version of modernist *ostrenenie*, which the Russian formalists and futurists saw as art's primary function. In their various formulations, "laying bare the device" exposes the routinized, conventional (today we might say "constructed") character of daily existence. Victor Shklovsky notes that habitual acts such as holding a pen or speaking in a foreign language become automatic, devouring individual objects and turning signification into an algebraic function. Art exists to "recover the sensation of life; it exists to make one feel things, to make the stone *stony*" (12). The technique of art "is to make objects 'unfamiliar,' to make forms difficult, to increase the difficulty and length of perception" (12). The formalists designate defamiliarization as the ethos of the aesthetic, a "making strange" that recuperates a world too familiar to notice. Adapting this view to our concerns with embodiment, we might say that disability becomes the ethos of the social insofar as it exposes cultural assumptions about the corporeality of the social body.

A good example of such defamiliarization can be seen in a recent French ad for Electricité de France (EDF) that shows a series of able-bodied persons negotiating an urban landscape designed entirely for persons in wheelchairs or who are deaf and blind. A woman is jostled on a sidewalk by persons speeding by in wheelchairs; a man stoops in the rain while attempting to use a payphone at wheelchair height; a woman asks directions from an attendant who only speaks sign language; a sighted man becomes frustrated by attempting to read library books entirely written in Braille. The concluding epigraph, *Le monde est plus dur quand il n'est pas conçu pour vous* (the world is harder when it is not conceived for you) offers a nice variation on commercials promising greater access and accommodation by making the able-bodied consumer the minority figure. EDF's claim, *Désormais, le monde les espaces EDF sont accessible à tous. Quand votre monde s'éclaire* (From now on, the spaces of EDF are accessible to all. When your world lights up: EDF), resonates powerfully for disabled persons who have benefited from new electronic technologies such as Internet, TDY telephones, and voice-recognition software. Unlike ads that signal inclusiveness by adding a person in a wheelchair to a crowd of able-bodied models, EDF's ad imagines a world where change is not supplemental but structural.

Essays in this book define various ways in which disabled bodies, far from occupying roles at the margins of aesthetic discourse, are constitutive of cultural productions in general. In this respect, I am following a common thread within disability studies that understands disability not as a medical condition or bodily infirmity but as a set of social and cultural barriers to full participation in social life.[6] If disability is treated strictly as a medical matter, confined to specific regimes of therapy, rehabilitation, and social services, then the disabled subject is reduced to his or her impairment, not unlike the ways that racialist discourse reifies individuals around phenotype and pigmentation. Viewed through a social model, disability becomes a marker of social attitudes about bodies and cognitive ability in general, located not in the body but in society itself. As Rosemarie Garland Thomson says, disability is "not so much a property of bodies as a product of cultural rules about what bodies should be or do" (*Extraordinary Bodies* 6). The work of disabled and Deaf artists such as Terry Galloway, Peter Cook, Aaron Williamson, Homer Avila, Lynn Manning, Larry Eigner, Carrie Sandahl, Derek Jarman, Evgen Bavcar, and Clayton Valli suggests that what it means to be disabled or deaf may depend less on the impairment than on adjustments made to social rhetorics and formal genres in which disability is framed.

Despite the recognition of disability as embedded in social attitudes, reception of disability in the arts has never been easy, despite the presence of blind, deaf, or disabled figures (Homer, Milton, Beethoven, Kahlo) as signifiers for artistic genius. Even when a critic approaches a disabled artist with sympathy, there is often the anxiety that such art must, at some level, be a form of advocacy rather than a productive element of innovation. In a review of a dance performance by Homer Avila at the Merce Cunningham Studio in February 2002, dance critic Jennifer Dunning acknowledges her "considerable trepidation" at seeing Avila's performance in his inaugural program following the loss of a leg and part of a hip to cancer. Her review is devoted not to what Avila *does* in the program but to her "trepidation" at seeing a one-legged dancer. She imagines that the experience will be "rough going for anyone who, like me, feels faint at the sight of a paper cut," but she is reassured that the "solo did not attempt to make up for the absence of Mr. Avila's leg" and that he displayed "few of the expected, dreaded hops" (8). Dunning does worry that his movements "veered close to the kind of tricks beloved of ballet pyrotechnicians," but on the whole she feels that such movements "have a rightful place in his vocabulary." Dunning concludes with a caveat: "Understandably but regrettably, Mr. Avila seems intent on doubling as a spokesman for the disabled. His use of a hearing-impaired composer for 'Not/Without Words' suggested that he means to make a point, as he did with his charming insistence on lifting the dancer who had just lifted him in the improvisational audience participation piece that ended the evening." Such qualified rhetoric ("charming insistence") and faint praise is reminiscent of Arlene Croce's similar judgment of Bill T. Jones's *Still/Here,* a performance that deals with chronic illness. Croce, who did not see Jones's performance, nevertheless felt obliged to complain, "I can live with the flabby, the feeble, the scoliotic. But with the righteous I cannot function at all" (qtd. in Dunning 8). Dunning agrees: "I'm with her there." Such attitudes remind me of intellectuals of the 1940s and 1950s who acknowledged the technical skills of Richard Wright or Gwendolyn Brooks only to qualify their praise with the caution that by writing about black experience they would remain merely "Negro artists."[7] Dunning and Croce ask for a disinterested dance, one curiously divested of bodies. They criticize "righteousness" in dance, but exhibit a righteousness of their own by assuming that the disabled body must not speak of (or by means of) its condition.

My emphasis on the aesthetic in this book is not to create a safe haven for disabled artists but to counter the prevalent view in cultural theory that views matters of form, design, and structure as inherently ahistorical and apolitical. As I will point out, matters of aesthetics are deeply implicated in social attitudes toward disabled persons. As Martin Pernick shows in *The Black Stork,* it was precisely the use of aesthetic values that drove early proponents of eugenics and racial science to argue for sterilization of mentally retarded children, and to establish "ugly laws" to protect society from unsightly physical specimens (22–24). In this sense, the aesthetic was used to validate and reinforce the so-called objective science of heredity by declaring what should or could be seen in public.[8] Artists, fully cognizant of how those values apply to them, have taken the aesthetic not as a means of transcending the body but as a means of thinking through it.

Thinking through the Body ∽

Thinking through the body has been an important component of cultural studies, from Michel Foucault's theories of bio-power to Judith Butler's theories of performativity, Donna Haraway's formulation of cyborg identities, Michael Omi's and Howard Winant's ideas about racialized bodies and eugenics, and Eric Lott's, Gayle Wald's, and Michael Rogin's work on racial cross-dressing. In such cases, female, queer, and racialized bodies challenge categories of normalcy and expose the degree to which bodies are constructed within narratives about deviance, abjection, and difference. Given the importance of nontraditional bodies and sensoriums in cultural theory, it is surprising that disability is seldom mentioned within such venues. The reasons for this absence may be related to the importance of certain identity categories (race, class, gender, sexuality, and nationhood) that have been the centerpieces of social movements and that dominate cultural studies and minority discourse. Although as disability theorists have pointed out, such categories are deeply imbricated in ideas of physical and cognitive impairment, the idea of expanding identity categories to include disability may threaten an already embattled territory. Critics on the left fear a dilution of hard-won political positions and civil rights legislation by expanding the category of oppressed persons too broadly. Critics on the right fear the economic impact of expanding the class of potential plaintiffs in legal cases filed under the Americans with Disabilities Act (ADA) and worry about alliances with more militant political movements. The fact that disabled persons have historically been identified with the institutional and carceral systems that have defined racial and sexual otherness makes alliances between disability and minority populations problematic.

Another significant reason why disability has been left out of cultural and social theory is the problem of definition. It is difficult to forge a social movement around such a wide spectrum of impairments and conditions. The World Health Organization defines disability as "[any] restriction or lack (resulting from an impairment) of ability to perform an activity in the manner or within the range considered normal for a human being" (Barnes and Mercer 13). Under this definition, does a person with an invisible impairment or chronic disease qualify? What about persons whose disabilities are controlled by medication, dialysis, or pacemakers? Do persons who are HIV-positive fall into the same category as other blood-borne diseases such as hemophilia or other autoimmune disorders such as kidney disease? What about mental illness? Are persons with Down syndrome or bipolar disorders disabled in the same way that a quadriplegic or person with cerebral palsy is? Early activists often accompanied political protests that led to the passage of the ADA with the chant "We're not sick," thus alienating persons with chronic diseases or mental illness. Deaf persons often repudiate the disability label, preferring to think of themselves as a linguistic minority, but even here, the definition is complex. A hearing child of deaf adults (CODA) may be considered culturally Deaf through his or her fluency in ASL, whereas a person who becomes profoundly deaf late in life, however fluent in ASL, will never be considered a member of Deaf culture. Such differences exemplify the problem of trying to define a unified "disability community" held together by common social goals and shared beliefs.

To some extent the very diversity and pervasiveness of disability argues for its centrality as an identity position that destabilizes identity categories altogether. In Lennard Davis's terms, disability "dismodernizes" modern narratives of genetic improvement and social normalization that were formed in the nineteenth century. If postmodernism dissolves the grand narratives of modernity and its humanist core through an emphasis on social construction and performance, it may, in Davis's view, leave nothing upon which to build a social movement. Dismodernism deconstructs modernist narratives based on the body and negotiates the wandering rocks of essentialism and social constructionism by calling attention to the "differences" we share:

> What dismodernism signals is a new kind of universalism and cosmopolitanism that is reacting to the localization of identity. It reflects a global view of the world. To accomplish a dismodernist view of the body we need to consider a new ethics of the body. (*Bending* 27)

I flesh out some of the implications of Davis's thesis in the chapters that follow, but I would observe here that what Stuart Hall sees as a need for "conjunctural knowledge"—situated, historically specific understandings of phenomena—in cultural studies complicates a dismodernist view that might collapse identities into some global category.[9]

It would be relatively easy to point out that each of the identity categories I have mentioned as central to cultural studies has a specific coefficient in some aspect of disability discourse and that the historical emergence of class, race, gender, sexuality, or nationality coincides with taxonomic and scientific attempts to contain and control certain subjects during modernization. A class analysis of disability discourse, for example, would observe that the great majority of disabled persons in the world are poor (it is estimated that worldwide, two-thirds of the disabled live below the poverty line), are often diseducated, and can be found at the lowest levels of the workforce. The labor movement in the United States is written around struggles for a workplace that provides adequate disability insurance, accessible workstations, medical care, and protection from workplace accidents. Feminist disability scholarship has pointed out the degree to which gender has been defined through various nervous disorders and psychological categories (neurasthenia, castration anxiety, hysteria) that are the product of a male medical and psychoanalytic establishment. Similarly, one could point to the historical linkage of homosexuality and mental illness, a proximity that has led to various forms of incarceration, sterilization, and, in times of ethnic cleansing, genocide. The same could be said for late-nineteenth-century constructions of race through eugenics and comparative anatomy in which minority populations and immigrants were often linked to persons with cognitive impairments. The condition now known as Down syndrome was originally called "mongolism" in order to equate persons with mental illness with the weakening of the Aryan gene pool by immigrations coming from East Asia. As I point out in chapter 3, Deaf persons often find themselves in a colonial relationship to hearing culture that repudiates manual sign language in favor of oralist education. Oral pedagogies in the postbellum period were often motivated by attempts to naturalize deaf individuals into U.S. citizenship by making any gestures of separatism—such as the use of ASL—a threat to national cohesion. What such connections suggest is not a universal category of disability so much as a spectrum of discrete convergences of hegemonic social attitudes and discrepant psychological and somatic conditions.

Some sense of the imbricated relationship between cultural production and disability can be seen in recent controversies over assisted suicide. The case of Theresa Schiavo, a young Florida woman, who suffered severe neurological damage in 1990 and who remained in a coma for fifteen years, became the site of a culture war between civil libertarians, on the one hand, and an unlikely coalition of religious conservatives and disability rights advocates on the other. Similarly, critical response to films such as Clint Eastwood's *Million Dollar Baby* and Alejandro Amenabar's *The Sea Inside* has brought issues surrounding euthanasia and medical ethics into conflict with disability activists. In each case, basic questions about the "quality of life" and the "right to die" have been debated through representations of a disabled body and its ability to respond to social agendas formed around it.[10]

The case of Theresa Schiavo may not appear to have anything to do with aesthetics or cultural production, until one realizes that much of the controversy surrounding her concerned the question of images and the ability of others to interpret them. Critics and pundits on the left and right have understood that the meaning of Schiavo's condition was a synecdoche for tensions in the culture over the question of "quality of life." Feminist legal scholar Patricia J. Williams noted that Schiavo's "inscrutable silence has become a canvas for projected social anxieties" (1). Katha Pollitt described the "Terri Schiavo freak show [as] deeply crazy, so unhinged, such a brew of religiosity and hypocrisy and tabloid sensationalism" (1). And Tom DeLay, speaking at the Family Research Council in Washington, saw a redemptive message in the Schiavo case; the "one thing that God has brought to us is Terri Schiavo, to help elevate the visibility of what is going on in America." Prior to her cardiac arrest in February 1990, Schiavo had not indicated what special procedures should be implemented in the case of extreme trauma. As a result, interpretation of her wishes was left to her husband, who claimed she would have rejected any extreme measures and who therefore wanted her feeding tube removed, and to her fundamentalist Catholic parents, Robert and Mary Schindler, who fought to maintain life supports. Television images showed Schiavo interacting with her parents and doctors, and these pictures were subjected to minute scrutiny to verify if, as her parents claimed, she was responding to stimuli or whether her eye movements and facial expressions were simply reflexes. The fact that she maintained normal sleep-waking cycles, breathed on her own, and occasionally smiled and blinked her eyes made it seem as though she was responding to her parents' presence. Furthermore, there was the matter of terminology. Doctors and Florida circuit judge George Greer (the primary judge in her case), for the most part, described her as "brain dead," living in a "persistent vegetative state," and recommended the removal of life-prolonging feeding tubes. Michael Schiavo, on the other hand, sought to end her "suffering with dignity."

In order to assign blame for the 1990 incident that caused Schiavo's cardiac arrest, critics began to look at her early life as well as at her husband's actions in the intervening years. Right-to-life advocates accused Michael Schiavo of wanting to cash in on her illness, citing an earlier medical negligence suit for $1.1 million that he received in 1992. The fact that he had taken up with another woman with whom he had fathered two children was adduced as evidence of his weak moral character. On the other side, critics of the Florida Department of Children and Families that sought to gain custody of Schiavo claimed that the neurologist from the Mayo Clinic hired to evaluate her condition was a conservative Christian and therefore could not deliver a disinterested opinion. As Joan Didion points out, in the absence of a clear diagnosis of Schiavo's physical condition, public opinion tended to search for clues in Schiavo's "bad habits." She quotes Patricia Williams, who, in *The Nation* noted that Schiavo's "bulimic aversion to food was extreme enough to induce a massive systemic crisis that left her in what doctors describe as a 'persistent vegetative' state" (61). Didion concludes that "in this construct [Schiavo] had for whatever reason played a role in her own demise, meaning that what happened to her need not happen to us" (61). Commentators defined the political importance of the case as a "right-to-die" issue, or, more subtly, a "personal choice" matter," yet in the absence of legal documents by Terri Schiavo claiming those rights, the case became one in which the disabled body was interpreted by others.

This latter issue is important for disability studies insofar as, once again, the body of a disabled woman was deemed a "life not worth living" and therefore disposable. Not Dead Yet, the activist group that opposes euthanasia and assisted suicide, protested alongside fundamentalist Christians at Schiavo's home, yet their rather different reasons for supporting

Schiavo's parents were often left out of the discussion.[11] Katha Pollitt ignores disability implications in her *Nation* article, seeing the Schiavo case as an example of a slippery slope leading to the reversal of *Roe v. Wade* and the elimination of all civil rights. Pollitt segues quickly from Schiavo and euthanasia to abortion and to stigma leveled against "bad girls" who get pregnant. Theresa Schiavo becomes merely a point of departure. Even a balanced report such as that of Joan Didion mentions Not Dead Yet's protest only in passing, thus avoiding the implications of the case for disability rights advocates. As persons who have been historically vulnerable to medical interventions, a large majority of persons in the disability community knew very well what commentators meant by Schiavo's life being one "not worth living": one not like theirs. That life became the site for a national debate about medical ethics, abortion, stem-cell research, "activist judges," Supreme Court nominees, and the future of the filibuster. The U.S. House of Representatives and Senate's attempts to block the removal of the feeding tube—ordered by Judge Greer—and their subsequent attempt to create a law pertaining only to Theresa Schiavo (with George W. Bush's support) brought chills to many Democrats and members of the Left who saw such actions as the beginning of a conservative Armageddon. Whatever Schiavo may or may not have wanted for her mortal remains became obscured by secondary and tertiary narratives about the future of civil liberties, *Roe v. Wade,* and the Supreme Court.

My second example, Clint Eastwood's film *Million Dollar Baby,* offers a more obvious object for cultural analysis, having been the site of extensive media debate over its representation of euthanasia. It joins a rather large number of disability-themed movies made in recent years, including *Elephant Man, A Beautiful Mind, Ray, The Sea Inside, The Station Agent,* and the documentary *Murderball,* that have raised the presence of disability issues in the public arena. The almost unanimous positive critical acclaim (and financial success) that the film received when it was first released was countered by the almost unanimous complaint from the disability community over the film's seeming advocacy of euthanasia for persons with spinal cord injuries. The complaint was less concerned with the dramatic and cinematographic qualities of the movie than with the way it made assisted suicide seem the logical result of those qualities.[12] As in the Schiavo case, the question of a nondisabled person's ability to speak for a disabled person generated a public debate far beyond the movie.

The film concerns a spunky, working-class woman, Maggie (Hillary Swank), who enlists an aging boxing trainer, Frankie (Clint Eastwood), to coach her so that she can win a title match. Frankie's taciturn character and lined face bespeak a checkered past whose ghosts he attempts to assuage by vigorous pursuit of his Catholic faith. He is reluctant to train a "girl" boxer, having lost his own daughter to some unexplained parental error, but when his top fighter leaves him for a more lucrative shot at a title, Frankie gives in and takes Maggie on as his charge. He is encouraged in this act by his gym manager, Eddie (Morgan Freeman), a former boxing champ who lost his eye in an early fight for which Frankie feels responsible. Eddie is the movie's Sybil, offering sage opinions on boxing and life that resonate with Maggie's dream. Eddie muses,

> If there's magic in boxing, it's the magic of fighting battles beyond endurance, beyond cracked ribs, ruptured kidneys, and detached retinas. It's the magic of risking everything for a dream that nobody sees but you.

This dream of self-fulfillment, despite the odds, has implications for Eddie as a disabled African American that rhyme with Maggie's own "disability" as a poor woman from the rural South.

The first two-thirds of the movie constitute a straightforward boxing movie, tightly acted and brilliantly shot in dusty gyms and smoky boxing rings. Maggie's boxing improves under Frankie's careful, if cranky, tutelage. She becomes a formidable athlete, winning fight after fight by knocking out her opponents in the first round. The final third of the film switches direction dramatically when, in the women's welterweight championship match, Maggie sustains a serious head injury and becomes paralyzed from the neck down. Now the "true" drama of *Million Dollar Baby* begins; what had been a story of triumph over class and gender limits becomes a triumphalist parable about disability. After being immobile for a time, relying on a ventilator to breathe, and sustaining bedsores that require a limb to be amputated, Maggie decides that she wants to terminate her life.[13] Inexplicably, she does not ask her doctors to remove life supports but wants Frankie to do the job. He wavers for some time, consulting with his Catholic priest, who urges him not to accede to Maggie's wishes, but in the end decides to euthanize her by injecting her with a fatal dose of adrenaline and then disconnecting her ventilator. Maggie dies quickly, and Frankie leaves town, never to return. In the film's last scene, we see a grainy shot of a lonely rural cafe—one that Frankie in an earlier scene hinted he might buy one day—with Morgan Freeman's voice-over reciting what appears to be a letter to Frankie's absent daughter. At this moment we realize that Eddie's voice-over has been an extended epistle to the estranged daughter, trying to explain to her "what kind of man your father was." Eddie's monologue reinforces the fact that although Maggie is essential to the film's pathos, the real drama is about Frankie. In Mitchell and Snyder's terms, she serves as a prosthesis for a narrative about Frankie's tragic fate, his Lear-like burden of familial, religious, and ethical burdens.[14]

Like many disability-themed movies, the disabled figure is terminated in the end in what John Hockenberry calls a "crip ex machina," providing the able-bodied viewer a measure of compassion for the victim while permitting an identification with the able-bodied hero who survives. As members of Not Dead Yet and the National Spinal Cord Injury Association pointed out, the ending avoids the legal fact that in the United States, Maggie could have requested the removal of life-sustaining treatment and did not need Frankie's assistance (see Weiss, "Boxing Flick"). Critics also point out that as the film's director, Eastwood, does not provide alternatives to assisted suicide that might have modified Maggie's ultimate decision. Frankie does offer to buy her an electric wheelchair and enroll her in college, but Maggie refuses any amelioration. As doctors reported of Schiavo's condition, Maggie's life is deemed "not worth living" and therefore disposable. Film critics and commentators dismissed the disability complaint, saying, as Maureen Dowd did in the *New York Times,* the "purpose of art is not always to send messages. More often, it's just to tell a story, move people and provoke ideas. Eastwood's critics don't even understand what art is" (Davis, "Why Disability Studies Matters" 3). But one might turn Dowd's remarks around and say that although Eastwood may know about boxing and male angst, he doesn't know much about disability, and what he does know is influenced by his own personal legal difficulties through a suit filed by one of his employees under the ADA.[15] As in cases we have already encountered, an appeal to a disinterested "art" trumps content that calls the terms of interestedness into question.

As Lennard Davis points out, had *Million Dollar Baby* been a film that denigrates gays or women, the progressive community would speak out against "films, novels, plays or any artwork that demeaned people of color, gay people, or any oppressed group" ("Why Disability Studies Matters"). But because the film was viewed as a compassionate look at "personal choice," it was read as a civil rights document, in this case an appeal to an artist's right to make a movie as he sees fit and a woman's right to commit suicide. For people with disabilities, the message was viewed not as a matter of choice but one of untenable ethical alternatives. They saw that given the chance, society, reinforced by films like *Million Dollar Baby,* would terminate their lives as well. The fact that the film was also criticized by Christian conservatives on moral grounds helped create an alliance that blurred the differing reasons for the film's detractors.

To return to my initial concern with what it means for cultural studies to think through the body, we could see the debate that surrounds Theresa Schiavo and *Million Dollar Baby* as a limit case for the binary opposition that organizes disability studies. A too strict reliance on impairment as biological rejects the social meanings that Schiavo's or Maggie's conditions produce and consigns their bodies—as the popular press seems to have done—to regimes of rehabilitation and medical treatment, on the one hand, or euthanasia on the other. By denying them agency and treating their bodies as inert, neutral elements, medical science may then impose agency on them from without. At the same time, strict reliance on a *social* model of disability may jettison the physical impairment altogether and focus on social and material obstacles. As Tom Shakespeare says, "The social model so strongly disowns individual and medical approaches, that it risks implying that impairment is not a problem" (200). What is missing, as Sharon Snyder and David Mitchell have pointed out, is a *cultural* approach to disability that would take into account the experiences and meanings that disabled people have constructed about their bodies. The divide between medical and social models needs to be retheorized as an "interactional space between embodiment and social ideology," and in the process needs to take into account the social meanings that bodily differences assume by disabled individuals (7). To anticipate the subject of my next section, disability studies needs to bring into alignment what the world sees as the disabled subject and the world through which the disabled subject sees.

Performing Visibility ⌒

If everyone in the world were blind, perhaps touching would be
called seeing.
    —JOSEPH GRIGELY

A picture held us captive. The convergence of ethics and disability that I
have been discussing depends on an image, the picture of a disabled person that, to continue my use of Wittgenstein, "lay in our language, and
language seemed to repeat it to us inexorably" (48e). Theresa Schiavo's or
Maggie's bodies become disabled in discourses that swirl around their
public presentation and reception. Their physical bodies are forgotten in
the attempt to recuperate them as metonyms for what "we" don't have or
don't wish to have. Visibility, as Lennard Davis points out, is the modality
within which disability is constructed: "The person with disabilities is vi-
sualized, brought into a field of vision," and as such monitors (or polices)
the field of embodiment for the "normal" viewer (*Enforcing Normalcy* 12).
Because the gaze is so powerful in constructing claims of truth and reason,
it is often the hardest condition to "see," provoking Joseph Grigely in his
"Postcards to Sophie Calle" to wonder what would happen if everyone
were blind. In that case, would "touching be called seeing"?[16]

Such a condition is elaborately developed in José Saramago's *Blindness,* a novel in which the entire population of a city—and eventually a nation—becomes blind. Saramago may have been creating an allegory about
Fascism during the Salazar regime in Portugal—the blind leading the
blind, perhaps—but in the process he imagines a world no longer dependent on sight, one in which "touching becomes seeing." Characters in the
novel (who have no names) begin to rely on other senses for communication, location, locomotion, and survival. Early on, the government tries to
contain this contagion by incarcerating the blind in an asylum, but soon
their guards also become blind and the prisoners escape, rendering the
need for prisons and asylums moot. Only one character retains her sight,
the wife of a doctor, and she functions as a guide and helper for the blind,
although there is the possibility that she could in time become a leader (or
a despot) because of her sensory advantage. At the end, people gradually
regain their sight, and one character seems to speak for the author: "I

don't think we did go blind, I think we are blind, Blind but seeing, Blind people who can see, but do not see" (292). The idea that we are all prisoners in Plato's Cave, seeing only shadows, suggests how powerful the connection between sight and knowledge has been from the outset. It also reminds us how convenient blindness has been as a metaphor for personal misfortune and social disorder.

We could see Saramago's novel as offering yet another example of aesthetic prosthesis in which disability serves a master narrative of normalcy and wholeness. It also reminds us of the importance of scopic regimes as agents of personal and national identity. The medical gaze, as Michel Foucault defines it, is a technology of power that naturalizes bodies through consensus and agreement, whether the gaze is directed at a movie screen or at a sonogram monitor.[17] Erving Goffman observes that the term *stigma* referred originally to bodily signs that "expose something unusual and bad about the moral status of the signifier" (1). That association of visible marks, cut or burned into the body, continues in categorizations of bodies that are "disfigured" or "deformed" or "freakish." But the stigmatization of certain bodies through visible signs belies the extent to which the idea of a "normal" body is naturalized around those signs. In Robert McRuer's terms, a disability analysis reveals "compulsory able-bodiedness" as the condition for visibility, as that which must be asserted and affirmed. Of course, my use of the binary opposition *visibility/invisibility* reveals an ableist agenda of its own that becomes problematic when the subject is blind. The very fact that knowledge is represented through ocular metaphors ("I see what you mean"; "he was blind to the facts") testifies to the difficulty of stepping outside of disability in order to gain a critical perspective on it.

Viewed through a Foucauldian frame, disability becomes visible historically through various medical and scientific discourses emerging in the late eighteenth century, in which power relations of the dominant are inscribed on a body rendered "docile" so that it may assist productive apparatus of capitalism. From nineteenth-century freak shows and carnival acts, through the photographic displays of eugenics textbooks to Jerry Lewis telethons, disability has been synonymous with the theatrical display of "different" bodies. At the most immediate level, disability is constructed through complex rituals of staring and avoidance that occur when people confront a person with an empty sleeve, a prosthetic limb, a scarred face, a stutter. These social pragmatics are double-edged: the able-bodied viewer averts the gaze or looks clandestinely, the disabled subject "performs" invisibility—acts as though invisible or else compensates in some way to make the viewer feel comfortable. Disability memoirs are filled with descriptions of what we might call a crip double consciousness in which the individual in a wheelchair must simultaneously "act normal" while negotiating an inaccessible and sometimes hostile environment. The late actor and playwright John Belluso, who used a wheelchair, describes the theatricalization of disability as a continuous public performance: "When I get on a bus, all the heads turn and look, and for that moment, it's like I'm on a stage. Disabled people understand the world in a different way. You understand what it's like to be stared at, to be looked at, and in a sense you're always performing your disability" (Breslauer 4).[18]

Performance artist Mary Duffy, who is armless, makes this performative aspect of disability the site of many of her works. She merges the act of staring with the act of aesthetic appreciation by posing nude in the posture of classical sculptures. Appearing as what Rosemarie Garland Thomson calls "the Tableau Vivant Venus" ("Dares" 36), Duffy's monologues expose the gendered character of staring, making herself into an object of scopic interest (a nude, armless woman) and then addressing—even hectoring—an art establishment that wants to keep its distance. By this act, Duffy deconstructs a pictorialist aesthetics based on the Horation formula *ut pictura poesis,* by making sculpture speak. She also deconstructs ideals of feminine beauty by exposing her own armless body as the object of the gaze through which beauty is framed.

Thomson has taken the transgressive act of staring as a key issue in her recent work. She describes the ways that social relations are created out of acts of staring, looking, and gazing that offer, to the able-bodied viewer, a form of guilty pleasure. Unlike glancing, scanning, or glimpsing, staring at a disabled person "registers the perception of strangeness and endows it with meaning" ("Dares" 30). Staring is a "potent social choreography that marks bodies by enacting a dynamic visual exchange between a spectator and a spectacle. Staring, then, enacts a drama about the people involved" (31). Although modern philosophers like Sartre and Levinas have formulated intersubjectivity around a constituting look, they do not address the politics of embodiment articulated through that look.[19] For Sartre, the constituting "look" *(le regard)* engages two presumably neutral subjectivities on either side of a keyhole; for Levinas, the "face" of the other exposes the contingency and vulnerability of the one looking.[20] Neither philosopher imagines that the encountered other is blind. As Thomson points out, cultural theory has diagnosed the social implications of such staring through scopic regimes that include feminist gaze theory, which studies the formation of the patriarchal gaze, materialist critiques of consumerism and control, and ethnographic treatments of the colonizing gaze. All three of these regimes reinforce staring as a visual practice "that materializes the disabled in social relations" ("Dares" 32).

As Thomson and others have shown, disability performance like that of Mary Duffy has made the multiple levels of staring into a primary issue, turning the disabling gaze back on the audience and forcing its members to confront their own discomfort at the sight of the disabled body. She cites the work of Cheryl Marie Wade, for example, who foregrounds her "claw hands" in the video documentary *Vital Signs:*

> Mine are the hands of your bad dreams.
> Booga booga from behind the black curtain.
> Claw hands.
> The ivory girl's hands after a decade of roughing it.
> Crinkled, puckered, sweaty, scarred,
> a young woman's dwarf knobby hands
> that ache for moonlight—that tremble, that struggle
> Hands that make your eyes tear.
> My hands. My hands. My hands
> that could grace your brow, your thigh
> My hands! Yeah!
>
> (Qtd. in Thomson, "Dares" 35)

Wade stares back, acknowledging the social anxiety that her hands evoke, while reclaiming them for acts of tenderness and intimacy. Rather than perform invisibility by hiding her hands, Wade brings them forward, both physically on stage and verbally in her performative rhetoric. We are refused the passive gaze that maintains the observer's authority and forced, instead, to violate that childhood adage, "It's not polite to stare."

A further complication of the disability/visibility rhyme can be seen in Terry Galloway's performances, which often merge discourses of deafness, queerness, disability, and gender through references to popular media and film. As a performer she wonders

> how to have a voice in theatre. How to be heard. How to be a poor, queered, deaf, unbeautiful girl and still make a claim on that empty space. Everything I do is autobiographical, but I'm trying to code it differently. ("Making a Claim" 51)

Deaf since a young age, Galloway creates memorable, often hysterically funny, performances that interrogate a wide range of cultural signage— from noir radio dramas and movie melodramas to celebrity telethons. As the preceding quotation implies, Galloway seeks a "voice" in a theater that has little room for deaf actors, but she also seeks a form of autobiography that uses the "empty space" of an inaccessible theater for a "queered, deaf, unbeautiful girl." She wants to "code it differently," by acknowledging limit as a constitutive force:

> What if your whole performance is predicated on the fact that you are not: not the usual performer, not the usual beauty, not what is usually seen. And that you are deliberately not saying the same old things about art and life that are usually said. ("Making a Claim" 51)

One might add to this list of negatives the fact that Galloway does not present herself as a member of Deaf culture with a basis in ASL, having been mainstreamed as a child in public schools. Although her oral basis removes her from more traditional venues of Deaf culture, it permits her access to a wide range of acoustic environments, including film, radio, verbal monologue, and standup poetry, on which she draws with caustic wit and broad satire.

In her video performance *Annie Dearest,* Galloway takes on a sacred text of disability literature, Helen Keller's autobiography and its representation in the 1962 film *The Miracle Worker.* The first part of the performance features a black-and-white reenactment of the moment in the film when Keller (Patty Duke) makes the verbal connection between the word "water" and the water being pumped out of a well by Annie Sullivan (Ann Bancroft). Galloway parodies the sentimental framing of this moment—

the swelling music and epiphanic discovery by Keller of language—by linking Sullivan, Keller's patient teacher, to Joan Crawford as the abusive mother represented in her daughter's memoir, *Mommie Dearest*. In Galloway's version, Annie Sullivan, the patient, heroic, hearing teacher, is transformed into a demonic oralist instructor who forces Helen to endure various forms of water torture until she pronounces the acceptable phonemes: "wa . . . wa . . . wa . . . water!" *Annie Dearest* is a parody not only of sentimental portrayals of disabled persons but an exploration of sensationalist human interest stories (of which Crawford's memoir is an example) through which disability is represented.

In an afterword to the film, Galloway appears—now in full color—as the cocreator of *Annie Dearest* and, most importantly, as an "authentically deaf person." She explains that despite her hearing aids and deaf accent (lateral lisp), she is technically not supposed to be in a film about deafness since she does not use ASL in her performances. In her faux documentary voice, she avers that if she were an "authentically deaf person" she would sign her remarks, but fortunately she has a stand-in—or "hand in"—in the form of her interpreter Stevie, who stands behind her and signs across her chest. This irreverent coda has, at its heart, a serious subtext: the claim for an authentic Deaf identity marked by exclusive use of manual signing. Galloway's controversial critique of official Deaf culture focuses on the exclusions of cultural nationalism by acknowledging her awkward relation to both hearing and deaf worlds. Her coda is also about the fragile trust between the deaf individual and the oral world that interprets experience for her. The more Galloway claims to be authentically deaf, the more unstable becomes the claim. She "performs authenticity" while acknowledging her marginal status among deaf persons. But while she is critical of the official hierarchies of Deaf culture, capital D, she is also aware of the insidious role that audism plays in performance itself—through the use of various forms of visual translation (voice-over, closed-captioning, and hearing ASL signer) that she deploys in *Annie Dearest*. At the end she asks Stevie if she (Stevie) has been "talking behind my back," and Stevie nods her head affirmatively. "I was afraid of that," Galloway concludes. Here, she foregrounds the complex and multifaceted implications of depending on others who may literally and figuratively wrest power from deaf persons by "talking behind our backs."

My second example of language mediated by sight is taken from the work of deaf artist and philosopher Joseph Grigely. As I point out later in this book, Grigely creates installations in which the walls are plastered with small slips of paper that he collects from his "conversations with the hearing," as he calls one of his installations. These ephemeral texts are the written half of dialogues that the artist has had with hearing interlocutors, the other half of these conversations completed by Grigely's voice or by gestures. What we see in the gallery or museum space is a rough patch-work of tiny texts, ephemeral post-its and bar napkins that become—quite literally—a wall of words. Affixed to the walls are brief descriptions of the circumstances of each conversation that become, in themselves, metaconversations with the viewer. Grigely wants to turn the docent commentary on the artist's work into the work itself, while debunking the "authoritative" art commentary on the work's origins.

Grigely's interest in the interface between the visible and the textual can be seen in his "Postcards to Sophie Calle," a series of responses to the French photographer from 1991. Calle's exhibition *Les Aveugles* was featured at the Luhring Augustine Gallery in New York and involved photographs of blind people who had been asked to respond to the question of "what their image of beauty was" (31). In addition to printed responses to this question, the exhibition featured photographs of the blind respondents and the "beautiful" objects to which they refer. Grigely's postcards are an extended meditation on the sighted viewer's gaze at the blind face and on the sighted artist's ability to render the blind experience. Grigely admits to being "taken in" by the written responses as they describe touching bodies and sculpture, but his pleasure is "mitigated by something troubling" about them:

> They [the blind subjects] do not apologize for the fact that it is the body, the engendered body particularly, that must be touched to be seen. This is the tactile gaze of the blind. It is a gaze unconditioned by whatever feminism and sexual politics have taught us about touching. The terms and conditions by which this tactile gaze exists thus cannot be judged by our own standard, where the actions of the blind become rendered . . . into *our* vocabulary of tactile violence. This touching is not about feeling, not about touching even, but about seeing. Touching itself is elided; it is a semantic projection of our own physiology, not that of the blind. If everyone in the world were blind, perhaps touching would be called seeing. (33)

I will return to the idea of tactile seeing in chapter 6, but here I would observe that Grigely questions the presumed erotics of tactility—and the sexual politics that limits its meaning. He compares the blind person's touching of sculpture in the museum to the deaf person's use of sign language, the latter of which is not a "pretty way of communicating—it's language, language pure and simple" (33). Of course language is never "pure and simple," as his epistolary pretense makes clear, but he wants to differentiate a romantic view of the blind—as simple, naive, sensual—from an ontological view—as subjects for whom touch is a form of communication. Our inability to imagine alternate configurations of sensation stems from ingrained attitudes about what constitutes perception, the "inevitable effect of an imposed transmodality: it reconfigures our physiological conventions and the language with which we describe those conventions" (33).

This "transmodality"—what I have been calling defamiliarization or what Terry Galloway calls "coding it differently"—lies at the heart of a critical disability aesthetics in which practice—performance, textuality, visuality—redirects epistemological questions onto the body. If classical aesthetics has been based on a theory of disinterested contemplation, what does this disinterest mean for those who do not see and who become the objects of another's contemplation? Grigely admits to feeling profoundly disturbed by such questions because Calle has permitted no reciprocity to the gaze. The blind are asked to respond to beauty as subjects, but their faces become the objects of the sighted gaze:

> I am arrested by the fact that these images do not, because of their visual modality, return themselves to the blind. *Since your face is not available to me, why should my face be available to you?* (34)

Sophie Calle's camera captures the face of the blind but leaves her own face out. The panoptical gaze of the camera keeps everyone in sight, yet protects the seer from view. As a deaf viewer, Grigely understands what it means to be looked at strangely and provides his own disability perspective on the act of looking: "I am able to gaze, look, stare into the faces, into the eyes, of faces . . . I feel I am in the presence of a social experiment. I feel I am being watched, feel as if I am a part of this experiment. Alone and not alone, I am uncomfortable" (34).

Although Grigely's postcards are critical of Calle's project, they nevertheless recognize the compelling nature of her attempt to give a place to
blindness visitors to the museum, her interest as "social archaeologist" in
the ordinary details of blind response.[21] The problem, however, is that it is
not an exhibit for the *blind* but for the *seeing viewer,* a form of colonization similar to ethnographic scrutiny of primitive peoples or the modernist's fascination with non-Western art ("What difference is there between gazing at the eyes of the blind or the labia of the Hottentot Venus?"
36). He notes that progressive critics often use negative stereotypes of disability to refer to those who are "blind" or "deaf" to cultural diversity, even
though these same critics are acutely sensitive to the ways that sexism or
racism are encoded in language. Such obtuseness to the material reality of
blindness is reinforced by an image that Grigely finds most arresting in the
exhibit, a photograph of a Braille text by Claude Jaunière. It is the ultimate
oxymoron of display—a text meant to be touched that has been flattened
into a photograph, encased in plexiglass. As Grigely looks more closely at
the image, he realizes that the text has been printed upside down, the epitome of disregard in an exhibit designed to represent blindness. Grigely's
"monospondence" (as he calls it) with Sophie Calle engages the artist in a
dialogue about the aesthetic use of disability. By writing his response to
Les Aveugles in the form of postcards, Grigely signifies on Calle's own vernacular, exploratory form. Since she does not include her face in the exhibit, Grigely does not represent himself, but in his final postcard, he offers a solution: "Perhaps, Sophie, you might some day return what you
have taken, might some day undress your psyche in a room frequented by
the blind, and let them run their fingers over your body as you have run
your eyes over theirs" (58).

Siting Disability ↪

As the work of Terry Galloway and Joseph Grigely indicates, disability may
be a theater or a museum, a place where something is seen. If disability is
a matter of sight, it is no less one of site, a series of locations and spaces
where political economy, bioregional differences, cultural representations,
and medical bureaucracies converge. I am not speaking metaphorically
here. Anyone who has gone to a hospital for even a minor procedure

knows what it means to enter the labyrinth of waiting rooms, doctors offices, pre-op wards, and operating theaters while wearing a hospital gown that ties badly in the back. And there are other kinds of spaces—the chilly warren of insurance documents, liability waivers, and postoperation directives that map the body's passage through the new HMO-driven medical bureaucracy. The site itself—doctors in green scrubs, clots of medical residents appearing at any hour of the day, strange noises in the hallway, and lights turned on in the middle of the night—creates a phantasmagoria that is unnerving for an adult patient and terrifying to a child. Whatever physical ailment brings one to the hospital is quickly displaced onto regimes of diagnosis, cure, and analysis. These are the sites through which the body becomes medicalized, the subject becomes object.

Medical anthropologists have begun to study the etiology of disability in such phantasmagoric spaces, observing that when disability is located in society, rather than individual pathology, the diagnosis of a condition is always driven by factors beyond the information contained in an MRI scan or platelet count. In terms that Homi Bhabha uses to describe the hybridic nature of global culture, we might ask, what is the "location of disability," and how does consideration of space alter the meaning of impairment? Does HIV exist in the individual's cell structure or in the compromised immune system or in the social attitudes toward persons deemed at risk in a given cultural frame? Is HIV-positive the same for a white male in the United States as it is for an African woman in Botswana? Is menopause a natural hormonal change in middle-aged women or a disease, invented by pharmaceutical companies to promote hormone replacement therapy?[22] Do diseases such as silicosis, carpel tunnel syndrome, or "Gulf War syndrome" exist in patients or in the workplace environments where these conditions have historically emerged? Feminist scholars have noted that S. Weir Mitchell's famous "rest cure" for women who in the late nineteenth century suffered from nervous disorders was as much an attempt to impose a spatial constraint on the sexually and economically emancipated "new woman" as it was to solve her nervous disorder.[23] As Charlotte Perkins Gilman's short story about the ill effects of Mitchell's cure on one woman demonstrates, the space of what used to be called "hysteria" may be the prisonlike nursery in which the female narrator of "The Yellow Wall Paper" is incarcerated.

In one of his talk performances, David Antin describes the patient's interaction with a doctor as a kind potlatch:

> . . . a patient comes to a doctor with a complaint   not
> with a disease and what the doctor offers him is a disease   a
> disease is the doctors prospective gift to the patient   which is
> then followed by other gifts   since one gift leads to another
> a course of therapy   drugs surgery   who knows (281)

The idea that a patient is "given" a disease and that such a "gift" leads to further exchanges reinforces medicine's anthropological associations with myth and ritual. This counternarrative complicates the usual model of disease as something that one "has" and resites it onto something that others interpret. This hermeneutic activity, as I point out in chapter 1, has been especially important to hematological diseases because of the symbolism that attends blood within national narratives of patriotism and sacrifice. In his study of the blood distribution industry, Richard Titmuss notes that in the early days of transfusions, blood donations were thought to be a "gift relationship" since they were given without thought of payment. When blood could be sold for profit, the "gift" of blood was no longer an appropriate model and was replaced by a commodity relationship between seller and client. The ill effects of the commodity model were evident in the infection of thousands of individuals with HIV/AIDS in the early 1980s through transfusions from pooled blood products.

In a similar vein, Keith Wailoo has pointed out that the diagnosis of certain diseases such as sickle-cell disease or Tay-Sachs, by their identification with African American and Jewish populations, become visible less by the particular biological features of the disease and more by questions of race and heritage. He notes that such racialized diseases "are not so much new inventions of the science of genetics; they are rather, reinterpretations that draw on particular notions of group history, identity, and memory" ("Inventing the Heterozygote" 236). Wailoo points out that early studies of sickle-cell disease emphasized the recessive traits inherited from the parents. The heterozygote or carrier of the recessive gene became as important as the one afflicted; the focus of medical research was redirected from curing the afflicted patient to containing of the spread of disease and contamination of others. The importance of the carrier "high-lights how new technologies gave rise to new forms of identity, and to widespread anxieties about social interaction and new methods of surveillance" (237). The biological definition of the heterozygote and the carrier's identification with the diseased population became a social issue that often attends the arrival of new migrant populations. In such examples, the siting of blood extends to the economic and spatial forces of modernity in which racial identity was often measured by the "one-drop rule."

If we think of disability only in terms of an unitary physiological or sensory limit, we will fail to understand the complex matrix of sites that are brought into play, making it impossible to say where a disability ends and the social order begins. As I say in my final chapter, if we imagine that disability is something pertaining only to bodies, then we restrict the term to a medical frame, but if we imagine that disability is defined within pharmaceutical exchange, blood donation centers, labor migration, ethnic displacement, epidemiology, genomic research, and trade wars, then the question of the location of disability must be asked differently. Does disability exist within a cell structure, a caregiver, a trade agreement, an insurance claim, a special education program, or, as the recent devastation caused by hurricane Katrina exemplifies, a disaster preparedness plan?

If we consider disability as a series of sites, then we would have to include those places in which awareness of disability emerges, in which the "handicapped" population becomes empowered as a political entity. The independent-living movement often charts its origins to the ward at the Cowell Hospital on the University of California, Berkeley, campus where Ed Roberts and other disabled students lived and pursued an education previously deemed inaccessible.[24] Their relationship to the campus's then-active antiwar and free speech protests was instrumental in gaining a site for their assisted living and ultimately in launching a social movement that shifted the rehabilitation model of impairment to one based on communal, self-sufficient living. The same might be said for the history of Deaf culture, which is written around residential schools, clubs, and camps where deaf families have historically placed their children and around which thriving Deaf communities have emerged. The importance of such educational venues for Deaf people is reflected in two ASL signs that could be translated, "Where do you live?" One version means, "Where are you currently living?" (WHERE-LIVE-YOU?) and another means,

"What residential school did you attend?" (WHERE-FROM-YOU?) (see Padden and Humphries, *Learning* 7). In this sense, Deaf identity is linked as intimately to the sites of instruction as the site of local habitation.

Michael Bérubé has provided a case study of how disability exfoliates within multiple locations and discourses. *Life as We Know It* is a memoir of his son Jamie, who was born with Down syndrome, a chromosomal imbalance in the fetus that leads to delayed mental and physical growth. Bérubé surveys the ethical and philosophical challenges raised by forgoing amniocentesis and chancing the birth of a child with what are usually described as "birth defects." The primary question he asks is "defects" for whom and by what definition? Answering this question turns out to engage major bioethical problems of the current period. When they became pregnant, Bérubé and his wife, Janet, decided against prenatal screening, believing that it is an "invasive procedure that would only 'catch' things we didn't think we wanted caught, and that might induce a miscarriage to boot" (46). Jamie's birth and early life were admittedly difficult, but, as the book chronicles, he gradually emerges into a curious, funny, and engaging four-year-old child. His parents' obvious pleasure in Jamie and their acceptance of his idiosyncrasies challenge easy ethical choices around "pro-choice" and "pro-life" positions, although the passage between these Manichaean poles is fraught.

The memoir is also a bioethical study of social attitudes about persons variously labeled "mongoloid idiots" or "retards" as well as the more benign "special needs" or "differently abled" children. Such labeling becomes as much a part of Down syndrome as the undivided twenty-first chromosome that is its genetic cause since it marks in advance what procedures will be considered inevitable for parents. As Bérubé observes, "[After] Jamie had been in the ICU for two weeks or so, he started becoming a narrative" (40). He is referring to the daily reports on Jamie's development that he delivers to friends and relatives, but he is also referring to his child's status as a medicalized entity, subject to stories around which parental choices and public policy are made. Bérubé recounts how difficult it would have been if, upon receiving the results of amniocentesis, he and his wife had been told that their baby would "never be able to live a 'normal' life" or that he would never be a "conscious being, never learn to talk, read or recognize his parents," the sorts of things that parents have historically been told about Down's children (47). Such attitudes from medical professionals often leave parents with few alternatives to abortion. The fact that Bérubé is writing his memoir some years after Jamie has been born at a moment when the (now) four-year-old boy does talk, does read, and does recognize his parents makes this book a cautionary tale about the wonders of genetic engineering.

Among the narratives that Berube wants to redirect is the American individualist version that says that having a "defective" child is a form of narcissism, that bringing a "less than normal child" into the world is a social burden. He worries about a functionalist society that bases childbearing decisions on eugenicist ideas about nontraditional fetuses combined with cost-accounting criteria. But he is no less critical of pro-life constituencies who lump all matters of childbirth into a single, all-purpose definition of "life" without making distinctions around who best to define that life. Social libertarians and conservatives who oppose special programs, parental leave laws, and school lunch programs may be willing to defend the rights of the unborn, but they pay little heed to life beyond the womb. Bérubé feels that his decision not to have prenatal testing in no way contradicts his and his wife's pro-choice beliefs but is, in fact, an extension of them insofar as both are based on a woman's right to control what happens to her body (46).

As Bérubé makes clear, issues like abortion or neonatal testing are a matter of framing. If the case is defined in terms of the state's ability to override a woman's right to choose, then the issue is about the right to privacy protected by legal precedent. This means something very different than if the case is framed in terms of whether a woman has a right to kill an unborn child. As the Genome Project nears its goal of mapping the DNA of every individual, the question of framing becomes all the more significant as we debate the pros of biological engineering against the cons of biological determinism and neoeugenics.

A similar debate is already occurring within the Deaf community over the use of cochlear implants. These electronic devices are surgically implanted in the brain where they stimulate the cochlear nerve to receive certain sounds that have been sent by a transmitter located in the ear. While they do not restore full hearing, cochlear implants do permit a spectrum of sounds to be recognizable, permitting persons who become deaf later in life to retain a degree of connection to hearing friends and family. Persons with hereditary deafness, however, do not fare as well. They have fewer nerve cells in the cochlea and thus receive fewer auditory signals, thereby limiting the effectiveness of the implant.[25] Harlan Lane describes a series of tests performed on deaf children before and after implantation showing that ability to recognize words improved only slightly and that deaf children wearing hearing aids fared better than those wearing the cochlear implant (220). In order to channel novel sounds into recognizable words, an extensive regime of speech therapy and training must follow surgery, posing, as Carol Padden and Tom Humphreys have observed, an ominous return to the days of oralist education if such therapies are predicated on prohibitions against signing (*Inside Deaf Culture* 168).[26]

The documentary film *Sound and Fury* attempts to provide a balanced overview of both sides in the debate and illustrates the importance of considering the role of space in disability. It explores the fears expressed by many Deaf people that the implant poses a kind of technological genocide designed to eliminate Deaf culture altogether. *Sound and Fury* shows the lives of two Long Island families in which genetic deafness extends across several generations. When the hearing son, Chris Artinian, decides to have cochlear surgery for his deaf son, his deaf brother, Peter, is profoundly upset at what he interprets as his sibling's rejection of Deaf culture and family. For the hearing brother and his wife, the decision to have surgery for their child is self-evident; why wouldn't they want their son to hear? Why would anyone, given the opportunity, choose to remain deaf? Their strident arguments in favor of surgery are accompanied by a more troubling condescension toward their deaf parents and toward deaf people in general.

Despite his anger over his brother's unqualified endorsement of the hearing world, Peter and his wife, Mari, contemplate a cochlear implant for their deaf daughter, Heather, when she tells them that she wants one in order to participate with other hearing children. Peter and Mari consult a number of families with children who have had the surgery, but they see how antipathetic the hearing world is to deaf children and how qualified the results of the device are. They also worry that their daughter will live in a cochlear implant limbo, neither a full member of Deaf world, nor of the hearing world either. They also visit an oralist school in which neither Deaf culture nor ASL are mentioned as a component of deaf experience. As a result of these forays into a hearing world, they decide against implantation and move to another city where there is a larger deaf community and a more extensive network of deaf schools and social services. Al-though the two brothers deal with their deaf children in opposite ways, the rift that the film exposes between the two families goes beyond deaf-ness to issues of family and community.

In terms of my concern with the location of disability, *Sound and Fury* suggests that cultural deafness is very much a matter of class, generation, and education. The deaf parents of the sons are fiercely protective of their Deaf heritage and cannot understand why anyone would want to perform an operation that is both physically invasive and culturally destructive; they experience the operation as a personal rejection of them and the ex-tensive network of deaf families that we meet in the course of the film. They are clearly less affluent and less educated than either of their sons, re-lying on cultural traditions and heritage as hedges against what they see as cultural suicide. Their more affluent, hearing son and wife see their par-ents' culturalist definitions as outmoded and think of the cochlear im-plant as a sign of forward-looking progress, an opportunity to utilize tech-nology to integrate their daughter into the hearing world. What is most interesting, however, is that their deaf son has moved firmly into the mid-dle class and has a managerial job, permitting him a degree of movement between hearing worlds (his colleagues are hearing) and deaf culture. The two sons must negotiate a complex set of responsibilities to their children, their class affiliations, and their parents.

These two examples suggest that the local conditions that produce Down syndrome or deafness are profoundly linked to social attitudes that are reinforced and naturalized by medical science, genetic engineering, and media. For disability studies to study disability adequately, it must sit-uate a physical or cognitive impairment in a landscape larger than either the individual or the impairment. The ADA defines a disability as some-thing that "limits one or more major life activities," which, of course, means defining in what environment such activity occurs. Recent chal-lenges to the ADA have been fought precisely over whether a person with a correctable disability can claim redress under the law—whether a pilot who wears glasses can sue for being denied an opportunity to fly or whether a person with repetitive stress injury who can do some household chores is therefore ineligible for damages because she cannot work on a factory assembly line. Such examples suggest that defining disability will always include the place where disability becomes visible.

Living in the Hurricane ∽

What we might conclude from the preceding discussion of sight, site, and space is the idea that disability is a matter of barriers, both physical and attitudinal, that prevent an individual with an impairment from participating in all forms of social life. But as my example of Ravel's Concerto in D suggests, those barriers may be as culturally productive as they are socially limiting. Political movements and aesthetic innovation that emerge in response to sexual or racial difference may be motivated all the more for what they *fail* to recuperate, for what they *refuse* to resolve. When the deaf performance artist Aaron Williamson was asked by a student, "When did you lose your hearing," he responded: "I choose not to say when I *lost* my hearing but rather when I *gained* my deafness; everything I do as a performer begins with that."[27] A disability politics needs to respect such choices and remain cautious about substituting for the impaired or deaf body a hypostatized healthy or hearing body that, were it not for social barriers, could serve as the horizon of identity.[28] The concerto that Ravel created for Paul Wittgenstein is significantly different from *Bolero* (some might say, for the better), just as Beethoven's late quartets, written while the composer was becoming deaf, pushed harmonies and rhythms into levels unimaginable in the age of Mozart and Haydn. One might say that Beethoven "triumphed" over adversity, but a disability perspective might add that adversity made the Grosse Fugue possible.

While I have described the defamiliarizing effects of disability on cultural objects and genres, I realize that such a formulation presumes that there is a "familiar" body that must be validated, a "young, married, white, urban, northern, heterosexual, Protestant father of college education, fully employed, of good complexion, weight and height, and a recent record in sports," as Erving Goffman famously described him (128). Such a figure is a necessary fiction in the enforcement of normalcy. Hence, one of the key tasks of disability studies is to take the ordinary out of ordinary language, the familiar out of defamiliarization, the ability out of disability in order to understand the essentialist and ableist core to our definitions of difference. Instead of insisting on a common humanity and a healthy body as a default to difference, what about making *alterity* a position from which to develop an imagined community?

The familiar was not long ago dominated by sights of devastation caused by Hurricane Katrina, the floods, fires, social displacement, and death that lay in its wake, the city of New Orleans transformed into a wasteland of abandoned, flooded houses and stranded refrigerators at the curb's edge. The media rightly focused attention on the fact that the population most affected in New Orleans and surrounding areas was, by and large, poor and black. Images of angry African Americans yelling at FEMA representatives, children and women looting stores, bloated bodies floating in flooded streets, black families hauling belongings in shopping carts—such graphic images are being compared to those in a third-world country. And indeed, the comparison reminds us of what social critics have been saying for a long time about the decline of social programs in favor of market-driven alternatives to everything from education to health care to infrastructure repair, to the ongoing war in the Middle East. If Katrina was a natural disaster "waiting to happen," as the experts say, the anticipated destruction of social levees like Social Security and Medicare are political disasters awaiting the aging baby boom generation.

Often unmentioned among the images coming from New Orleans are those of white *and* black people in wheelchairs, lying unattended on gurneys in hospitals, breathing through ventilators pumped by hand, dying from lack of pure water for dialysis, resting on crutches in food lines. Persons with disabilities who were trapped in the World Trade Center on 9/11 or those who drowned in their houses in New Orleans's Ninth Ward are protected by the most comprehensive disability law in the world, but the access guaranteed by the ADA is hardly adequate to the human and natural disasters of recent history. If our imagined national community is made strange by the eruption of an American third world into the public consciousness, it is no less defamiliarized by the sight of bodies left vulnerable to rising water and slow-moving relief efforts. Perhaps this new narrative of the United States as a third-world nation will spark a new debate about disability on a global scale, not merely as a matter of health care but as a matter of political economy and redistribution. At such a point, disability studies will no longer need to plead its case from a marginal position within cultural studies and civil rights legislation but will join the broad quilt of social movements in pursuit of truly equal access.

Chapter 1

Strange Blood

Hemophobia and the Unexplored
Boundaries of Queer Nation

Nominal Queers ⮌

In the late 1970s, the development of freeze-dried blood-clotting factors drawn from multiple donors dramatically affected the lives of persons with hemophilia.[1] Until this time, persons with chronic blood diseases had relied on transfusions from whole blood or cryoprecipitate (fresh frozen plasma) administered by a nurse or physician.[2] Such transfusions were both time-consuming and expensive, necessitating a ready supply of blood products and a clinical staff well versed in each patient's bleeding history and blood type. Since severe hemophiliacs require transfusions often—sometimes several times a week—patients need easy access to a clinic. Too long a delay following a bruise could result in joint bleeding or hematoma that would take weeks to dissipate. Hematomas are excruciatingly painful, and over time they cause severe cartilage and tissue damage to the joints, leaving many hemophiliacs crippled. In the case of bleeding to the cranial or neck area, delays in treatment could result in death. Without immediate blood transfusions, routine tooth extractions, nosebleeds, bumps, and bruises become life-threatening events. With the new freeze-dried product, hemophiliacs could infuse themselves at home, giving them a freedom that they had not enjoyed before.

The miracle of factor concentrate was a boon to patients, doctors, and blood-product companies alike. Patients could keep vials of concentrate in their refrigerators to be used at the first sign of bleeding. Children were especially aided by this new technology since they could be transfused at home or at school and thus participate in most regular play activities. Whereas prior to the development of cryoprecipitate in the mid-1960s persons with hemophilia seldom lived beyond teenage years, they could now live a full life.[3] By using home transfusion as a prophylactic or preventative form of treatment, they could avoid joint or muscle bleeds, thus eliminating the attendant orthopedic problems that crippled so many severe bleeders. Doctors and hematologists could spend less time administering transfusions and devote more time to the residual effects of bleeding disorders. And of course the profits of blood-product suppliers soared. A hemophiliac with severe Factor VIII deficiency will spend $60,000 to $150,000 annually for clotting factor alone, each vial of concentrate costing as much as $1,500.[4] Any further complications such as injury or surgery can boost medical expenses for blood products to $500,000. Blood ceased to be a "gift," in Richard Titmuss's phrase, donated by disinterested individuals for the purpose of sustaining life, and became a product that earned high profits for its producers.[5]

As it turned out, the miracle of factor concentrate was a death sentence. In January 1982 the Centers for Disease Control in Atlanta received word of a fifty-five-year-old hemophilic male who was diagnosed with *Pneumocystis carinii* pneumonia, the most characteristic and fatal of the opportunistic diseases suffered by AIDS patients. Although his case could not be directly linked to AIDS, two more cases in the summer of that year were diagnosed, and all three patients died. When the CDC alerted the Food and Drug Administration (FDA) that what was then called GRID (Gay-Related Immune Deficiency) might be spreading through transfusions, the agency did nothing, fearing a panic that would severely diminish the blood supply. Since factor concentrate is distilled from thousands of donors, chances of infection for hepatitis had always been a risk. Now, with the added danger of HIV infection, blood could be lethal. Without any restrictions placed on them by the CDC or FDA, the major blood-product companies continued to distribute infected blood.

The willingness of the major pharmaceutical companies to continue distributing blood products after their purity had been questioned has been the focus of numerous individual suits and one major class-action suit. The suit was filed against four blood-product companies (Rhone-Poulenc Rorer Inc., Baxter Healthcare Corp., Miles Inc. [now Bayer Corp], and Alpha Therapeutic) and the National Hemophilia Associations, the latter of which, according to the *New York Times,* "falsely advised hemophiliacs in the 1980s that the H.I.V. risk in taking the products was minimal. It [the suit] says the foundation gave this advice because it was financially dependent on the manufacturers" ("AIDS Suit" A18). A federal appeals court in Chicago, however, ruled that the thousands of HIV-infected hemophiliacs who joined in the suit could not file as a group since a class-action in a suit of this size could bankrupt the plasma-products industry ("Ruling Bars HIV-Infected Hemophiliacs" A 16).

In January 1983, the National Hemophilia Foundation asked that screening procedures be adopted to discourage blood donations from high-risk groups, specifically homosexual men. It was not until 1985 that AIDS antibody screening tests were approved, and nationwide testing of blood began. Between 1980 and 1986, more than 60 percent of the nation's twenty thousand hemophiliacs were infected with the HIV virus, and by 1988 90 percent of all severe bleeders had been infected.[6] With the advent of blood screening in 1985 and through the development of heat-treated and recombinant factor, exposure to HIV through transfusions dropped considerably. But for the thousands of hemophiliacs who were infected with the HIV virus in the 1980s this change offers little solace.

As a person with hemophilia I well remember the enthusiasm with which my doctors and clinical aids received the news of factor concentrate. I was instructed in the proper mode of home transfusion, given my precious bottles of powdered concentrate and infusion kit, and sent home to await my first bleed. Since I have a rather moderate form of Factor IX hemophilia (Christmas Disease), I never had to use the concentrate during the years it was contaminated, but visits to the clinic in the mid-1980s revealed a profound change in the hemophilia community. Now in addition to the more recognizably crippled hemophiliacs, I saw patients emaciated by various opportunistic diseases characteristic of persons with AIDS. Mailings from the various hemophilia organizations changed from being about new blood products and infusion therapies to information about HIV infection, AZT, hospice networks, AIDS hotlines, and, inevitably, memorial services. Persons with hemophilia who had been medically integrated into normal life activities were now ostracized from schools and businesses, their already fragile insurance policies canceled, and their access to life-sustaining blood products profoundly altered. Moreover, fears of AIDS contamination at the blood banks kept potential healthy donors away, thus diminishing the supply of fresh frozen plasma.

One of the most psychologically devastating effects of AIDS on the hemophilia community was its disruption of the codependent relationship between patients and the medical establishment. For obvious reasons, hemophiliacs had developed close ties with clinics, doctors, and pharmaceutical companies, and individuals often moved from positions as care-receivers to care-givers, working within hemophilia organizations and clinics and serving on the boards of blood-product companies. Spouses and parents of hemophiliacs often became professional nurses or clinicians themselves through their intimate knowledge of blood infusion processes. If the National Hemophilia Foundation (NHF) was reluctant to criticize pharmaceutical companies in the early stages of AIDS, it was because these companies were regarded less as corporate entities than as members of the family, as interested in the health of their consumers as in that of their profits. As David Kirp observes, so dependent were medical specialists on their "pharmaceutical patrons" that it was not until 1994 that the World Federation of Hemophilia permitted public criticism of the drug companies (66). As with other chronic diseases, patients developed long-term relationships with nurses and doctors, relationships cemented by the development of comprehensive care and family-oriented treatment. AIDS turned blood products into commodities and transformed medical professionals into antagonists. And after some delay, as I will point out, it turned hemophiliacs from patients into activists.

I rehearse this brief history to describe a multistage crisis in what I call "blood culture," one based on the transmission and circulation of healthy blood. By speaking of a culture of blood I am contrasting those constituencies bonded by shared bodily fluids, tissues, and genetic codes to those based on family, racial, or even national characteristics. Among the latter, blood is often used as a metaphor that stands for racial characteristics—as in the infamous "one-drop rule" by which individuals with even the slightest trace of African heritage were automatically marked as black. Since hemophiliacs—as well as other persons with genetically inherited disease—share the blood of others, they are linked as a group in ways that defy traditional cultural markers. The fear of blood or bleeders (hemo-phobia), then, annexes phobias about other constituencies for which the penetration of the bodily envelope is perceived to transgress boundaries of racial or sexual normativity. Cultural identities are often based on bi-nary terms (self/other, participant/observer, insider/outsider, hege-monic/subaltern), but one based on blood would have to be, in the most literal sense, fluid and porous.

The stages in this crisis within blood culture could be defined as fol-lows. First, the infection of clotting factor dramatically halted what had been a forward-moving, optimistic narrative in hemophilia research.[7] Second, it marked a shift in AIDS discourse from narratives about a dis-ease spread among "others" to one infecting "us."[8] If AIDS could be trans-mitted by blood (instead of sexual acts), then "we" heterosexuals were vul-nerable to penetration. Finally, by bringing an exclusively male community of hemophiliacs (as an X-linked disease, hemophilia is found almost exclusively among males) together with gay males, AIDS redefined the nature of homosocial community and forced a reconsideration of sex-ual identities among heterosexual bleeders.[9] This latter stage has impor-tant implications for current debates within queer theory and sexual pol-itics. The politics of Queer Nation, as Lauren Berlant and Elizabeth Freeman have pointed out, involves a carnivalization of gender roles that contests fantasies of American national unity. But the borders of Queer Nation, while open to transgressions of sexuality, are often closed to iden-tities not constructed *through* sexuality—identities that are interpellated into queer culture but which lack adequate documentation. In this respect people with disabilities—including hemophiliacs and persons with AIDS—cross multiple borders, beyond those of sex and gender.

In each of these levels, public fear of tainted blood annexed earlier na-tional anxieties about infection, placing hemophiliacs in subject positions that had been occupied by immigrants, people of color, and sexual mi-norities. Hemophiliacs who had devoted their lives to integrating them-selves into "normal" life now found themselves in clinics and support groups with nonmainstream, marginal populations. At the same time, by their proximity to a gay-marked disease, hemophiliacs were forced to cre-ate new positionalities in relation to their sexuality that contradicted their pursuit of normalcy. Such migrations of identity suggest that designations for medically impacted minorities such as *disabled* or *challenged* are inadequate to the social complexity of a genetically inherited or chronic diseases. Furthermore, the blurring of medical and sexual binaries raises a problem for social-constructionist theory in that models of queerness based upon gender performance and theatricalization may have to accommodate subjectivities based upon the most essentialized of categories: genetics, epidemiology, and blood.

Cindy Patton observes that once "perceptions of HIV risk were linked to social deviance, literally anyone or any category of people deemed epidemiologically significant could be converted into nominal queers" (*Last Served* 19). As an "epidemiologically significant" group, hemophiliacs were interpellated into homophobic, racist discourses for which they were ill prepared. Their political focus had traditionally been directed at medical research and health delivery systems, beginning with coagulation studies in the 1940s and the formation of the National Hemophilia Foundation in 1948.[10] Now, as "nominal queers," hemophiliacs had to confront a gendering process that had always attended their disease and that had resurfaced through homophobic responses to AIDS. What we might call the "queering of hemophilia" did not happen overnight through a Stonewall riot or social movement; it involved a gradual restructuring of a largely male homosocial culture and the support networks upon which it had been based.[11]

By speaking of hemophiliacs as "nominal queers" I am adapting Patton's phrase to describe figures who in acquiring AIDS iatrogenically (e.g., through a medical procedure) also inherited discursive features of social Others. They became high-risk individuals whose sexual lives were scrutinized, whose employment was endangered, whose spouses became medical pariahs, and whose relationship to the blood-product industry upon which they depended became adversarial. In numerous cases they were subject to direct harassment, most famously in the case of the Ray family, whose hemophiliac sons were taunted at school and whose Florida house was burned down in a KKK-like attack, forcing them to relocate in another city. In more recent years and through contact with gay AIDS activists, hemophiliacs have developed an activist posture toward blood-product companies that sold infected blood, filing a class-action suit and sponsoring a congressional bill (the Ricky Ray Relief Act) that would provide compensation for HIV contamination.

This interpellation of hemophiliacs into gay culture was hardly a seamless process. With the entry of AIDS into their community many he-mophiliacs closed the door to their medical closets in order not to be associated with gays or not to be subject to the same prohibitions that gay people with AIDS were facing. Many were resentful of gay men whose sexual liberation had transformed their medical liberation into a nightmare. The media played up conflicts in between the two communities, creating what one commentator calls "hemo-homo wars."[12] By serving as the "innocent victims" of a "gay plague," hemophiliacs became unwitting allies of the religious Right in shoring up a homophobic agenda—not exactly a scenario designed to win friends among gay AIDS activists. In France, as David Kirp points out, Jean-Marie Le Pen's National Front used hemophiliacs as foils in its anti-immigrant, antigay policies, linking the French acronym for AIDS, SIDA, with *Socialisme, Immigration, Deliquance, Affairisme* (69). The National Hemophilia Foundation's attempt to screen out homosexual men as blood donors in the early days of AIDS was regarded as scapegoating by various gay and lesbian groups. The screening of blood donors was linked by many gays and lesbians to racist practices of the nineteenth century. The San Francisco Coordinating Committee of Gay and Lesbian Services said that "donor screening was reminiscent of miscegenation blood laws that divided black blood from white blood and was similar to the World War II rounding up of Japanese Americans in the western half of the country to minimize the possibility of espionage" (qtd. in Shilts 220).

As I have already indicated, the role of hemophilia in AIDS discourse coincides with debates about family values and heteronormalcy during the Reagan-Bush era. Hemophiliacs, by association with a "gay-related" disease, were subject to homophobia on the one hand and what one commentator has called "hemophobia" on the other.[13] If hemophilia means "love of blood," its phobic counterpart refers to the anxiety felt by health care workers, employers, teachers, and parents over the threat of infected blood. But hemophobia also taps a more ancient prejudice against bleeders—from Talmudic prescriptions against circumcision to warnings about Dracula to the eugenics movement to germ theory and immigration reform.[14] As a specifically modernist trope, "hemophobia" resuscitates an earlier semiotics of the bleeder as aesthete or neurasthenic female, weakened by aristocratic privilege and threatening to democratic institutions. Bleeding disorders raise concerns about the porousness of boundaries, the vulnerability of the bodily envelope, the infection of bodily fluids—concerns that parallel phobias about sexual deviance and racial mixing. Hemophobia, in other words, represents the merging of two discourses—one of blood, the other of sexuality—in which anxieties about bodily boundaries in one are articulated through anxieties about gender binaries in the other.

Unfortunately, access to the origins of hemophobia is limited. Lacking an adequate cultural history of hemophilia, we must turn to histories of race and sexuality to find analogues of cultural threat and moral panic based around blood. As I will suggest by reference to William Faulkner's *Absalom, Absalom!* anxieties about impure blood appear in even our most canonical literary sources, although like the fluid itself, the subject lies beneath the skin. While I am not suggesting that hemophiliacs have been subjected to the same social opprobrium as blacks, gays, and lesbians, I am arguing that their relationship to homophobia and social othering has forced them to create a "medical closet" that, like the sexual closet, has had to be renegotiated in an era of AIDS. In a newspaper report, Ryan White, the Indiana hemophiliac boy whose HIV infection through blood products made him the "poster boy" for AIDS research, was called a "homophiliac," a journalistic slip of the typewriter whose implications I want to explore.[15]

Blood Culture ⌐

The division I have outlined between hemophilia and hemophobia is one anticipated by Michel Foucault in *The History of Sexuality.* Foucault describes a shift from a "society of blood," based on the divine right of the sovereign, to a "society of sex," based on the medicalization of the body in the late nineteenth century. In the case of the former, blood relations inform the maintenance of social order throughout every level of society. A monarch's authority is vested in a lineage established by blood, while citizens are willing to shed blood for the privilege of the sovereign's protection. Power, in a society of sanguinity, speaks "through blood; the honor of war, the fear of famine, the triumph of death, the sovereign with his sword, executioners, and tortures; blood was *a reality with a symbolic function*" (147). In a society of sex, on the other hand, power is based on maintaining the health of the larger social body, of which individual biology becomes the fetishistic focus. The policing of the body, the categorizing of its functions, ardors, and excesses—what Foucault calls bio-power—becomes the central concern of health and medicine. Hemophobia in this scenario would refer not only to a fear of bleeders but also of residual aristocratic features in the new scientific, rationalized society.

Blood and sex cultures meet in Bram Stoker's *Dracula,* a novel in which the vampire's need for fresh blood is often identified with sexual and racial transgressions. Dracula's aristocratic appearance and behavior—pale skin, pale complexion, polite manners, elegant dress—become a monstrous perversion of eastern European refinement. As Judith Halberstam points out, he is also identified with anti-Semitic attitudes of the late nineteenth century, linked to George du Maurier's Svengali, Dickens's Fagin, and other representations of the predatory Jew. As such, Dracula marks an anxiety over "foreign" or "ethnic" insemination into Christian life that, as Halberstam says, "weakens the stock of Englishness by passing on degeneracy and the disease of blood lust" (95). Since Dracula drains the blood of others, he is linked to anti-Semitic economic theories by which "true" value is weakened by usurious interest rates and in which the liquidity of capital is diverted into unhealthy investments. As a consumer of the healthy blood of citizens, Dracula contributes to eugenicist fears of national pollution and miscegenation. The health of the vampire depends, by an inverse logic, on the waning of empire since he saps vital fluids that could serve the national interest. And because Dracula's bloodlust is gender blind, he is linked to homoerotic discourses, for which his effeminate and aristocratic qualities serve as markers.

A second narrative of the shift from sanguinity to sexuality is one represented by the decline of the czars, a shift that significantly revolves around a hemophilic child. According to the well-known story, the young czarevitch Alexis Romanov is the answer to Russia's dreams, the long-awaited heir to the throne of Nicholas and Alexandra following the birth of four girls. But the visitation of hemophilia upon the child, through genes spontaneously mutated in his grandmother, Queen Victoria, alters the course of Russian history. In Robert Massie's now-canonical account, the "blessed birth of an only son" provided the mortal blow to the imperial state: "Along with the lost battles and sunken ships, the bombs, the revolutionaries and their plots, the strikes and revolts, Imperial Russia was toppled by a tiny defect in the body of a little boy. Hidden from public view, veiled in rumor, working from within, this unseen tragedy would change the history of Russia and the world" (114).[16]

If we were to read Massie's romantic rhetoric through a Foucauldian optic, we might see an alternative historical genealogy to his more elegiac version: the noble code of blood has been polluted, thinned out by intermarriage with non-Russian subjects. Rasputin, vestigial remnant of archaic religious traditions, is engaged by Alexandra ("that German woman") as court advisor. Practicing the black arts of hypnotism and mesmerism, he miraculously clots the czarevitch's blood, earning him Alexandra's devotion and purchasing access to the inner court circle. His proximity to Alexandra leads to the public perception that he has become her consort; his sexual excesses among court ladies mime the degradation of royal blood in general. The restive proletariat, anxious to differentiate itself from the noble code of blood, focuses on the sexual activities of the royal family and on the absent body of the future heir. The overthrow of the Romanov dynasty replaces weak, feminized authority with the blood of the people in a bloodless coup. Scientific socialism replaces cosmopolitan aristocracy and mystical religious traditions of the decadent Romanovs; Russian Moscow replaces European Saint Petersburg.

Essential to this change is the restoration of racial and national purity, the repudiation of foreign forces and ethnicities by nationalist values of soil and folk. Foucault notes that a primary vehicle in the transition from blood to sex is the discourse of eugenics, the science of racial purity, which served in the formation of modern nation-states. Founded by Francis Galton in the mid–nineteenth century in England and based on Darwinian theories of evolution, eugenics gained a powerful foothold in the United States as justification for immigration reform, racial exclusion legislation, and antimiscegenation statutes. In many of its formulations and uses, genetic inheritance is figured through the metaphor of blood. This linkage between genetic infection and polluted blood is stated baldly by Robert Allen, Democratic congressman from West Virginia in 1922: "The primary reason for the restriction of the alien stream . . . is the necessity for purifying and keeping pure the blood of America" (Kevles 97). Allen's reference to pure blood and uncontaminated bodily fluids resonates throughout racist discourses of the Progressive Era. One result of such attitudes was the 1924 Immigration Act, signed into law by Calvin Coolidge, who, as vice president, declared that "America must be kept American. Biological laws show . . . that Nordics deteriorate when mixed with other races" (Kevles 97). Although concern for pure bloodlines had informed earlier debates over immigration, beginning with the second wave of colonists to the new world, it achieved a special importance in antimiscegenation legislation of the Reconstruction era, the attempts to identify racial features through the "one-drop rule" and in various germ theories in public health for which blood was the dominant trope.

Blood provides one of the three colors of the national flag. As articulated through eugenics discourse, it dominates what Lauren Berlant has called an American national fantasy or imagined community. This national fantasy is figured as an anatomy that links individual bodies of citizens with a corporate body of "embedded racial and gender inflections" (5). Blood, to adapt Berlant's formulation, circulates through this national fantasy as a metaphor of democratic possibility and potency that must be contained within the channels for which it is intended. Unlike the Russian national fantasy mentioned above, with its royal lineage of biologically linked leaders, the American version of national succession must be based on the symbolic replacement of blood shed on the revolutionary battlefield with the new blood of democratically elected leaders—a kind of political transfusion that perpetuates the founding fathers' authority.

When blood is allowed to mix with other races, it threatens more than the purity of the white race; it pollutes the exceptionalist character of the American errand. For John Adams, slavery posed a threat to the Constitution because it threatened the normal orders of nature, defined as such by the circulation of blood. In an essay on Shakespeare's *Othello,* written in 1835, Adams says that the tragedy is not that the Moor kills Desdemona out of irrational jealousy but that her blood could be quickened by a Moor. "The blood must circulate briskly in the veins of a young woman, so fascinated, and so coming to the tale of a rude, unbleached African soldier" (qtd. in Saxton 89). As Alexander Saxton points out, Adams believes that when Othello smothers his wife on stage, audiences are denied the cathartic emotions of pity and terror proper to tragedy. Instead, their emotions "subside immediately into the sentiment that she has her deserts" (89). Saxton relates Adams's reading of *Othello* to more general remarks on the ill effects of slavery as it was determining the growth and expansion of American interests in the 1830s. Events such as the annexation of Texas, according to Adams, had turned the Constitution into a "menstrous rag," a phrase joining misogyny to racism through the metaphor of blood as it was used to define national integrity and unity (88).

The Brother Who Is Other ⟆

Founding fathers like Adams created more than a national imaginary of white succession; as in the case of Jefferson, they produced biological offspring from slaves whose stories were not incorporated into the national fantasy. The scandal of miscegenated blood is a topic to which numerous American literary works turn, especially in stories of racial passing *(The Tragic Mulatto, Pudd'nhead Wilson, Of One Blood, The Marrow of Tradition, Passing)* that mark the continuing effects of sexual violence during slavery into the present. Such works, as Russell Castronovo points out, are as much about blood as about race since both figure in the genealogical narrative of national purity. "Revolutionary 'blood' does not always follow predictable pathways and instead gets lost in questions of race and dismemberings of the fathers' law" (3). One work that gathers together themes of patriarchal succession, racial purity, and sexual contamination most powerfully is William Faulkner's *Absalom, Absalom!* The story of Thomas Sutpen's "grand design" to create a dynasty in Yoknapatawpha County is based on a southern heroic ideal of uncontaminated, white inheritance. Sutpen's project is doomed, not only because of his own lower-class roots in tidewater Virginia, but by the potential presence of black blood in his own children. Prior to his arrival in Jefferson, Sutpen had married the daughter of a Spanish creole woman while working as a plantation overseer in Haiti. Realizing that the presence of (real or imagined) African blood in her background would thwart his dynastic plans in the southern states, Sutpen leaves her and his young son behind. When that son, Charles Bon, turns up at college with his son from his second marriage, the threat of miscegenated blood resurfaces. Furthermore, Bon's subsequent intention to marry Judith Sutpen, his father's daughter from that second marriage, adds incest to miscegenation in an exfoliating cycle of familial pollutions. In order to prevent this tragedy of infections, Sutpen's son, Henry, kills Bon to preserve the patriarchal line.

Much of the novel's drama revolves around the "spot of negro blood" that may or may not be carried by Bon into the Sutpen family. The details of Bon's racial background, his intentions toward Judith, his oedipal anxieties about his biological father—these issues are mediated by the various narrators who tell the story, all of whom have some personal stake in the historical meaning of Sutpen's design. We never learn definitively whether or not Bon has that fatal drop of blood since he is never given a chance to narrate his own story. But it little matters since blood in this novel is not a biological or chemical agent; it is a discursive feature of a southern genealogical imperative. One's genetic or racial origin must be searched and codified, its origins subjected to the same scrutiny to which earlier Puritan preachers subjected the lives of New England saints. This speculative endeavor verifies Foucault's thesis concerning sexuality: that its medicalization during the nineteenth century creates it as a subject for speculation and discussion. The murder of Charles Bon is a futile attempt by his brother to stop not only the perpetuation of Negro blood but the endless questioning of blood's contamination, its circulation as a sign within a racist society.

The element that links the various themes that I have adumbrated—blood culture, eugenics, hemophobia—is the role of the Caribbean in Sutpen's past. It is in Haiti that Sutpen earns the money that permits him to build his dynasty in the South and participate in the national fantasy. But that money is made on the backs of African slaves whose blood ultimately returns to "infect" Sutpen's dynastic plan. It is also money made while protecting Haitian plantations from slave revolts that historically served as warnings to southern plantation owners about the spread of dissent to the southern states. Bon's return to his father represents a more subtle form of slave revolt, a return of repressed violence, now practiced under the guise of filial piety and brotherly love. The tainted blood of Sutpen's Haitian sojourn is mixed with the moral taint associated with his megalomaniacal pursuit of southern respectability. One of Faulkner's narrators, Quentin Compson, describes Haiti as "the halfway point between what we call the jungle and what we call civilization, halfway between the dark inscrutable continent from which the black blood . . . was ravished by violence, and the cold known land to which it was doomed" (202). Although *Absalom, Absalom!* is usually seen as an epic of the rural South, it is equally a novel about the Caribbean, "a soil manured with black blood from two hundred years of oppression and exploitation" (202). Thus while the narrative of racialized southern capital takes place in Jefferson, a second narrative of sexual and racial origins takes place in the "other" south of the West Indies. It is in this subsidiary narrative that Blood Culture, the dream of pure, white biological succession, supercedes American Culture.

Haiti not only provides Sutpen with offshore capital; it introduces an alternative sexual economy to the heterosexual code of southern homosociality. Bon is potentially black and potentially incestuous, but he is also regarded as feminine and aristocratic. To Quentin Compson's father, Bon is a kind of dandy:

> the slightly Frenchified cloak and hat which he wore, or perhaps (I like to think this) presented formally to the man reclining in a flowered almost feminised gown, in a sunny window in his chambers—this man handsome elegant and even catlike and too old to be where he was, too old not in years but in experience, with some tangible effluvium of knowledge, surfeit: of actions done and satiations plumbed and pleasures exhausted and even forgotten. (76)

Although Mr. Compson does not speak of homosexuality, his indirect reference to an "effluvium of knowledge" and obscure "actions done" and "satiations" suggest acts that, in his heterosexual economy, have no referent. And as Mr. Compson often points out, Henry's interest in Bon is more than filial: "Yes, he loved Bon, who seduced him as surely as he seduced Judith" (76). As Barbara Ladd notes, Bon represents the "return of a tragic history to the American South—in the guises first of white creole decadence, then of blackness and in the form of retributive justice" (357).

Most commentators have noted the racial threat that Bon poses to Sutpen's dynastic ideal. What is less often observed is that Bon's feminization challenges the heterosexual lineage upon which that dynasty depends, a lineage stressed by the novel's title (Absalom as the firstborn, favorite son of David). This feminization threatens the novel's metaphorics of blood, rearticulating racial otherness as sexual unassimilability. The gendering of Bon as feminized aesthete turns a narrative about filiation into one of same-sex and (potentially) homosexual bonding among brothers. Henry's murder of Bon serves not only to eliminate the threat of African heritage in his family but to stifle Henry's own homosexual desires for the brother who is other. Bon's Haitian background is no small feature in this series of transformations, just as the Caribbean plantation culture functioned as a site of racial danger and revolt throughout the antebellum period.

Absalom, Absalom! revives an earlier version of American anxiety about germs and infection among immigrants, one that returns with AIDS. We could read Bon as the unassimilable hemophiliac, aristocratic and feminine, bearer of a "weak" or recessive gene through his mother, retainer of a tragic and aristocratic, Europeanized past. His threat to southern patriarchal society, based on a genealogical principle among fathers and firstborn sons, is related to his combining two immigrant cultures: Creole (Mediterranean French and Spanish) and African (Haitian). In the media's treatment of AIDS, Haiti often functions as an entry point for the disease, the place where the disease originates or else the point of transition from Africa to the United States. In each case, AIDS comes from outside, entering the national body through unprotected borders. Haiti is a site for infected blood and acts that, like voodoo, challenge American Judeo-Christian identity. In the history of American national fantasy, Haiti functions as a colonial tinderbox where unspeakable revolt may fester and erupt. Furthermore, those eruptions, like the revolt of Toussaint-Louverture, can serve as a moral proof for southern plantation owners that any failure of resolve in maintaining discipline among slaves could lead to disaster. As Faulkner makes clear, social revolt and chaos are carried in the veins as much as in the individual acts of ex-slaves.

"None of Us up Here Have Boyfriends" ⌐

The coalescence of blood, race, and sexuality in Charles Bon raises important questions about the integrity of blood as a marker of national identity. Although he is not a hemophiliac, Bon's threat to the postbellum South—and ultimately to Reconstruction America—is the fiction of racial and sexual pollution that will corrupt patrilineal descent. His identity is articulated through a cultural imaginary that includes figures at the heart of American romance, from Poe and Hawthorne to Anne Rice and Jewell Gomez: feminized invalids, aristocratic recluses, and vampiric predators. Hemophiliacs have historically occupied a similar realm, threatening fixed gender codes in significant ways. Their vulnerability to physical trauma keeps them from participating in the normal indices of heteromasculinity—contact sports, physically demanding work, regular working schedules. Their particular genetic configuration as males who receive a recessive gene through their mothers has traditionally identified them as sissies or mama's boys. As men who bleed internally on a regular basis, hemophiliacs share biological similarities with menstruating women; as men who depend on the blood of others, they occupy a passive or "receptor" position with respect to health delivery systems. As cripples and invalids they contest the American masculine cult of action and energy. The fact that hemophiliacs are, in fact, obsessive risk-takers and exercise addicts has not altered the pervasive image of them as emaciated invalids.

An ad for Helixate FS, a recombinant antihemophilic factor, reinforces the latter by its promotion of the product in *Bloodlines,* a local newsletter of the National Hemophilia Association: "The game is over when it's too dark for them to see. . . . The best of times are on the muddiest fields. . . . Wearing clean clothes is okay when it's a uniform. . . . *Because boys will be boys.*" The gendering of bleeding disorders exposes the degree to which hemophilia is a cultural as well as a medical formation. As such it can be used as a lens by which to view normalcy and national health. The medical model that regards genetically inherited diseases as matters of treatment and rehabilitation fails to represent the gender trouble that accompanies homosocial communities in a homophobic society. The fact that Aventis Behring, which makes Helixate FS, must market its product by projecting a Tom Sawyer version of boyhood testifies to the power of cultural forms in reproducing biological subjects. "Boys will be boys" assures the parents of bleeders that their children will grow up to be real men, and we know what that means.

Within a national AIDS narrative, hemophiliacs played (unwittingly in some cases) an important role in securing an image around which legislation, research, and public policy could be made without having to engage issues of homosexuality and homophobia. Nationally recognized persons with AIDS (PWAs) like Ryan White or the Ray brothers were routinely brought out at public functions to serve as signs that the government was concerned. Yet this concern was expressed in ways that denied gays, Africans, spouses, and partners of PWAs and others infected with

HIV the element of personhood. In its obituary for Ryan White in 1990, *Time* magazine claimed that White "first humanized the disease called AIDS. He allowed us to see the boy who just wanted, more than anything else, to be like other children and to be able to go to school" ("'Miracle' of Ryan White"). The fact that White "humanized" a disease that, by the time of his death, had already killed thousands of humans reinforces Paula Treichler's contention that AIDS is an "epidemic of signification" as well as a lethal disease, perpetuated as much by discursive markers as by the exchange of bodily fluids (32).

Essential to the enforcement of normalcy among hemophiliacs has been the perceived threat to the family as a result of AIDS. Sander Gilman notes that press representations of hemophiliacs with AIDS show the child in the family setting, which contrasts radically with the imposed isolation of the gay man or intravenous drug user with AIDS. "The presence of the family serves to signal the 'normality' of the child and the low risk of transmission, in spite of the child's radical stigmatization" (105). In the case of hemophilia there are institutional reasons for this identification of the bleeder with the family. The earliest medical support groups for hemophiliacs were based on children. The Crippled Children Services (CCS), established in the 1960s, served as advocates for hemophiliacs' orthopedic needs. Their efforts led to passage of the Genetically Handicapped Persons Program (GHPP) in 1974, which provided funding to families for blood products. The Bureau of Maternal and Child Health (MCH) was also formed by the U.S. Public Health Service to monitor federal funds relating to hemophilia. Much hemophiliac socialization was provided for children at special "hemo camps" that provided a positive environment for children whose medical exigencies could be easily accommodated and monitored. In most cases advocacy efforts have been sponsored by parents of hemophilic children.[17] Since hemophilia was, until the 1970s, largely a pediatric disease, it is not surprising that early funding efforts should have been directed at children. Yet this association of hemophilia with children played into the New Right's family values agenda, even in the most innocuous cultural venues.

Nowhere is the discourse of normalcy within hemophilia better illustrated than a talk show of October 1, 1993, in which the host, Phil Donahue, interviewed HIV-infected hemophilic boys along with their mothers. The absence of fathers on the show reinforced the genetic links between mothers and sons, leaving Donahue to serve as the all-purpose nongenetically linked dad to provide the "difficult" questions. In the give-and-take, Donahue stresses the boys' ordinariness by calling attention to how healthy they look or how active they are in school. Most significant for our purposes is that Donahue treats the boys' appearance on his show in the very terms of queer politics—as a coming-out narrative:[18]

> DONAHUE: All right, what's going on here? Are you coming out today?
> MR. BLAND: I came out when I . . . was on a panel in St. Louis with Jeane White [mother of Ryan White], so . . .
> . . . .
> DONAHUE [to Eric Benz, Age fourteen]: You're fourteen and you're going public here for the first time, huh?
> MR. BENZ: Yes.
> DONAHUE: You're in a regular—you go to school every day and—"
> . . . .
> DONAHUE: Josh Lunior—Accord, New York. You're twelve. You're in the sixth grade. Yes, you are HIV-positive. You went public this spring, huh?
> MR. LUNIOR: Yeah.
> DONAHUE: No longer a big secret.

"Coming out" or "going public" as a metaphor for hemophiliacs with AIDS is tolerated in this program because, as Donahue is at pains to emphasize, all of the boys are "normal."

> MR BLAND: I have full-blown AIDS now.
> DONAHUE: You don't look full-blown sick to me.
> MR. BLAND: You can't tell by looking, Phil.
> DONAHUE: You can't? Well, how do you feel? Do you feel any symptoms? Don't you feel weak or—
> MR. BLAND: No, I feel like a normal person.
> DONAHUE: You do? You look like a normal person . . . Very clear of eye.

This sort of banter is conducted with each of the boys. Donahue stresses the fact that despite their illness they don't "look" sick; they have "normal" friends and they all play sports. Speaking to Grant Lewis, age thirteen, Donahue asks, "How about your gang? Everybody understands and they're not, you know, looking at you, waiting for you to . . ." To which Lewis answers, "All my friends have been real supportive." Donahue concludes: "Really? And you lead a normal life? You play any sports . . . ?" The incessant references to sports throughout the interview suggests that it becomes the single index for heteromasculinity, as important for a boy's cultural assimilation as any biological factor.

Although the occasion for the boys' appearance on the show is hemophilia in the AIDS community, Donahue makes their heterosexuality a primary issue:

> AUDIENCE MEMBER: Hi. Do any of you have girlfriends and do they—and what do they think of you?
> . . . .
> DONAHUE: . . . Sure, they do. They have girlfriends, boyfriends and—
> Yes? And enemies, too, I'm sure.
> PANELIST: [off camera] Boyfriends!
> RANDY RAY: None of us up here have boyfriends.

Donahue's intentions may be to alert the public to the hostility faced by hemophiliacs with AIDS, but in order to do this he must differentiate the ostracism these boys have felt from that affecting homosexuals. "None of us up here have boyfriends" is a given on this show, and Donahue reinforces the joke by not mentioning the gay community at all, even though it makes its covert appearance in his responses: :You don't have any—nobody's starting to walk around you, you know, oh, you know, like you're . . ." Donahue's difficulty in completing his sentence, his inability to supply a word for what the boys "have," testifies to the queerness of a dialogue in which disease and sexuality intermingle. What we see in the *Donahue Show* and other such public forums (congressional hearings, talk shows, public rallies) is an attempt to screen off persons with hemophilia as innocent victims whose normalcy as heterosexual males must be preserved. Sexual Otherness is enacted as an inexpressible sentence, something you wouldn't want your son to complete. All of the tropes of masculine normalcy—participation in sports, homosocial contacts with other heterosexual males, interest in girls—are trotted out for public consumption.

And it is the *consumption* of heteronormalcy that is very much at issue in the portrayal of hemophiliacs in AIDS discourse. Since AIDS is, above all, a complex associated with wastage and loss, it challenges consumerist notions of economic health and productivity. The bleeder with AIDS is a double specter of capitalist decay—a male unable to capitalize and retain vital fluids; a sexual body infected by "foreign" and "unsafe" investments. Donahue's desire to produce normal boys out of infectious diseases is underwritten by an economic scenario designed to reassure worried investors.

Queer Coalitions ⌐

In my introductory remarks I mentioned that the emergence of hemophiliacs into AIDS discourse represented a crisis in queer identities as much as in hematology. I want to elaborate this point with reference to the status of the hemophiliac body made visible through AIDS. The public outing of hemophiliacs in forums such as the *Donahue Show* illustrates the extent to which AIDS demands an anatomy, preferably that of a young boy, around which to create public policy. Yet if hemophiliacs have become increasingly visible as they are enlisted in appeals for federal research funding, they remain invisible in AIDS discourse. I have already outlined some of the reasons for their marginalization among gay activists, but given the fact that among severe bleeders HIV infection reached almost 90 percent, it is hard to understand why they have not been more prominent in the debate. In primary books and essays about the culture of AIDS by Douglas Crimp, Paula Treichler, Cindy Patton, Simon Watney, Kenneth MacKinnon, Douglas Feldman, and others, hemophilia is seldom mentioned, if at all. In the index to Cindy Patton's otherwise excellent book *Inventing Aids,* hemophiliacs are referred to as "blood product consumers"—as if their only identity as persons with AIDS is their economic dependency on a product. This is a disservice to persons whose lives were shattered by a debilitating and painful disease and then by AIDS. It also fails to recognize activists within the hemophilia community, some of them gay, who fought this very consumerist relationship and who forged coalitions between the gay and hemophilia AIDS communities. Finally, it reinforces the idea among many cultural critics that issues of disability and disease are medical problems, tied to specific regimes of treatment, not to civil rights or identity-based politics.

The reasons for the marginalization of hemophiliacs in AIDS discourse may attest to the success of the normalization effort mentioned earlier. It may also suggest some limits to the critique of identity politics being waged in the name of Queer Nation. If the concept of queer was mobilized to call into question the identitarian character of post-Stonewall sexual politics, then its more radical implications would be to accommodate a wider network of constituencies than those usually defined by "gay" and "lesbian." If so, these constituencies might include figures usually (but not exclusively) defined as heterosexual. Can a medical condition or disability be construed as queer? Can we know in advance what forms the linking of medical and sexual minorities will take? Is queer an identity or a set of practices? The answers to such questions must first appeal to the performative aspect of queer identities, the extent to which any individual occupies a position from which to subvert or carnivalize gender binaries. In addition, one would have to attend to the interpellative activity by which any individual is enlisted into a given zone of social pathologizing—the extent to which someone called "queer" recognizes herself or himself as the object of such a speech act. I have argued that in certain instances, hemophiliacs have been the subjects of such interpellations, both as feminized men and as medicalized Others. Yet hemophiliacs have also been interpellated into a heterosexist economy in ways that makes their identification with queer politics difficult. What makes hemophiliacs as a group problematic for queer theory is their conflation of an essentialist discourse of blood and a constructivist discourse of feminized masculinity.

Judith Butler observes that the materiality of the body is not a base upon which ancillary performances can be hung, a prediscursive sex that predates gender. Even the most biological of conditions—the absence of a certain protein in red blood cells for example—manifests itself in gendered form. If we cannot fix identities to a material body, we cannot fix "queer" specifically to gay and lesbian identities. If we do, we replicate the very binarist logic that queer theory deconstructs. Butler recognizes that *queer* has a history, and that this should be honored. Yet she understands that the term sometimes represents a "false unity of women and men." She observes, "Indeed it may be that the critique of the term will initiate a resurgence of both feminist and anti-racist mobilization within lesbian and gay politics or open up new possibilities for coalitional alliances that do not presume that these constituencies are radically distinct from one another" (*Bodies* 229). Among those "possibilities for coalitional alliances" would be figures whose material bodies have been the sites of normalizing discourses and who, in order to claim authority over their own bodies, have had to emerge from closets they never knew they inhabited. One could think of numerous groups similarly positioned: African Americans with sickle-cell disease (whose dependency on transfusions places them in a conditions analogous to hemophiliacs), deaf persons, the homeless, quadriplegics, the visually impaired, welfare "mothers" (insofar as persons on financial assistance are usually seen as women)—all such groups and persons occupy multiple positions with regard to gendered and socialized norms.[19] In the terms introduced earlier, they are nominal queers whose cultural marginality has been articulated through narrow venues of medical and social advocacy. And in most cases their social marginality to heteronormal society results from processes of gendering that feminizes in order to disempower. At the same time, if these coalitions are going to place their new queerness in service to larger social goals, they must mobilize as much against antihomophobic and antiracist agendas as against the corporatization of medicine, social services, and health care.

The current upbeat prognosis for AIDS treatment—the success of protease inhibitors in combination with AZT, the success of sex education programs—gives one cautious optimism about a possible decline of the pandemic.[20] But these advances must be set against the high costs of combination therapies that limit access to such treatments to those who have adequate means. Gains made in restricting the spread of AIDS must be qualified by one's awareness of increasing federal and state initiatives curtailing the rights of gays and lesbians, denial of health care to immigrants, and attacks against public assistance to the poor—all in the name of family values. And most significantly, the diminishment of new AIDS cases must be measured against the huge increase in AIDS throughout the developing world, especially in Africa, China, and India. Hemophiliacs may breathe a collective sigh of relief that the safety of the blood supply has been assured, but they must be wary of retreating into a "clot closet" where bleeding is treated strictly as a matter of genetics and medicine. The lesson we, as hemophiliacs, should derive from AIDS is that, as a syndrome, it is spread by more than bodily fluids; it is spread by prejudice and stereotype, paranoia and phobia, diseases over which science has little control. AIDS activists have made such categories the subject of a powerful social critique, but unless the boundaries of Queer Nation include citizens of Blood Culture, such a critique will remain a relatively sectarian affair.

Chapter 2
Phantom Limbs
Film Noir's Volatile Bodies

They had the crutches to stare at. They never really
looked at the man.
—Barton Keyes in *Double Indemnity*

Specular Distractions ↩

In Jacques Tourneur's film *Out of the Past* (1947), a deaf boy (Dickie
Moore) protects Jeff Bailey (Robert Mitchum) from police and gangsters
who, for differing reasons, are pursuing him for his role in a murder. Jeff
is subsequently killed by the femme fatale, Kathie (Jane Greer) when she
discovers that he is handing her over to the police as the killer. When Jeff's
current girlfriend, Ann (Virginia Huston), asks the deaf boy whether Bailey had intended to return to Kathie, the boy nods, telling a lie that frees
her from her emotional dependence on the hero and permits her to marry
a local policeman. In *The Fallen Sparrow* (1943), Kit (John Garfield), having been tortured in prison during the Spanish Civil War, is haunted by
one of his tormentors, a man with a "dragging foot" who has followed him
back to the United States. The sound of the man's dragging foot reduces
the shell-shocked Kit to shuddering hysteria until, faced with evidence
that his pursuer is a Nazi spy, the hero confronts him in a final shootout.
In *The Blue Dahlia* (1946) Johnny Morrison (Alan Ladd) has returned
from World War II to find that his wife, Helen (Doris Dowling), has been
unfaithful to him. After an argument between them, Helen is killed, and
suspicion points to Johnny, but more particularly, to his wartime buddy,

Buzz (William Bendix), who was injured in the war and suffers from what we would now call post-traumatic stress syndrome. Buzz's mental disability, although not evident all the time, causes him to become violent whenever he hears certain kinds of loud music.[1]

These examples from classic film noirs could be expanded to include numerous films from the 1940s and 1950s in which a person with a disability plays a supporting role, serving as a marker for larger narratives about normalcy and legitimacy.[2] The deaf boy in *Out of the Past* mirrors Jeff Bailey's flawed, yet stoical integrity, providing a silent riposte to the flashy glamor of and tough-guy patter between the other males in the film. The figure of the limping Nazi spy in *Fallen Sparrow* enables the director, Richard Wallace, to use disability to shift Kit's problematic leftist collaboration with Republican Spain to World War II patriotism. Buzz's disability in *The Blue Dahlia* annexes the era's concern about soldiers psychologically damaged in the war. In the latter case, the U.S. Navy and the film Production Code censors vetoed screenwriter Raymond Chandler's original ending for the movie in which Buzz is the killer of Johnny's wife. They felt that in 1945, representing returning navy vets as psychotic killers was not in the interest of national healing.[3] In most cases disabled figures play cameo roles, much as black, Latino, or Asian figures provide a racialized counternarrative to the hero's existential malaise. In Eric Lott's terms the proximity of a racially marked character assists in "darkening" the white hero, linking him to more subversive or morally suspect forces within the society at large. A similar troping of able-bodied disability appears in films based around a male who, although internally wounded, must nevertheless be physically able to walk down the mean streets of cold war America.[4]

This phenomenon can be partially explained by what David Mitchell and Sharon Snyder call "narrative prosthesis," the use of disability to enable a story. The disabled body serves as a "crutch upon which literary narratives lean for their representational power, disruptive potentiality, and analytical insight" (49). If narrative closure depends on restoration of the able-bodied individual (to health, society, normalcy), the disabled character represents a form of deviance necessary for marking the body's unruliness. But disability may often facilitate other narratives not so easily represented. Moreover, it may utilize the disabled body as a site for social panics about volatile bodies in general, diverting the public gaze from one stigmatized identity onto another. Hence my title, "Phantom Limbs," refers to the residual sensation of narratives that the film cannot represent or reconstitute. We might say that the phantom limb phenomenon is the affective response to narrative prosthesis, the way that trauma is experienced after the limb has been surgically removed and therapy undergone.[5]

The phantom limb phenomenon is especially prevalent in film noir, a genre that emerged during a period of cold war consensus when the maintenance of normalcy and national health coincided with geopolitical imperatives at large. Cultural representations of sexual or personal excess, from Elvis's gyrating hips to Beat bohemians and motorcycle outlaws, were dismissed by consensus intellectuals, on the one hand, or heavily monitored by congressional investigating committees and the Motion Picture Production Code, on the other.[6] Film noir sometimes supported those goals by celebrating returning war heroes or crooks that go straight, yet many of them (often made by black- or gray-listed directors) achieved their ends by presenting dystopian views of marginal social types: the criminal, the disgraced detective, the wrongly accused fugitive. The noir hero is a tough loner who is flawed but who has integrity in a corrupt world. He fights on his own terms, even though he is haunted by a dark past. Although he is usually described as prey to the femme fatale, his non-domestic status and bachelorhood mark him as a sexually indeterminate figure. His shadowy relationship to the dominant culture is established by a range of cinematic techniques that destabilize the viewing experience. Expressionist camera angles, high-contrast lighting, disjunctive scores, voice-overs, and flashbacks stylistically reinforce an atmosphere of anxiety and paranoia. Lost in an anonymous bureaucratic system or suffering from trauma of events incurred during the war; the noir hero must discover a code of honor based on contingent necessity rather than sanctioned authority.

To historicize the phantom limb phenomenon with regard to cold war culture, one might look at the ways that physical disability served as a marker of gender trouble. Film noir is usually described as a masculine genre, marked by its literary origins in the hard-boiled detective novel, but it is often characterized by anxiety over the stability and definition of gender roles. Although the Production Code severely limited what could be shown of "deviant" passions, noir films created unforgettable gay icons— the fussy, effeminate Joe Cairo (Peter Lorre) in *The Maltese Falcon* (1941);

the effeminate drama critic Waldo Lydecker (Clifton Webb) in *Laura* (1944); the butch masseuse in *In a Lonely Place* (1950); and the "malignantly fey" Bruno Antony (Robert Walker) in *Strangers on a Train* (1951)— that have earned the genre a high status in queer culture (Russo, 94). These thinly veiled figures of gay and lesbian identity serve to show, through their metonymic relationship with him, that although the noir hero is often conflicted sexually, his heteromasculinity is never in serious question. In Richard Dyer's terms, such sexually marginal figures "remind us of how far [the noir hero is] removed from that sort of thing" (69).

"That sort of thing" may help shore up a normative sexuality, but it also provides a conflicted specular site that complicates the viewing of film noir generally. Robert J. Corber notes that in Otto Preminger's 1944 film *Laura*, Clifton Webb's portrayal of the homosexual theater critic Lydecker reinforces a "transgressive form of visual pleasure film noir offered spectators." According to Corber, "Webb's willingness to make a spectacle of his homosexuality hindered the spectator's absorption in the diegesis, which was one of the primary goals of the classical system. It encouraged a mobile and ambulatory gaze that was easily distracted by the surface of the image" (56). Although Lydecker is not disabled, he occupies a place of specular "distraction" often occupied by such figures. When the detective, Mark McPherson [Dana Andrews] interviews him in a bathtub, for example, McPherson's sexual obsession with Laura is disrupted and redirected at the naked male body. The fact that the body belongs to a drama critic reinforces the theatrical character of such distractions throughout the film.[7]

In numerous film noirs, a physical or cognitive disability marks a sexual inscrutability, otherwise unspeakable within terms of 1940s and 1950s Production Code directives. Film theory has focused extensively on the mantis-like features of the femme fatale, but less has been said about her husband, whose disability serves as a camera obscura upon the noir hero's existential wounds. In *Double Indemnity* (1944) Phyllis Dietrichson's husband is on crutches; in *The Lady from Shanghai* (1948), Elsa Bannister's husband wears braces and uses a cane; in *Walk on the Wild Side* (1962), Jo's husband's legs have been amputated, and he pulls himself around on a dolly. In all three films, the husband's crippled condition contrasts with the noir hero's phallic potency, but it also surrounds the body with a visual spectacle that exceeds the narrative's ability to contain it. The presence of a disabled figure complicates the triangular gaze among viewer, noir hero, and femme fatale and provides a means of representing perversity that cannot be solved by reference to the film's diegesis.

By speaking of the femme fatale's husband, I am speaking metaphorically about a figure, male or female, whose disability thwarts the smooth functioning of a heterosexual gaze. Because psychoanalytic gaze theory has been based largely on an oedipalized dyad, it has not been able to address the ways that other subjectivities are constructed and contested through acts of looking. In Robert Aldrich's 1963 film *Whatever Happened to Baby Jane,* for example, a former child star, Jane Hudson (Betty Davis), has been forgotten by Hollywood, while her disabled sister, Blanche (Joan Crawford), is still remembered, despite being a paraplegic. In the film's visual rhetoric, Blanche is the stoical, beautiful former actress who is now tragically crippled, while Jane is the able-bodied but mentally deranged, alcoholic shell of her former self. Much of the film's drama is based around the ways that Jane's heterosexual gaze is mediated by a Hollywood studio system that promotes ideals of youthful beauty against aging and physical decay. Jane fantasizes that she is still Baby Jane until she looks into the mirror and sees her decrepit, older self, a rather uncanny filmic revision of Wilde's *Portrait of Dorian Gray.* She then looks into the "mirror" of her disabled sister and sees the success that she never had. Both gazes intensify her growing insanity. The film demonstrates how heterosexual desire is constructed through institutional contexts that disability makes strange.

A cinematic phantom limb provides a diversion for a more subtle subplot about same-sex alliances. In the first of these films, Walter Neff's (Fred MacMurray) appropriation of Mr. Dieterichson's (Tom Powers) crutches diverts attention from the affectionate relationship between Neff and his insurance coworker, Barton Keyes (Edward G. Robinson); in the second, Arthur Bannister's (Everett Sloan) crutches, braces, and exaggerated pelvic thrust mediate his queer relationship with his law partner, George Thirsby (Glenn Anders); and in the third, Jo's (Barbara Stanwyck) husband's amputated condition frames her erotic desire for the female lead (Capucine). Each of these examples illustrates how the disabled body reinforces a normative heterosexuality embodied by the noir hero even as it allows another sexuality to "pass" before the eyes of the Breen Office censors. Filmic passing is performed when homosexual content is con-tained by the period's "compulsory homosociality," in which same-sex al-liances and power are reinforced by excluding women and in which the threat of genitalized contact is replaced by official forms of male bond-ing.[8] Such formations become important in a society in which certain types of homosocial association (Neff's and Keyes' loyalty to the insurance firm, Bannister's and Grisby's participation in the law) are essential to the perpetuation of capitalist hegemony. When women get together, as in *Walk on the Wild Side*, such associations, instead of providing a socially (and economically) redemptive community, are signs of lesbian attach-ments and prostitution.

A particularly lucid example of this double vector of sexualities and disabilities is Andrew Niccol's 1997 *Gattaca*, in which the genetically "in-valid" but physically able-bodied main character, Vincent Freeman (Ethan Hawke), must appropriate the genetically "pure" DNA of the paraplegic, Jerome Morrow (Jude Law), to participate in a specialized space pro-gram.[9] The fact that the relationship between the two men is thematized as queer by, for instance, their sharing of bodily fluids, spaces and identi-ties reinforces the close link between narratives of genetic perfection and sexual pollution. Jerome's self-immolation at the end of the film provides an all-too-typical Hollywood denouement for both queers and disabled figures. Here Vincent's crippled condition is the prosthesis that supple-ments the film's allegory of physical perfection; his queerness supple-ments the film's allegory of heterosexual normalcy, figured in the main character. Although the film was made in 1997, its cinematic techniques and themes of alienation and social control are similar to many aspects of film noir.[10]

It would be reductive to see the disabled figure in film noir merely as a surrogate for queer identity, but it is safe to say that these films build on a well-established connection between disability and sexuality that can be found in cultural texts from *Richard III* to *Fight Club*. Representations of a king, "rudely stamped," or a man with dissociative identity disorder (DID) manifest themselves through narratives about nonnormative sexu-ality;[11] the perceived weakness (in these cases) of masculine power seems impossible to express outside of sexual difference. As Robert McRuer defines the phenomenon,

The system of compulsory able-bodiedness that produces disability
is thoroughly interwoven with the system of compulsory heterosexuality that produces queerness . . . compulsory heterosexuality is
contingent on compulsory able-bodiedness and vice versa. ("Compulsory Able-Bodiedness" 89)

Finding the historical specifics of compulsory able-bodiedness is an important task for disabilities and queer studies, but such scholarship is often limited by residual medical and psychoanalytic models that generalize
the connection of bodies and sexualities around narratives of loss and
lack. What, then, is the body of theory that the phantom limb remembers?

Disabling Theory ↩

Midge, do you suppose many men wear corsets?
—Scottie Ferguson, in *Vertigo*

Before looking more closely at my filmic examples, I want to frame my
readings by considering feminist psychoanalytic film theory, for which
film noir is often a test case for how subjects are enlisted in dominant
structures of desire. Because such theory has been important for understanding how cinema structures acts of looking through gendered spectacles, it has disabled the disability narrative of many films by treating acts
of looking and gazing as defined by castration. For Slavoj Žižek, the fantasy object creates an "immobilizing, crippling effect" upon the subject
who must transform his "impotence into power by means of the gaze"
("Hitchcockian Blot" 126). Claire Johnston notes that *Double Indemnity*'s
title sequence, showing a man on crutches, places the movie "under the
sign of castration" (90). By equating visibility and acts of looking with castration, by equating feminine "lack" with physical difference, this theoretical approach always renders the missing limb as a missing phallus.
Whether one agrees or argues with this reading of visual pleasure, it is
defined by an Oedipus whose blindness must always be seen as fatal loss,
whose insight must be purchased through self-mutilation. Since much
film noir criticism is indebted to this tradition, it serves as a kind of theoretical gaze itself, creating the terms by which films suture the "incomplete" body onto the "incomplete" woman.[12]

In her influential 1975 article "Visual Pleasure and Narrative Cinema," Laura Mulvey proposes that phallocentrism "depends on the image of the castrated woman to give order and meaning to its world" (746). This Freudian truism is embodied in classical narrative cinema in which the camera adopts the position of the male protagonist as active viewer of a passive female subject. Through "looking" or scopophilia, the male seeks to gain erotic control of that which he finds threatening. The fear of castration drives the male protagonist, often a detective or police inspector, to establish his authority by fixing the female's actions through voyeurism and fetishization. Film noir's extensive use of flashback and voice-over to interpret the diegetic material reinforces such male control by framing threatening (libidinal) events from the past in the voice of authority who may provide a "rational" and "truthful" narrative.[13]

For Mulvey the films of Alfred Hitchcock embody this fetishized gaze since they invariably center on a wounded protagonist's anxiety about the reality of the female object of his desire. In *Rear Window* (1954) Jeff Jeffries (Jimmy Stewart), wearing a cast and confined to a wheelchair, compensates for his inactivity by speculating on the lives of his neighbors from the vantage of his window. His detection of a murder in an apartment opposite his follows from his perceptiveness as a photographer, but it is facilitated by his girlfriend, Lisa Fremont (Grace Kelly), whose erotic interest for Jeff increases as she becomes involved in the detection process. Jeff's interest in the murder is also stimulated by the fact that the crime is committed against a bedridden woman, Mrs. Thorwald, who is thus an "invalid" like himself. Although she is confined to her bed, Mrs. Thorwald is capable of haranguing and provoking her husband, Lars (Raymond Burr), thereby providing Jeff with a negative example of domestic life that seems to confirm the wisdom of maintaining his bachelorhood, despite Lisa's marital designs on him. Jeff's identification with the feminized invalid is complete when, at the end of the movie, he is attacked by Mr. Thorwald and must defend himself by using the flash attachment from his camera to temporarily blind his attacker. The idea of the impotent male warding off the able-bodied attacker by blinding him with an empty camera would seem to complicate Mulvey's idea that the castrating gaze must always be directed at the female protagonist.

Once Lisa moves—quite literally—into Jeff's line of vision by entering the perpetrator's apartment, Jeff's scopophilic desire increases and he begins to regard her as a possible companion and sexual partner. In terms made familiar by Mulvey, Jeff overcomes his physical limitation—his impotent position in a wheelchair—by focusing his gaze on solving a crime and by controlling Lisa's actions in his line of sight.[14] Although Lisa, a high-fashion model, has presented herself to Jeff's (and the viewer's) view in various seductive outfits, it is only in his fantasy of murder and marital intrigue across the courtyard that her performance of femininity achieves its required erotic element.

In Mulvey's second example, *Vertigo* (1958), former police detective Scottie Ferguson (Jimmy Stewart) is disabled by a paralyzing fear of heights. Now retired, he agrees to help an old friend, Gavin Elster (Tom Helmore), by keeping an eye on his wife, Madeleine, who, he claims, has become obsessed with a long-dead female relative, Carlotta Valdez. It turns out that the woman Elster tells Scottie to follow is not Elster's wife but his mistress (Kim Novak) whom he has made over to resemble Madeleine in a plot to murder her. While tailing the impersonator around the streets of San Francisco, Scottie gradually becomes obsessed with her and, more significantly, with *her* supposed obsession with a dead ancestor. Finally, she leads him to a mission south of the city where, seemingly under Carlotta's sway, she appears to leap from a tower to her death. But the woman Scottie sees falling is, of course, the real Madeleine, Elster's wife. Elster, expecting Scottie's vertigo to keep him from climbing the tower to save her, has counted on his taking what he has seen for a suicide. In despair over the apparent loss of (and inability to save) the woman with whom he has fallen in love, Scottie meets another woman, Judy Barton (Novak), who resembles Madeleine. In a series of brutally demeaning scenes in fashionable boutiques and hair salons, Scottie makes Judy over into Madeleine, much as her former lover, Elster, turned her into his wife. It turns out that Judy *is* the impersonator of Madeleine, and she, responding to what she imagines as Scottie's desire for her, seizes his reappearance in her life as an opportunity to rekindle their romance. But her hopes are doomed since Scottie, who eventually realizes who she is, actually loves the dead Madeleine, for whom the working-class Judy can only be a simulacrum. In the climactic scene, Scottie takes Judy, dressed as Madeleine, back to the mission bell tower to reenact the deception. There, after Scottie confronts her about her role in deceiving him, Judy falls to her death.

As Mulvey notes, Scottie's obsessive pursuit of Madeleine and his equally obsessive desire to re-create her in Judy are seen from "our" point of view; there is no room for Judy's perspective. "Apart from one flashback from Judy's point of view, the narrative is woven around what Scottie sees or fails to see" (755). Scottie's fear of heights is transferred onto his ability to control the image of Madeleine, and we become complicit in this act of coercion. In both *Rear Window* and *Vertigo*, Hitchcock represents the attempt of a male to overcome a disability, coded as impotence, by re-creating the woman into the object of his own fantasy. Lisa, the object of society's desire as a fashion model at first, must be made into the object of Jeff's binocular gaze; Judy, the working girl from Kansas, must be made over into the aristocratic Madeleine.

Mulvey's article launched a broad critical attempt to develop a theory of female spectatorship. The work of Teresa de Lauretis, Claire Johnston, Karen Hollinger, Tania Modelski, Linda Williams, and others retrieves a feminine gaze from Mulvey's scopophilia. Modelski, for example, notes that Scottie's former girlfriend, Midge, possesses important knowledge that Scottie lacks, her spectacles bespeaking clear insight into the constructed nature of gender as against his mystified vision. Modelski also criticizes Mulvey's failure to consider the crucial scene in *Vertigo* in which Judy does gaze back at the camera, recognizing her own complicity in Scottie's fantasy, and, by acknowledges the camera's presence, placing us in command of knowledge that Scottie lacks (87).[15]

What is disturbing about both Mulvey's and her critics' responses to Hitchcock and noir films generally is the ease with which they accept castration as a definition of the disabled protagonist's relation to woman. Rather than call into question Freud's theory of castration anxiety—which is a theory of sexual differentiation based upon lack—these critics redirect their focus from the Lacanian symbolic, the realm of language and law, to the imaginary, the child's preoedipal ties to the mother. The heterosexual relationship between protagonist and femme fatale is not altered; the power dynamics are merely readjusted between genders. This approach has implications for our reading of the disabled figure in film noir since it fails to recognize his links to female characters around him. Although such links are often pathologized (Norman Bates [Anthony Perkins] in *Psycho* is an obvious case in point), they are complicating factors in any treatment of gender. When Scottie asks Midge if many men wear corsets, he is also asking about the role he must assume when wearing clothing usually identified with women—and by extension when placed in a culturally disabled position vis-à-vis normative bodies. To see Scottie here as representing his castrated state in relation to a maternal figure seems beside the point. To see him recognizing the ways that disability in a compulsorily heterosexual and ableist world is figured as feminine helps explain his obsessiveness over Madeleine. Midge, as a designer of women's underwear, knows something about male fantasies as well as about the construction of bodies according to male designs (she claims that the brassiere she is drawing in this scene was designed by an aircraft engineer). Scottie's inability to live within his "darned fear of heights" is also his inability to live in a world that expects certain actions of each gender. Vertigo is equally a fear of gender uncertainty when the normative body is no longer normal.

Noir Bodies ↶

You know, a dame with a rod is like a guy with a knitting needle.
    —FISHER IN *Out of the Past*

In shifting my focus to film noir I would like to build on Mulvey's important idea that cinema constructs its viewers through the gaze but add that the viewer is neither unitary nor necessarily a heterosexual male. Furthermore the "gaze" in film noir is not so simply a reincarnation of some primal scene—the child witnessing his parents *in flagrante delicto,* the mother revealed as castrated. The gaze occurs in highly specific historical contexts that frame what the act of seeing means. In the period during which film noirs were being made, specularity often implied acts of surveillance and political scrutiny that had specific geopolitical implications for national security.[16] As I will point out at the end of this chapter, the ahistorical reading of the wounded hero in psychoanalytic film noir theory needs to be contextualized by reference to the historical fact of disability in the postwar period, particularly through the many disabled veterans who returned from World War II and the rise of prosthetic technology to address their impairments.

    For Mulvey, the invariable object of the protagonist's gaze is a woman, but what happens when the protagonist is himself the object of scrutiny—

when his or her crippled body is no less a spectacle than that of the femme fatale? Such is the case with Billy Wilder's *Double Indemnity*. Most theorists of film noir regard *Double Indemnity*, based on James M. Cain's thriller, as the ur-noir film where many of the terms for the cycle were invented. The opening credits foreground the importance of disability in the film by superimposing titles over a man with crutches who moves menacingly toward us until his shadowy form covers the entire screen. Given the film's setting within an insurance company, the credits announce not only the physical but economic impact of that menace.[17] The film opens with Walter Neff driving erratically through the early morning Los Angeles streets, arriving at the Pacific All-Risk Insurance building and staggering to the office of his coworker, Barton Keyes. There, he starts a Dictaphone and confesses his role in an insurance scam. Neff's confession—which becomes the intermittent voice-over for the entire movie—begins by identifying himself through the rhetoric of an insurance affidavit: "Walter Neff, insurance agent, thirty-five years old, unmarried, no visible scars . . . [he glances down at his wounded shoulder] . . . until a little while ago." The visible scar refers to the bullet wound recently inflicted by Phyllis Dietrichson, but it also refers to the film's thematics of visibility and invisibility in which the couple has had to maintain the appearance of normalcy ("no visible scars") in order to conceal their role in a crime.

Neff is erotically attracted to Phyllis Dietrichson when he first encounters her wearing only a bath towel and an anklet in her Los Feliz home, but his ardor diminishes once he becomes inveigled into her plot to kill her husband and collect on an insurance policy. The risky nature of their scheme initially heightens their mutual sexual attraction, but once the deed has been done, erotics is diverted onto its cover-up. The couple becomes edgy and short-tempered, their meetings more fugitive. The erotic charge that prompted Walter to collude with Phyllis in a murder plot is transferred to his associate, Keyes, an investigator whose relentless pursuit of insurance malfeasance is inspired by what he calls a "little man" inside him. His belief in actuarial odds leads him to suspect that the insurance claim filed by Mrs. Dietrichson is a fraud and that she has colluded with a shadowy lover to murder the husband and make it look like an accident. Keyes' accuracy in pinpointing the fraud earns Neff's respect and establishes the terms of male competitiveness and camaraderie that drive the movie, a bonding reinforced by witty repartee shared by the two men. At one point, after Neff lights Keyes's cigar, Walter says, "I love you, too," a remark repeated at the end of the movie, but given emotional force by the fact that Neff is now dying of a bullet wound. While Keyes comforts him Neff says, "[You] know why you didn't figure this one, Keyes? Let me tell you. The guy you were looking for was too close. He was right across the desk from you." To which Keyes replies, "[Closer] than that, Walter." "I love you too," Neff says, in his final line before dying. This final scene of male consolation is a good deal more intimate than most of the scenes between Neff and Phyllis, leading some critics to suspect that Neff's voice-over is more of a lover's confession than a report.[18]

The homosocial desire between the two men is framed in terms of professional respect against the brittle ambition of the female lead. But unlike the homosocial triad diagnosed by Eve Sedgwick, in which males form alliances *through* the female, there is a second triad in which Neff and Keyes' relationship is bound to the husband (1–5). Mr. Dietrichson, who has become disabled in a construction site accident, is scheduled to attend his homecoming football game by traveling on a train. On the way to the station, he is murdered by Neff while Phyllis drives the car (in Cain's novel, Dietrichson is strangled with his own crutches). Neff impersonates the husband by adopting his crutches and catching the train for which Dietrichson had bought tickets. Neff's plan involves faking a fall from the back of the train, whereupon the previously murdered husband would be placed on the tracks, making the murder seem like an accident. Here, Neff's prosthetic crutches join him to a male who is both literally and symbolically disabled: literally through an accident and symbolically through his relationship to a scheming wife. But such filmic depictions are less about persons with disabilities than the role such persons play in a corporate world dependent on defining and restricting plausible forms of injury. When Billy Wilder changed the name of Cain's insurance company, from Fidelity to All Risk, he pointed to the instability of bodies that must be "covered" by actuarial odds. But he pointed to other, sexual risks that occur when the domestic frame is broken and the wife begins to take out her own policies. Wilder makes pointed reference to Keyes' being "married" to his job and to the idea that by being unmarried, he may have more time to pursue his passion for work. Neff, too, is unmarried, spending his bachelor hours in bars and bowling allies, and while one might see both as examples of the corporate-driven, other-directed individual diagnosed by sociologists of the period, they are also figures whose indefinite sexuality is covered by a pair of crutches.

The links between wounded husband and lover are highlighted by the shadowy person on crutches slowly advancing into the foreground in the opening credits. Because he is shot entirely in black, he could be either Neff or Dietrichson. The links are reinforced by the fact that once the murder is completed, Neff assumes a paternal role in relation to Dietrichson's daughter from a former marriage. This role places him in direct conflict with Phyllis as the evil stepmother and replicates the exact circumstance of the Dietrichson family romance. And just as she schemed to get rid of her husband, so Phyllis intends to kill Neff once he becomes squeamish about the insurance fraud aspect of the crime. Finally, Neff is literally "crippled" at the end of the film by Phyllis, whose bullet causes him to bleed into the fabric of his coat as he recites his confession to Keyes. Thus, the "visible scars" that mark Neff's fatal attraction for Mrs. Dietrichson link him to her disabled husband in ways that ultimately prove fatal.

Double Indemnity is framed, fore and aft, by the sign of disability. From the opening credits, with its menacing man on crutches, to the finale, with Keyes leaning over the bleeding Neff, men are wounded. It has been common to interpret such wounds as psychosexual—the ill effects of momism and liberated women. I see the metaphorics of disability differently, located not in the individual on crutches but in a climate of normalized gender roles measured, as Keyes brilliantly displays in one scene, by actuarial tables and probabilities. As Michael Szaley observes, Cain's novel was conceived among a number of New Deal works—including *The Postman Always Rings Twice* (1934), Betty Smith's *A Tree Grows in Brooklyn* (1943), Kenneth Fearing's *The Big Clock* (1946), and, as we will see, *The Lady from Shanghai*—which deal in some way with insurance. What Wallace Stevens called "the age of insurance" continued well into the 1960s, and Billy Wilder acknowledged the fact by repeating Neff's second-floor view of anonymous clerical desks in the insurance company in the *The Apartment* (Szalay 11). In this 1960s movie, as in *Double Indemnity*, the risk attached to bodies in normalized roles is directly linked to male alienation in a homosocial corporate environment. Between Cain's novel and Wilder's movie we move from Fidelity to Risk, from New Deal social programs like Social Security to postwar private sphere competitiveness. The threat that bodily injury might not be "covered" takes on a sexual cast in a movie in which female sexuality is trumped by Keyes' "little man," a kind of intuition that defies both corporate hierarchy and actuarial logic.

A variation on triangulation between lover, disabled husband, and femme fatale occurs in Orson Welles's *The Lady from Shanghai*, between Elsa Bannister (Rita Hayworth), her husband, Arthur (Everett Sloan), and a tough Irish sailor and aspiring novelist, Michael O'Hara, played by Welles. As in *Double Indemnity* the wife involves the male protagonist in a scheme to murder her husband, but the plot goes awry, and Bannister's partner, Grisby is killed, with Michael set up as the fall guy. Much of the movie involves establishing the erotic relationship between Elsa and Michael, but there is a second, queer connection between Arthur and Grisby that has never been discussed. Although he is Bannister's law partner, Grisby is also inexplicably included in a yacht trip from New York to San Francisco, suggesting more than professional connections with the family.

Arthur Bannister walks with crutches and braces, a sign, for any viewer of the 1940s, of the virulent poliomyelitis epidemic that affected thousands of people in the postwar era and that was ameliorated by development of the Salk vaccine in the mid-1950s. Although Bannister is not disabled in the novel upon which the movie is made (Sherwood King's *If I Die Before I Wake*), Welles made him a polio survivor presumably in order to link him with a virus associated in the public mind with impotence and physical wastage. Polio was seldom fatal, but it disfigured the limbs and limited physical activities severely. Daniel Wilson notes that the disease had a profound impact on young men in the highly masculinized postwar period, creating "an infant-like dependency: temporary loss of control over bladder and bowel and of sexual function, confinement to bed and dependency on others for the most basic necessities" (9).[19] The disease was initially called "infantile paralysis," but even when the name was changed, polio continued to be associated with childhood diseases and childlike conditions. Such infantalizing associations with polio drove FDR to hide all signs of his disability throughout his four terms as president. Fred Davis's 1963 sociological study of polio survivors and their families points out that in the United States, "crippling not only signifies a relative loss of physical mobility but also suggests social abnormality, isolation, and in the eyes of some, visible manifestation of inherent malevolence" (qtd. in Gould 219). By displaying Bannister's crutches and braces, Welles built upon several layers of 1940s social stigma: fear of contagion, often identified with immigrants who first manifested the disease in the early part of the century, anxiety about physical emaciation and wastage in a productivist economy, and paternalist philanthropic responses to the disease, manifested by the March of Dimes' fund-raising effort. All of these associations figure Bannister as an "unfit" husband for Elsa, but they also blend into his effeminate manner and theatrical courtroom gestures.

One scene that points up the queer connections among characters occurs at a fiesta that Bannister has arranged. While sailing up the coast of Mexico, the ship's passengers and crew go ashore. Bannister and Grisby carry on a drunken conversation that mocks Michael's macho toughness and Elsa's seductiveness, while establishing a collusion between them that is more than professional. Many of their references to Michael's heterosexual prowess are coded in terms of disability. Bannister says that if Michael wants to compete in their verbal sparring, he'll need a "handicap" (earlier, at the seaman's hiring hall, Bannister asks Michael if he is "able-bodied"). Responding to the news that Michael might be quitting the ship, Bannister retorts to his wife that "George likes to have [Michael] around, Lover; Michael's so big and strong—makes a good bodyguard for you . . . a big strong bodyguard with an Irish brogue." The bitchy repartee between Bannister and George over Michael's body sets up a speech by the latter about sharks that devour each other, a remark that applies to the Bannisters and their moneyed idleness but also to the homoerotic interchange we have just witnessed. Elsa is the focal point of the interchange— her beauty and youth counterpoised to Michael's strength and virility. She is shot in soft lighting and gauzy filters, gazing upward at Michael, in sharp contrast to Grisby and Bannister, who are shot in harsh, low key-light and unflattering close-ups showing their sweaty faces and grotesque grimaces.

Grisby's presence in this and other scenes is one of generalized sexual threat. He leers at Elsa in a bathing suit, attempts to seduce Michael into a complicated insurance scam, and whines in a sycophantic way at Bannister. Although his threat is not overtly homosexual, Grisby's effeminate manner and unspecified links to both Bannisters create narrative ambiguities that have plagued most readings of the film. While critics have attempted to resolve these ambiguities by focusing on the triangle of the

Bannisters and O'Hara as primary players in a heterosexual drama of sexual intrigue, they have ignored Grisby's odd presence as O'Hara's provocateur and nemesis.[20] Furthermore, Grisby's ambiguous sexuality combines with his right-wing political allegiances (he served on a pro-Franco committee, in contrast to O'Hara's participation in the Lincoln Brigade) and cold war paranoia. He is obsessed with the threat of nuclear annihilation and wants to escape to a desert island where he will be safe. In these scenes, Welles wears his leftist sympathies broadly on his sleeve while demonizing the idle, right-wing rich.

Grisby's nuclear paranoia is embodied in the telescope that he carries with him to spy (for no apparent reason) on various members of the yachting entourage. He uses the telescope to capture Elsa in a bathing suit, sitting on a rock in a perfect imitation of a *Photoplay* magazine pinup.[21] He later trains his optic on Bannister lurching up the beach with his braces while others carry heavy hampers around him. The first shot reminds us of the camera's specular potential within the Hollywood "star" system—Rita Hayworth as well-known "bombshell" and sex goddess, made famous from her role in *Gilda*. Welles critiques this system broadly in this film by showing Hayworth in pinup poses and then cutting to a close-up of Grisby, sweating and grinning, while holding his telescope. But just as Welles participates in the system by fetishizing Hayworth's pose, so he uses her physical perfection in contrast to Bannister's disability in these matching shots. Both "good" and "bad" bodies are viewed through the optic of the sexually (and politically) tainted Grisby. The message is about contagion, Elsa's physical perfection tainted by her proximity to a camera lens and crippled husband. The fact that Welles and Hayworth were themselves going through a difficult divorce at the time that the film was being made adds yet another layer to the film's thematics of specular control.

Bannister's disability performs several functions in the film. As I have said, on a historical level, it reminds us of the pervasive impact of polio during the postwar period. On another level, prosthetic signs of Bannister's polio metaphorize his sexual inadequacy as a husband in relation to the macho Michael O'Hara. He uses his rolling gait and halting movements as part of his courtroom manner to gain dramatic effect, alternately gaining sympathy from the jury for his disability and creating comic moments as a "helpless" lawyer forced to take the stand in his own defense.

Welles reinforces the importance of his disability in several scenes by focusing on Bannister's crutches first and then panning away to show his entire body—as though the crutches are a synecdoche for the entire man. These theatrical representations of physical weakness combine with his racialized Jewishness (in contrast to O'Hara's Irishness and Elsa's nordic blondness) to create a figure of ambiguous racial and physical threat.[22] Finally, Bannister's prosthetic and theatrical elements reference his unspoken homoerotic attachment to Grisby and, ultimately, to O'Hara.

All of these elements come together in the famous shootout in the mirror room of the funhouse that concludes the movie. Bannister is first represented by his crutches reflected in multiple mirrors as he enters the mirror maze, then by a full image of him, cane in one hand, gun in another, juxtaposed to head shots of Elsa. His ensuing speech to his wife attempts to unravel the various plot threads, but Welles's violent montage and crosscutting undermine visually what the speech tries to resolve thematically. Bannister admits to Elsa that "killing you is killing myself. It's the same thing, but you know I'm pretty tired of both of us." The shootout that follows is verification of these remarks; husband and wife blast away at each other, destroying one illusion while opening another. This final scene is a spectacular send-up of the film's metaphorics of illusion and reality, but it is also a destruction of both sexual and medical threats in an act of mutual self-immolation, permitting the hero to walk out at the end, wounded but wiser. Disability and sexual transgression are eliminated within mirrors that, rather than confirm identity, replicate it in an infinite regression of partial identities.

The compulsory homosociality in the first two films discussed in this chapter undergoes a change in the case of Edward Dmytryk's *Walk on the Wild Side*, a film in which same-sex alliances are among women. In his autobiography, Dmytryk refers to the film as "a woman's picture," made as such by transforming the depression era hobo camps and slum shacks of Nelson Algren's novel into a Mexican café and a brothel, both presided over by women (246). The film was made in 1962, placing it slightly outside of the noir cycle, but it deploys many of its stylistic stocks-in-trade: a dislocated, lonely drifter, a tragic femme fatale, a dark, underworld milieu, and occasionally cinematic effects involving odd camera angles, low key-lighting, and a violent conclusion. Its more overt depiction of (thwarted) lesbian desire shows how the authority of Production Code censorship had diminished. Dmytryk changed Algren's original novel considerably, adding Jo's lesbianism and transforming one of her customers, Schmidt, into her husband. In the novel, Schmidt is a former freak show and carnival giant, whose physical prowess is brought to an abrupt end when he loses his legs in a train accident. In the film, Jo and Schmidt are married in order to link two kinds of freaks, sexual and physical, to preside over a dysfunctional family of wayward girls in a brothel called the Doll's House.

The hero is Dove Linkhorn (Laurence Harvey), a Texas drifter searching for his lost girlfriend Hallie (Capucine). He discovers her working in a New Orleans brothel, whose madam, Jo, is clearly in love with Hallie and who does everything in her power to prevent Dove from intervening. Her husband Schmidt's lost limbs provide a convenient metaphor for male subordination and weakness, against Dove's and Jo's desires for Hallie. The husband moves around the brothel on a wheeled dolly, his proximity to the ground enhanced by Dymytryk's camera, which hovers over Jo's shoulder as she looks down upon him. In one scene, this filmic perspective heightens the links between the husband's disability and Jo's problematic sexuality. Schmidt has just learned that Dove intends to take Hallie away from the brothel, thus eliminating the sexual barrier in their marriage that has been created by the distracting younger woman. "Will things be different?" he asks Jo. "No, things will be the same," she responds, to which he adds,

> That's what you said after the accident—the one that took away my legs. Are things the same? Am I still your husband? Let her go. I know what's going on inside him. I know what it's like, loving somebody and not being able to do anything about it.

But Jo dashes his hopes and repudiates the husband's declaration of affection:

> Love! Can any man love a woman for herself without wanting her body for his own pleasure? Love is understanding and sharing and enjoying the beauty of life without the reek of lust. Don't talk to me about love. What do you know? What does any man know?

As an expression of Jo's sexuality, this speech is unusually explicit for its time, yet it trades in a stereotype that, as Vito Russo observes, "attempts to explain—but not excuse—her man-hating lesbianism" (144). Love of life "without the reek of lust" may sound odd coming from the proprietress of a whorehouse, but it is what she *must* say to reinforce lesbian stereotypes and enlist the viewer's sympathy in her marital plight with a crippled husband. The fact that, as the husband admits, "everything changed" between him and his wife as a result of his accident recycles a disability stereotype in which the castrated male produces the phallic female, a transference of sexuality across phantom limbs.

To reinforce this transfer, the scene that follows displays the husband taking revenge on both wife and heterosexual hero by butting his head into Dove's groin while the latter is held by the brothel's bouncers. The scene between husband and wife heightens the film's linkage of disability and emasculation, but it also stresses Jo's butch authority over a world of women. Capucine's weary femme posture and Dove's attitude of resignation stand in stark contrast to Jo's drive and determination as well as her command of a mock-domestic household. As with *The Lady from Shanghai*, deviant sexuality is punished in the end in a final shootout that leaves Hallie dead and Jo criminally indicted for running a whorehouse, while the heterosexual hero remains alive to continue his lonely odyssey.

Volatile Bodies ⟲

What can we learn from this (admittedly slight) evidence for a crossing of medical and sexual closets during the early cold war? For one thing, we may observe the close intersection of the two that always attends representations of the nonnormative body. What is Tod Browning's *Freaks* (1932) if not a film that exploits "extraordinary" bodies by imagining them as sexual? In Elizabeth Grosz's terms, such bodies are "volatile" in their challenge to models of physical wholeness and heterosexuality. But they are volatile because they make visible the field of sexuality itself, not as a set of drives toward an object but as a multifaceted field of positions, desires, acts, and practices. The disabled figure in film noir is a phantom haunting cold war society, never given star billing, yet necessary for assisting the narrative of sexual containment embodied in the noir hero.

Whereas discussions of the phantom limb usually involve nostalgia for a prior "whole" body ("a libidinal memorial to the lost limb," as Grosz says [41]), based on Freudian lack, I would posit a cultural phantom limb that imagines bodies still under construction.[23] In a society that figured the struggle between superpowers as one between "healthy" Protestant capitalism and "invalid" or diseased Communism, such bodies played a vital role in representing national insecurity. George Kennan, in his famous "Long Telegram" of 1946, begins a tradition of identifying Soviet expansion as a form of disease. According to Kennan, Soviet leaders put forth a dogma that presents the outside world as "bearing within itself germs of creeping disease and destined to be wracked with growing internal convulsions until it is given a final *coup de grace* by rising power of socialism that yields to new and better world [*sic*]" (54). Later in the document, Kennan inverts his disease metaphor, stating that future world stability depends on the "health and vigor of our own society. World communism is like malignant parasite [*sic*] which feeds only on diseased tissue" (63). The fact that he issued this foundational document of cold war containment while recovering in a sickbed in Vienna is a significant fact in the metaphor of contamination that he uses.[24]

In referring to the limits of feminist psychoanalytic film theory I noted the ease with which in such work the disabled male in film noir is generalized as the castrated Oedipus. For films made in the long shadow of a world war, the phantom limb was not a metaphor but a historical fact of everyday U.S. life. Even in films that do not depict returning veterans, like *Double Indemnity* or *The Lady from Shanghai*, the war makes its ghostly appearance. The development of prosthetic technology during the war announced the rise of what David Serlin calls "medical consumerism" and the growth of a rehabilitation industry that continues, in the ongoing Iraq War, to be big business. The effects of war trauma and disability were powerfully evident in postwar society, and their effects on masculine self-identity have been the subject of numerous treatments of the family and domesticity. Serlin notes that the advances in the science of prosthetics, the creation of ever more lightweight and flexible legs and arms, provided a counterdiscourse to the ensuing cold war. The "other arms race," as Serlin calls it, is one in which the attempt to normalize the prostheticized body was represented in *The Best Years of Our Lives* and other films about the difficulties of disabled soldiers attempting to reenter social and private life. Such social normalization through prosthetics and film have implications for heteronormalcy, but the dark doppelgänger of this restorative trend—what I am calling the phantom limb of cold war normalcy—is played out in film noir.

By studying a cycle of films created in the shadow of documents such as Kennan's "Long Telegram" and the recently ended "hot" war, we may see a moment when the discourses of national health and economic stability are geopolitical imperatives. In this regard, we may see some fraying in the fabric of national consensus. What sexual content could be kept out of films through Production Code censorship could be introduced through other doors. We may also see how a cycle of films described usually in terms of expressionist mood utilized those features to legitimate an ableist gaze. Orson Welles's spectacular mirror-room shootout may dash perspectives on reality, but it permits the "real" Welles (actor, director, heterosexual, able-bodied) to walk out into the sunlight at the end. Finally, by speaking of the phantom limb of cold war sexuality, we see how a moment of (albeit repressed) social agency for queer men and women, many of whom had formed homosocial communities during the war effort, was being formed through film. A broader look at films of this era—*Johnny Belinda, Gilda, Laura, Rebecca, Johnny Guitar, The Maltese Falcon, Mildred Pierce, The Manchurian Candidate,* and their retro versions in the 1980s and 1990s—shows that noir style is not just a set of surface features, but a venue for representing otherness in a culture of the same.

Chapter 3

Hearing Things

The Scandal of Speech in Deaf Performance

Think Hearing ↪

In the film version (1986) of Mark Medoff's play *Children of a Lesser God* (1980), James (William Hurt) is a speech instructor at a school for the deaf who believes that his students must be educated into oral culture by being taught to lip-read and speak. He falls in love with Sarah (Marlee Maitlin) who is Deaf but who refuses to participate in his pedagogical project. She signs throughout the film, insisting on her right to remain silent, until one climactic scene when, under James's badgering, she suddenly screeches out a stream of speech. It is a powerful scene because it is the first time the hearing audience has experienced her voice and realizes that she *can* speak but prefers not to. It is also powerful because instead of achieving the desired result, Sarah's vocalizing illustrates the coercive force of an educational system based around speech rather than manual signing. What James witnesses is a kind of deaf performative—a form of speech that enacts or performs rather than describes—its meaning contained not in the content of Sarah's words (most of which are unrecognizable) but in the results it achieves in shaking his oralist bias. In Henry Louis Gates's terms, it signifies "on" speech as a much as "by means of it" (44–88). For the hearing educator, speech is the key to normalization in hearing-based culture;

for the Deaf signer, speech is the sign of an alienating process that only performing can make evident.

I want to extend the concept of a deaf performative to describe the work of Deaf language-artists for whom the use of speech and vocalization is a kind of scandal and who utilize that scandal to critical ends. By *scandal*, I mean that the eruption of speech (or as we shall see, text) in Deaf performance challenges the conventional opposition of signing and speech and allows for more complex, hybrid combinations. In the wake of the Deaf President Now protests of 1988 at Gallaudet University and the launching of a powerful political movement for the empowering of Deaf persons, the use of speech-based pedagogies represents the continuing authority of hearing culture.[1] The attempt by audiologists, psychologists, educators, and legislators to reinforce oralist values has been combated by an increasingly politicized social movement of the Deaf who regard themselves not as a handicapped population but as a linguistic minority with distinct cultural and historical traditions.[2] As Dirksen Bauman, Harlan Lane, Douglas Baynton, Carol Padden, Tom Humphreys, and others have observed, audism—the ideological replication of humans as hearing subjects—has influenced treatment of Deaf persons from the outset. The incarceration of the deaf in institutions, the denial of ASL as a language, the imposition of medical aids (cochlear implants, hearing aids), mainstreaming in education, punishment of children for manual signing—all constitute what Harlan Lane has called a "colonial" subjugation of the Deaf (31–38). A postcolonial regime is very much under way, and performance is one of its key venues.

One of the (many) things that James in *Children of a Lesser God* cannot understand is that although Sarah may not speak, she certainly has a voice, and she uses it to communicate her agency and independence despite being surrounded by oralist instructors. If the use of speech is scandalous in some forms of Deaf performance, the idea of voice has a much nobler—if contested—pedigree. As Tom Humphreys and Carol Padden point out, within the deaf community, *voice* is a problematic term that combines two meanings: "the modality of expression in spoken language, but also as *being heard*" (*Inside Deaf Culture* 58). With the rise of oral pedagogies that associated "voice" with speaking, the Deaf community sought to "make themselves heard above the clamor of the demand for speech and the banishment of sign language" (59). The problem was "how to be heard on their own terms" (59). More particularly, how could they recuperate "voice" from the common assumption that deaf people are "mute" and therefore unable to communicate or, worse, "dumb" and therefore unable to reason. Humphreys and Padden describe turn-of-the-century sign language films made by the National Association for the Deaf (NAD) that were central to this recuperative project. The films showed distinguished senior members of the Deaf community like George Veditz and Edward Miner Gallaudet (son of Thomas Gallaudet, the founder of the first school for the deaf in 1817) lecturing and telling stories, thus providing examples of expressive signing at the moment it was most in danger of extinction. These films recorded the use of sign language by its most eloquent practitioners and provided a historical continuity with the first and second generation of signers in the United States. The films have subsequently been used by linguists to measure changes in ASL as well as in signing practices. As such, these films offered a "voice," here understood as a form of cultural transmission and empowering agency.[3]

Humphreys and Padden refer to the portmanteau ASL sign for "think-hearing" which transfers the sign for "hearing" (a finger rotating near the mouth) to the region of the head in order to describe someone who "thinks and acts like a hearing person" or who uncritically embraces the ideology of others (*Deaf in America* 53). ASL poets like Clayton Valli, Ella Mae Lentz, Debbie Rennie, and others have made "think-hearing" a subject of aesthetic critique while using ASL as a powerful counterdiscourse to phonocentric models for literature. In their work, "performing the text" means utilizing ASL signing to establish community (the Deaf audience understands a sign's multiple meanings) and politicize the occasion (the hearing audience cannot rely on acoustic prosodic models). Thus a key meaning in every Deaf performance is a set of shared cultural values implicit in the use of ASL. One might say that in addition to the four categories foregrounded in deaf performance—space, body, time, language—a fifth must be added: that of Deaf culture itself.

But to speak of "Deaf culture" as a single entity is to generalize a rather broad continuum of persons variously positioned with respect to deafness. The phrase would include children who are deaf but whose family is hearing or hearing children of deaf adults (CODA) as well as persons who have become deaf later in life or who still retain some hearing.[4] And in descriptions of Deaf performance, such differences often become obscured in a more general celebration of an authentic (e.g., soundless, text-less, ASL-based) poetry. The decision by some Deaf poets not to have their signed works voice-interpreted is an understandable refusal of hearing culture, but it has limited the venues in which they may participate and audiences they might reach. I would like to look at three deaf artists, Peter Cook, Aaron Williamson, and Joseph Grigely, who violate such authenticity and in doing so comment suggestively on issues of language and communication in general, insofar as they are based on a phonocentric model. In my conclusion I will suggest some of the implications that such performers pose for the intersections between performance, disability, and multiculturalism.

Exchanging Signs: The Flying Words Project ⌐

Peter Cook is the deaf half of Flying Words, a collaborative performance group, the other half of which is Kenny Lerner, who hears but also signs. The two create performances that draw on several vernacular Deaf traditions including mime, deaf ventriloquism, dance, and storytelling. Where Flying Words differs from Deaf poets like Clayton Valli and Ella Mae Lentz is in the use of sound and collaboration. Not only does Lerner occasionally vocalize (speak over) Cook's signs, Cook sometimes vocalizes while he signs. For Deaf nationalists, such collaboration with the hearing world is problematic, to say the least, but for the two of them, it is a way of extending the gestural potential of ASL into an immanent critique of audist ideology. Furthermore, Lerner's vocalization is seldom used to translate or interpret Cook's signing. Often, Lerner is silent while Cook punctuates his signing with words or parts of words.

Such is the case in *I Am Ordered Now to Talk,* a performance that dramatizes pedagogical tensions between oralist and manualist learning.[5] The two performers, standing on either side of a stage, render a poem by Cook recounting his oralist education at the Clarke School in Northampton, Massachusetts. Cook speaks the poem while Lerner signs, thus reversing the usual interpreter/interpreted role.[6] Cook's voice is, as Brenda Brueggemann points out, "loud, monotone, wooden, 'unnatural,' nearly unintelligible," while Lerner's signs are "a bit stiff and exaggerated as well"

Fig. 1. Peter Cook and Kenny Lerner in a Flying Words performance of *I Am Ordered Now to Talk*. (Reprinted by permission of
the photographer, Roy Sowers.)

(205). The unsettling nature of oral delivery is reinforced by the poem's violent denunciation of oral education, compared at one point to a kind of
lobotomy, "for the sake of Ma Bell." Cook's repeated version of the speech
instructor's refrain, "you / must / now / talk," becomes increasingly agi-
tated as the poem moves to its conclusion. At one point, the two performers come together, Lerner standing behind Cook, posing as the "speech
freako" who, in demanding vocal articulation from his deaf student, imitates a brain surgeon. Cook, as patient, warns

don't stare at me
I was on that cold metal table
that speech freako wants me
as example for the society
rip my brains with
peanuts buttered spoon
scream with blackboard trick:

B IS NOT P
D IS NOT T
S IS NOT Z

(Brueggemann, 206)

Like James in *Children of a Lesser God*, the oral instructor wants to make an example of the deaf student by asking him to pronounce phrases like "peanuts buttered spoon." Such phrases are replete with phonemes that, for a lip-reader, are difficult to distinguish. The oralist teacher's corrections, "B IS NOT P/ D IS NOT T / S IS NOT Z," are counterpoised to Lerner's signing, in which the verbal distinctions among phonemes become spatial and readable distinctions among manual signs. Cook's unintelligible speech suggests the limits of oralist education, while Lerner's signing, however tentative, provides a corrective. Both performers utilize a language "foreign" to their usual cultural milieu, and as such embody the very alienation thematized in the poem. The deaf student is forced to signify under orders; the hearing person "translates" into readable signs a speech that is all but incomprehensible.

Before beginning their performance, Lerner announces that Cook will sign briefly and without vocal interpretation to the Deaf audience. Lerner points out that Cook "will be focusing on hearing people. So, please, feel paranoid." Such framing of multiple constituencies creates a certain edginess that reverberates throughout the performance. It also foregrounds the *audio* in *audience,* the latter of which, for most performers, implies an homogeneous (hearing) entity. For Peter Cook to speak the poem is to show the ideology of think-hearing at its most flagrant. But by collaborating with Lerner, who remains silent, he does something more. He illustrates a fruitful comixture of sound and sign contributing to a critical as well as aesthetic performance.

The spatial dimension of Deaf performance is, of course, a direct result of ASL's visual character, for which interaction with a live audience is a given. The increased role of videotapes, DVDs, and other visual recording technologies is changing this feature, allowing Deaf performers to be seen beyond the performance venue. At its core, however, Deaf literature presumes a live audience and a body that moves in space. This aspect of signed poetry is a key feature of the Flying Words Project's best-known performance, *Poetry around the World,* in which Cook and Lerner play a series of variations (which they call "transformations") on signs for poetry and language. Their primary metaphor is the global extensiveness of poetry ("I can send language around the world," Cook repeats), but the means by which they develop this message suggests certain limits to a universalist aesthetics. In one segment, Cook quite literally throws the sign for "language" (the finger-spelled letter *l*)around the world like a baseball. He then waits for the letter to circle his body-as-globe, checking his watch from time to time, until language arrives in front of him again. Lerner stands behind him wearing a black hood and contributes to the signing in front of Peter's chest. Because both performers wear black against a black background, Cook appears to be signing with four hands.[7]

The two primary signs used here, "language" and "poetry," are given cosmic dimensions by being thrown through space, yet Cook recognizes the site-specific nature of his performance by acknowledging those who receive those signs. At one point, while he and Lerner bounce the hand shape *p* for text-based poetry among three of the performers' four hands, Cook waves at someone in the audience and suggests that they have a drink later. Although it is a small gesture, it breaks the circle in which signs are produced and acknowledges the larger space of signed communication. While Cook and Lerner construct a visual "text" on their bodies, they also gesture at the audience for which that text is a value.

To address his multiple constituencies, hearing and signing, Cook mixes three signs for poetry: the sign for ASL poetry, a gesture of the hand outwards from the heart; the sign for written English, based on the finger-spelled letter *p;* and, finally, the finger-spelled version, *p-o-e-t-r-y.* The three together indicate the Deaf poet's multilingual, multicultural identity. Cook suggests that if poetry is to achieve truly global resonance, it must utilize all the resources of language—including the cultural specificity of its dissemination. Cook also utters the plosive /p/ as he bounces the sign for poetry off Lerner's hands, a gesture that Brueggemann regards as a reference to an "oral school exercise" in which the deaf student is asked to pronounce the same sound over and over again. As she points out, this sound establishes a rhythm—"like a train gathering speed"—and thus enhances the metaphor of travel (207). It also frames the pedagogical implications of oral learning in which, for the deaf child, an abstract sound is molded into a word through rote repetition. Against this form of cultural coercion, embodied in Cook's utterances, the audiences experience the rich, multifaceted background of a poetry constructed through sign as well as site.

The heat generated by such transformations is illustrated by the way the two performers exchange signs, quite literally moving the finger-spelled *p* for "poetry" from hand to hand. Such sharing of signs is at the core of Deaf communication, but this performance literalizes the fact by displaying four hands signing. The links between hearing and deafness are established in the collaborative nature of performance, yet by occasionally placing the hearing Lerner behind in a mask, Cook stresses the ghostly presence of hearing culture—assisting but invisible. In this sense, Flying Words redirects the paternalist hierarchy of hearing to nonhearing persons by placing the deaf performer in front, reversing the spatial (and auditory) proximity. The spatial positioning of hearing and deaf, English and ASL, interpreter and interpreted, within Flying Words performances maps an indeterminate space between and within audist culture. Lerner and Cook utilize their bodies and their bicultural experiences to define and critique a world that must be spoken to be known.

Hearing Things: Aaron Williamson ↜

The Flying Words Project thematizes the authority of hearing culture by introducing speech into performance not as a transcription of sign but as a marker of a kind of authority or precedence. What would a world look like in which sounds *follow* rather than *precede* signs—in which individuals speak first and then learn what scriptural forms the words make? Such a world might, in Owen Wrigley's terms, "see a world built around the valence of visual rather than aural channels" (3). This is the subject of work by Aaron Williamson, a British performance artist who began to lose his hearing at a young age and who was profoundly deaf by his midtwenties.

Fig. 2. Aaron Williamson performing "Wave," from *Phantom Shifts*. (Reprinted by permission of Aaron Williamson.)

Fig. 3. Aaron Williamson performing *Hearing Things*. (Reprinted by permission of Aaron Williamson.)

Although he has been deaf for most of his adult life, he retains a strong connection to hearing culture and makes his bicultural condition a major theme in his performances. Like Peter Cook, he often collaborates with other performers, including musicians and drummers (he has appeared in punk bands since the mid 1970s).[8] But unlike many Deaf performers—including Flying Words—signing is not a prominent feature of his work. Rather, it is among the arsenal of gestures that he uses to confront the liminal situation of the late deafened: those with one foot in Deaf and the other in hearing communities.

A good introduction to Williamson's work is his 1999 performance *Phantom Shifts*, a series of lyrical reflections on the authority of the ear. In one sequence, the ear, in the form of a large plaster sculpture, is carried on the performer's back. Williamson has said that the inspiration for this image came less from an attempt to represent the burden of hearing than from an attempt to impede routinized movement. To some extent all of his work involves the imposition of limits to normalized action, constructing a "law of diminishing referentiality" that he shares with a wide range of contemporary performers (Williamson, lecture). The title of this segment, "Breath," refers to the sound track that features Williamson's labored breathing as he bears his physical (the plaster ear, is, in fact, quite heavy) and ideological burdens. But the soundtrack often cuts out, leaving silences that impose their own acoustic burden on the hearing viewer who expects some continuity between image and sound.

The second segment, "Wave," takes the metaphor of breathing another step by introducing vocalization in the form of a single syllable.[9] Thus *Phantom Shifts* defines a trajectory from breath to the beginnings of significant sound. The performer stands facing the viewer (or camera) at the end of a long room, wearing a white shift. Before him and extending toward the camera position is a long piece of translucent white material. In the foreground the plaster ear is faintly outlined beneath the material. It is, in British slang, covered by cloth or "cloth-eared," meaning mute or stupid. Williamson takes a series of deep breaths, approaches the white sheet, raises and suddenly lowers it, trapping air underneath the sheet and creating a wave that rolls from him to the ear in the foreground. The material is flexible enough to create a continuous unfolding wave or ripple the full length of the room. On one level, the wave seems to emanate from Williamson's breath, exhaled at the moment the material is lowered. On another level, the wave is a dramatization of sound waves traveling through space to strike the tympanum. Williamson's iconic gesture is about the separation of breath from sound, of sound from sense. The ear is less an extension of the body than a prosthesis toward which the body aspires. Williamson's breathing exercises resemble a kind of ritual gesture made toward the fetish at the opposite end of the room, but instead of animating the fetish with significant speech, Williamson's breath simply creates a wave.

In the final seconds of the brief performance, Williamson comes to speech, uttering a loud "ha" before lowering the sheet. This time, the ensuing wave uncovers the ear, permitting the performer to leave the performance space. In a discussion of *Phantom Shifts* Williamson has said that he uses this open-throated "ha" because it is the most expressive and primal of sounds, deployed equally in laughter and crying (Williamson, lecture). Thus the sound that lays bare the device of the ear is one that defies the purely semantic features of speech and calls attention to the body's expressive functions. If he cannot hear his own voice, Williamson can represent the scene of its emergence, the agon of its production. Moreover, by cutting the soundtrack off and on, he may embody for the viewer the discontinuity of images detached from their animating sounds.

What animates this and other performances by Aaron Williamson is a recognition of the constitutive force of speech and hearing in the production of knowledge. In Western theology and philosophy, the Logos or reason is represented as a voice, the spirit as breath. Such metaphors have been active in constructing much postwar poetics, from Charles Olson's projective verse and Beat testimony to the anthropological oralism of Gary Snyder or Jerome Rothenberg, to sound poetry and spoken word performance. For Williamson, the Logos is figured not as a voice but as an ear, the agent of reception in Saussure's communicational diagram. The poet short-circuits the Judeo-Christian model of the Logos as Voice by treating the ear as a fetish object, a stony recipient of cryptic messages that wash up on its shore.

This same deconstruction of a logo-and phonocentric tradition can be seen in Williamson's *Hearing Things* (1999).[10] This performance is a kind of cybernetic meditation on the oracle at Delphi as seen through a deaf optic. According to the story, the oracle purportedly delivered cryptic messages that were then decoded by her acolytes. Williamson's Artaudian version utilizes a technological interface to turn himself into a cyborg creature, half oracle, half scribe, part technology, part human. In order to effect this synthesis, Williamson utilizes voice recognition software to generate a text that becomes the focal point for the performance. In its most recent manifestation, *Hearing Things* uses software that picks up the sounds of audience members who are encouraged to speak into a microphone placed in the gallery space. In an earlier version, upon which I will focus here, the sounds are produced by Williamson himself, converted by the software into a text of recognizable English words. That text is then projected from the ceiling onto the floor and reflected in two transparent auto-cuing glasses behind the performer. Williamson moves around the text, gazing at the words and making a variety of whoops, cries, chatters, and moans—the indecipherable words of the oracle.

Although he cannot hear his own voice, he may see its representation in words generated by it, the computer acting as an interpreter of the deaf speaker's sounds. By a curious inversion of agency, Williamson may encounter his own words as alien—which for the deaf person living in an oral world is precisely the case. Moreover, he performs both "on" and "within" the text, the words occasionally projected onto his white shift, making him both the reflector and creator of the text to which he gives birth. His status as "Poet" is confirmed by the laurel wreath he wears on his head. And since he is wearing a dress, gender confusion reinforces the mixed nature of this originary word, half female oracle, half male amanuensis. Against the Judeo-Christian model of a male Jehovah, speaking from the whirlwind, we have a female oracle whose signs have yet to be learned by a patriarchal scribe.

The title *Hearing Things* is elaborately unpacked in this performance. On one level it refers to language as unreality—"I must be hearing things"—a phrase that refers to the phantasmal quality of words when encountered as foreign objects. For a late-deafened person, words have become wraiths of their former semiotic bodies. Williamson reinforces this aspect by seeing them projected on his body from some outside source. But at an epistemological level, "hearing things' refers to the binary opposition by which humans are measured in the hearing world—in which an originary Logos (the Oracle) must be heard in order to be incarnated in flesh. As Derrida has pointed out via Rousseau, hearing subjects are granted human status by their ability to hear, but as such, they become merely "things" that hear, objects whose only claim to identity is their possession of an intact auditory nerve.[11] The title fuses persons and/as things, made palpable by Williamson's use of a series of objects—a large plaster-of-paris ear, a navel stone and a metal tripod (as used by the Delphian Pythia)—which he attempts to animate. At three points in his performance he moves offstage to bring these objects into view, moving them around, fussing over them, much as Beckett's characters interrogate stones, bicycles, and biscuits. The objects become similar to the projected words themselves, inert, contextless, and foreign. Yet in Williamson's interrogation, they gain new life and function.

Williamson poses a number of problems for any consideration of Deaf literature, beyond the fact that he utilizes voice in his performances. The recursive manner by which text and body, computer and script, interact frustrates the idea of creativity as something that gives "voice" to some prior meaning. As an allegory of disability, such recursiveness embodies the ways that deafness is inscribed in what Foucault, in another context, has called "technologies of the self," the "truth games" or "practices of belief" that naturalize the self for any individual (15, 39). For Williamson, speaking of his use of technology, "The biological becomes fused with the digital as normal relations between cause and effect—between human and computer—are broken down. . . . As the digital and biological circulate with each other the boundaries of linguistic agency and textual authority erode as both components—computer and performer—desperately try to interpret, respond to and prompt each other's cracked, inauspicious stimulation" (*Hearing Things* 18). This "cracked" or fractured relation between human and machine suggests a fissure in the edifice of postmodern performance based, as it often is, on the authenticity of the body and gesture in an increasingly technologized world.

One dream of modernism was to return the text to its materiality, to make the text speak authentically by removing it from the instrumental purposes to which speech is linked. For postmodern Deaf performers, this materiality can no longer sustain its purely aesthetic focus. In this sense, Flying Words and Aaron Williamson could be aligned with Chicano/a interlingualists and feminist performance artists for whom performing or materializing the text always implicates the word as a problem, not a conduit, in which cultural identity is hybrid, not unitary.

Conversations with the Hearing: Joseph Grigely ᗑ

Thus far, I have treated speech as the presumed antithesis to manual signing, "scandalous" because complicit with audist or oral theories of communication. But as Derrida has made abundantly clear, speech defines less a phenomenon than an ideology of presence, a reification of signification within a phonocentric model. As such, the intrusion of textuality into deaf performance would pose the same threat, not unlike the use of vocalization to translate or interpret the deaf poet's signing. The use of printed

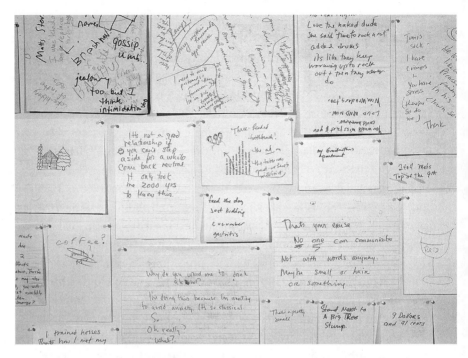

Fig. 4. *White Noise,* by Joseph Grigely, 2000, ink and pencil on pa-
per, 26.5′ × 19.5′ × 13.5′, installation view (detail), Musée d' Art
Moderne de la Ville de Paris and Whitney Museum of American
Art. (Reprinted by permission of the artist.)

English text to interpret the deaf person's intentions would once again co-
opt manual signs by linking them to English syntax and grammar. Since
there is no written representation of signs, communication among the
Deaf must be performed, as it were, in situ. For this reason, philosophers
of language since Rousseau have seen manual signing as primitive or narrowly iconic.

The intervention of textual communication into deafness is central to
the work of Joseph Grigely, a literary scholar and visual artist who has
written extensively on textual matters.[12] He has been deaf since childhood
and is fluent in ASL, although in his art installations, his focus is on written English and the conversation between deaf and hearing worlds.
Grigely diverges rather sharply from Peter Cook and Aaron Williamson by
stressing writing over sign or gesture, yet like both performers, he is interested in the strangeness of writing when encountered through a deaf op-

tic. My oxymoron—a deaf optic—describes a bicultural approach to communication in which hearing viewer must communicate with deaf interlocutor by nonacoustic means. Since 1994, Grigely has created installations out of the written notes passed between himself and hearing others. These bits of discursive flotsam—Post-its, bar napkins, gallery programs, sheets of notebook paper—contain partial communications between deaf and hearing worlds.[13] As such, they are metonymies of whole conversations rendered telegraphically through a few words: "Although it was no whiskey in it"; "Squid? oh my"; "What's your second best ideal." Not unlike most oral conversations, the content of such remarks is less important than their furtherance of communicational intentions. Because the remarks are written, they gain a materiality that spoken words do not. By displaying them on the walls of a gallery, Grigely refers to a lost site of communication, one that the viewer must complete by conjecture. And because the slips are placed next to each other, they create their own internal dialogues.

Unlike visual artists from the Dadaists to Cy Twombly or Arakawa, for whom writing and calligraphic elements are design features, Grigely's words are drawn from actual conversations. His scribbled messages are not *invented* but rather *collected* by him, displayed like archaeological finds whose origins are obscure. Occasionally he adds descriptive plaques—what he calls "story lines"—to explain circumstances of various meetings, creating a mock docent quality to his survey of ephemeral pieces of paper. As a collector he is interested in the materiality of ephemerality, the textures and color of paper, pen and handwriting, as they instantiate a moment of sociality. That such moments are often about Grigely's deafness is never far from their materiality: "Do you read lips?" one slip says, followed in the same hand by "Do you prefer written words?" Another reads, "I guess it's an *Economy of Words* that I'd like." Such metatextual remarks remind us that however immediate the exchange of conversation papers might be, the fact of one interlocutor's difference from the other can never be dissevered from the conversation.

Grigely titles his earlier exhibitions *Conversations with the Hearing*, reversing the ethnographic stereotype of the medical scientist who studies the deaf native. As an ethnologist Grigely collects the rescued written slips from various conversations and makes them the subject of his archive. His occasional descriptive plates provide a deadpan narration of a given meeting:

I met Tamara G quite by chance in New York, where she was spending a few months working on a project. She's from Frankfurt. During the time she was in New York we got to know each other a bit.
Occasionally we would go out together to have coffee or to go to exhibition openings—anything that would give us the opportunity to
talk about art and work in an informal context. Tamara has a very
nice and distinctive accent when she writes, and I often wonder if *her*
voice sounds like it looks. (Rubenstein 100)

Surrounding this card are the collected conversation papers between
Grigely and Tamara G, placed within an installation entitled *Lo Studio /
The Study,* which appeared at the Venice Biennale in 1995. The painterly
trope of the "artist's studio" has been retrofitted to include not only the
table on which the artist works but the written detritus of actual meetings,
conversations, and relationships. Instead of paints, models, and prints,
Grigely's studio features wastebaskets, piles of paper, and scotch tape—an
allegory, to paraphrase Courbet, of the artist's "real life" among hearing
people. As Raphael Rubenstein writes of this exhibition, "Grigely's messy
desk installations, which he carefully orchestrates, are not simply replays
of scatter art but his fullest attempt to render the complexities of human
conversation" (133).

At the core of this complexity is an exploration of metonymy, the way
that fragments of conversations point to larger utterances and social occa-
sions. In the absence of a descriptive narrative or full sentence, the viewer
must supply a context that can only be imagined. And as an allegory of
deaf relations to hearing world, every written mark instantiates a thwarted
relationship to the world that takes speech for granted. The phrase, "because you can't," printed on a slip of orange paper, could be a response to
a challenge ("Why can't I do such and such?") or a truncation of a larger
sentence ("Because you can't do such and such, therefore you must do
such and such"). By taking these partial utterances from their communicational conduit and placing them on walls in public spaces, Grigely calls
attention to the partial and attenuated nature of deaf/hearing communication when part of the utterance may be completed by lip-reading, body
language, or other gestures. And since many of these utterances were written on ready-to-hand documents—museum brochures, menus, match-
book covers—they point outward at a larger social nexus where private
conversation meets institutional space.[14]

The metonymic character of Grigely's art has an important bearing on what I take to be the artist's larger critique of audism. Speaking of this aspect of Grigely's work, Aaron Williamson notes that "writing in the presence of the reader produces a wide variety of reactions which may in themselves abbreviate the communication (for example, a realisation by the speaker that the lack of thought in a casual remark is about to become graphically apparent)" (Review 35). At another level, this metonymic aspect of communication refers to the construction of deafness itself, the marginalization of a population through medical, pedagogical, or eugenic discourses. While there is no direct correlation between marginal texts and marginal identities, there is always the sense that what is left *out* of a given remark ("is storytelling dying out?" one slip says) is the full presence guaranteed by spoken language—a speech that would, ironically, render such conversation slips unnecessary.

This critical aspect of Grigely's textual work can be seen in his pamphlet called *Deaf & Dumb: A Tale,* which consists of pages from books and treatises devoted to the study of deafness, dating from the late Renaissance to the present. Like his conversation papers, these pages have been separated from their original codex books, yet there is enough information in each page to indicate what the original book concerns. The pages themselves are facsimiles of actual pages, their antique fonts registering varying periods of print technology, and so have the same rhetorical status as his conversation slips—fragments of actual documents or conversations whose origins have been effaced. The "tale" of the pamphlet's subtitle concerns the ways that deaf persons have been infantilized, pathologized, or demonized throughout history. The cautionary aspect of the pamphlet is illustrated by its homely epigraph: "This little volume, although originally prepared for the Deaf and Dumb, will be found to be equally adapted to the instruction of other children in families, infant schools, common schools, and Sunday schools" (2). What may have begun as a scene of domestic instruction for deaf persons, in Grigely's republication, becomes a Foucauldian marker of carceral life in modern society.

Grigely's mock-serious pamphlet is indeed instructional, but to ends entirely different from the originals. Like Walter Benjamin's Arcades project, Grigely's pamphlet takes historical objects (books and pamphlets) and rubs them the wrong way, exposing racialist and ableist agendas in works with missionary intentions. Several pages are taken from primers in oralist education, including guides for pronunciation and proper elocution. Another text is drawn apparently from an eugenics treatise that warns against the dangers of deaf/hearing intermarriage:

> While there is still some doubt as to how large a part heredity plays in deafness, the indications of its influence are clear enough to make a person with a family history of deafness take all possible care to avoid conditions that favor hearing impairment. (24)

Many pages offer consoling accounts of deaf people who have been "converted" or "brought over" to the hearing world, through oral exercise. Other accounts suggest (wrongly) that deafness coincides with dumbness or muteness and is therefore a sign of insanity or feeble-mindedness. Perhaps the most telling page is drawn from Rousseau, who defines in brief the linguistic basis for many subsequent attacks on manual signing:

> Still, the speech of beavers and ants is apparently by gesture; i.e., it is only visual. If so, such languages are natural, not acquired. The animals that speak them possess them a-borning: they all have them, and they are everywhere the same. They are entirely unchanging and make not the slightest progress. Conventional language is characteristic of man alone. That is why man makes progress . . . and animals do not. (17)

A last example testifies to the economic marginalization by showing plausible trades that the deaf have entered at various "institutions for the deaf and dumb": cabinetmaking, shoemaking, bookbinding, gardening, and printing. In most cases, the page ends midsentence, leaving the fuller context empty. Although *Deaf & Dumb: A Tale* is technically a work of book art, it should be included in Grigely's art installations as a subtle interrogation of the links between textuality and marginalization, what he, in his critical work calls "textual eugenics."

Conclusion: Scandals of Speech ✍

It may seen that in describing Joseph Grigely's textual art I have swerved rather far from my initial concerns with deaf performance. Aaron

Williamson may eschew both English and ASL, but there is little doubt that he is "performing" at some level. Grigely's rather quiet installations hardly invite the same scrutiny of gesture and orality that are the hallmark of traditional performance artists, but they allow us to return to my use of Henry Louis Gates's idea of "signifyin(g)" as a vernacular act that creates meaning by gesturing at certain received traditions and canons of meaning-making. For Grigely to create a textual space based on truncated conversations is to comment on a broken relationship with hearing culture while making art out of that brokenness. By enlisting the hearing viewer in the difficulty of that conversation, Grigely may point to historical fissures that have kept the d/Deaf individual outside, as it were, of the gallery and museum—and outside of the epistemological discourse of art as a specific kind of knowledge.

As Grigely's art or that of the Flying Words Project or Aaron Williamson makes evident, alienation from the text—and textuality—is literal. Words appear on the ground or museum wall like exotic flora and fauna in some new, cybernetic Eden. Williamson may step on them, point at them, and give them meaning, but he is removed from their production. His nonsemantic roaring, like that of Sarah in *Children of a Lesser God*, is a speech act that challenges the ordinariness of ordinary language, making strange not only sounds but the discursive arena in which speech "makes sense." Similarly, the Flying Words Project, by treating the sign as a process of community-building, reinforces the collective qualities of meaning-production on a global scale. Peter Cook and Kenny Lerner's complex use of sound and sign, far from uniting the two in a gesture of multicultural unity, illustrates the continuing divide between speech-based and deaf pedagogies. Their metatextual references to both hearing and deaf audiences challenge the idea that ASL is an invented or iconic language, ancillary to English. Rather, in their hands, it becomes a rich, polyvalent structure, capable of containing the container. The "scandal of speech" in Deaf performance is not that it appears in concert with signing, but that its use calls into question the self-evident nature of speech-based communicational models. At the very minimum, such performers make *think-hearing* a phrase that once seen can never be heard the same way twice.

Chapter 4

Tree Tangled in Tree

Resiting Poetry through ASL

What Is Golf? ⤳

At a 2004 conference on disability studies in the university, Simi Linton spoke about Casey Martin, the golfer who was denied access to the PGA national golf tour because, as someone with a mobility impairment, he needed to ride in an electric cart. As Linton pointed out, his disability is not located in the game of golf—which he plays spectacularly—but in the rules by which golf tournaments are conducted. This prompted Linton to meditate on the seemingly unproblematic meaning of institutions and activities when they are limited to an able-bodied individual. The big question, she mused is, "What *is* the game of golf?" ("What Is Disability Studies" 519). This is a significant issue because it forces us to reevaluate impairment not from the standpoint of a physical condition but from the environment in which that condition gains meaning. Is golf radically different when it is played by someone who rides rather than walks from tee to tee? Who decides on the meaning of games and their rules?

The same questions could be asked of poetry when it is regarded from the perspective of poets who utilize American Sign Language—for whom poetry is no longer governed by the voice, page, or writing. Although poets often describe their work as emanating from the body and voice, these tropes mean something quite different when literalized by poets who sign their poems *by* and *on* the body and whose voice is removed from some interior space of the body and represented on its surface. Walt Whitman's claim that "my voice goes after what my eyes cannot reach" suggests a metaphoric expansion of poetry beyond its phenomenological origins and extended through the medium of print. But, as I have said in my previous chapter, when Peter Cook of the Flying Words Project sends language "around the world" by throwing the finger-spelled letter *l* into space, language ceases to be a metaphor for extension and becomes, visibly, a "flying word" in space. On the model of Linton's golf metaphor, we might ask the big question, *What is poetry?* when considered from the standpoint of sign language. And more particularly for our own era, what is modernist poetry when its ocularcentrism—its presumption of a transparent relationship between sign and object—is resited through sign?

This latter question requires some contextualization. Modernist ocularcentrism is manifested in the retinal aesthetics of a good deal of postimpressionist art. Cubism, futurism, constructivism, and fauvism all have, at their core, a critique of single-point perspective that has been in place since the Renaissance.[1] In its various modalities, painting from Cézanne and Pissaro to Duchamp fractures the unity of the object as well as the (presumed) perspectival integrity of the viewing subject. Whether attempting to render the play of light and shadow on the retina in impressionism or blasting the sculptural unity of an object into facets, as in cubism, modern artists subjected the ocular and painting's mimetic abilities to a severe challenge. Of course, like all attempts to characterize an epoch under a single rubric (mannerism, the Age of Reason, the Pound Era) this ocularcentric reading of modernism involves a reduction of a spectrum of pictorial gestures to a single emphasis. That emphasis is the product of a formalist aesthetic, whether one links it to Greenbergian abstraction or New Criticism, and this tendency has come under severe critique by Leo Steinberg, Martin Jay, Rosalind Krauss, Hal Foster, and others. Be that as it may, it is hard to miss the way that ocularity organized the construction and rhetoric of modern poetics. Literary counterparts to the visual arts—imagism, vorticism, objectivism—emphasize visual clarity and economy against the expressivism and rhetorical abstractions of late romanticism. The various metaphors for modernist distanciation, whether via Ezra Pound's ideogram, T. S. Eliot's objective correlative,

Louis Zukofsky's object "brought to a focus," or Gertrude Stein's repetition (based on film), privilege the eye as a way of achieving, as Pound said, "an intellectual and emotional complex in an instant of time" (4).

Emphasis on the ocular is reinforced by what Joseph Frank has called "spatial form" in modern literature. According to Frank, modernist literature aspires to the condition of the visual arts by creating the illusion of a simultaneous apprehension—as though the entire work could be read all at once. He adduces the philosophical *durée* of Bergson, Freud's theory of the unconscious, and the continuing influence of Paterian symbolism to show how poets and novelists solved problems of temporality and historicity. Whether in Joyce or Eliot's use of myth, Proust's epiphanic moments, or Woolf's stream-of-consciousness narration, modernist formal innovation jettisons linear, developmental narrative in favor of a "space logic" of simultaneity (13). Frank's ahistorical reading of modernism is symptomatic of his era's New Critical formal values, which, in an attempt to repudiate more biographical or historical contexts of literature, places emphasis on the literary work as a "verbal icon" (William Wimsatt) symbol (I. A. Richards), or "miraculist fusion" (John Crowe Ransom) of disparate particulars. Behind each of these formulations lies a profound distrust of quotidian reality—of temporality, mass culture, and the unruly body—in favor of what Martin Jay calls a "scopic regime" of detached observation and rationalism.[2]

The space logic of modernism is an aesthetic version of a much larger epistemological break within social modernity in which knowledge, far from being a disinterested arena, is aligned with forms of power based on sight. Michel Foucault notes that from the late eighteenth century on, the body becomes increasingly governed and scrutinized through forms of "bio-power," those technologies and institutions that categorize and discipline bodies. Statistics, hygiene, comparative anatomy, demographics, psychology—these are the new sciences of bio-power through which bodies are defined and measured. Not insignificantly, these are sciences that rely on eyesight and specular control in order to establish not only what the body *is* but, most importantly, how it can be monitored and controlled. Bio-power contributed to producing a statistical norm, an "average" body, against which others would be measured. The modern penal system or mental institution become the primary regulatory agencies for those whose bodies and behaviors that do not conform to the rule—or in Foucault's terms, made docile. Jeremy Bentham's panopticon becomes the epitome of regulatory power through visibility, a carceral architecture in which the control of authority is everywhere experienced yet nowhere visible.

Disability scholars have understood how Foucault's critique of biopower relates significantly to persons with physical or cognitive impairments. Shelley Tremain refers to the "asylums, income support programs, quality of life assessments, workers' compensation benefits, special education programs, regimes of rehabilitation, parallel transit systems, prostheses, home care services, telethons, sheltered workshops, poster child campaigns, and prenatal diagnosis" by which biopolitics makes disabled persons visible (5–6). Tom Humphreys and Carol Padden have discussed the regimentation and compartmentalization of deaf children in residential schools in Foucauldian terms. They point out that although these schools historically offered opportunities for community and shared signlanguage communication, they also participated in insidious forms of racism (by separating white and black students), communicational segregation (by separating signing and oral students), and audism (by separating deaf students from hearing instructors). As I have noted in my previous chapter, many Deaf poets and storytellers make the institutionalization of oralist education, the historical attacks on sign language, and the (presumed) linkage between deafness and mental illness a centerpiece of their work. In *I Am Ordered Now to Talk,* Peter Cook elaborates on a popular conflation of "deaf" with "dumb," for which the historical incarceration of poor and indigent deaf persons in asylums was often a social remedy.

The disciplining of deafness has had national implications as well. As Douglas Baynton and Jane Berger have pointed out, post–Civil War oralist education in the United States was directly tied to projects of national consolidation and citizenship. Deaf individuals, who in the antebellum period had created communities around residential schools in which ASL was encouraged, were now subjected to disciplinary action for using sign language. Manual signing became the visible representation of a deaf citizen's linguistic—and presumably characterological—deviance that had to be coerced back into the national fabric. In this respect, deaf persons joined Native Americans, immigrants, and ex-slaves whose visibility as noncitizen subjects was monitored by epidemiological and medical discourses. Against this historical background, the use of sign language becomes more than a vehicle of communication. Rather, it is regarded as a direct affront to progressive programs for consolidation and rehabilitation, unruly in its repudiation of speech and its insistence on cultural heritage and linguistic specificity.

Man Sees Horse: The Flying Words Project ∽

Having rehearsed two dimensions of modernist ocularcentrism, one aesthetic and the other sociohistorical, I want now to look at recent poets who utilize ASL's relationship to the visual to elaborate a politics of space and, in the process, critique hearing culture by representing—and satirizing—its presumptive claims to normalized identity. For Jim Cohn the defining moment for a rapprochement between the visualist imperatives of the Pound-Williams modernist tradition and deaf poetry occurred in a 1984 meeting of Allen Ginsberg and deaf poet Robert Panara at the Rochester National Technical Institute for the Deaf (NTID). Cohn sees the meeting as revealing the proximity of Ginsberg's Beat poetics of the clear, focused image to the visual aesthetic of his deaf signing poets. It also revealed that sign language poetics is not an isolated cultural movement but part of an international "poetic style based upon an awareness of the importance of the image" (*Sign Mind* 28). This awareness led to translations of Ginsberg's poetry into ASL and encouraged Cohn to form a collaborative poetry project involving deaf and hearing poets.[3] My only qualification of Cohn's important thesis would be to question whether the visual means the same thing for modernist poets in search of unmediated access to the thing in the world and for deaf poets whose visual language always bears the burden of its marginal relation to hearing culture. That is, a stress on the visual arises in response to specific cultural and historical needs; one poet's *ekphrasis* is a Deaf poet's common linguistic coin.

Among the foundational documents of modernism, Ezra Pound's rendering of the sinologist Ernst Fenollosa's essay on the Chinese written character occupies an especially privileged position. When Pound encountered Fenollosa's work in 1913, he used it to break with what he took to be a Western, rationalist epistemology. By adopting Fenollosa's (now discredited) theory of the Chinese character as a method for poetry, Pound was able to launch a number of poetic projects, including his the-

Fig. 5. From Ernest Fenollosa, "The Chinese Written Character as a Medium for Poetry." (Reprinted by permission of City Lights Books.)

ories of imagism and vorticism, and the historical methodology of *The Cantos*. What was particularly valuable for Pound in Fenollosa's essay was its emphasis on the visual character of the ideogram, its ability to fuse both temporality (the characters map a sequence of actions) and space (the character combines several discrete images) in a single sign. The Chinese character, according to Fenollosa, joins radicals into a compound or cluster that maintains connections to concrete objects yet permits a dynamic movement among them. Verbal language is based on an arbitrary relationship of word and thing, whereas Chinese pictorial language retains the image of the thing in the character, much as, in acoustic terms, onomatopoeia imitates natural sounds. When several characters are placed side by side, the visual, spatial properties of the objects are retained while permitting each to resonate with the other. As Fenollosa says, "A true noun, an isolated thing, does not exist in nature. Things are only the terminal points, or rather the meeting points, of actions, cross-sections cut through actions, snapshots" (10).

To show how the ideogram provides a "vivid shorthand picture of the operations of nature," Fenollosa uses two phrases (8). In the first, "man sees horse," each character emphasizes dynamic, forward movement. The character for "man" shows two legs striding forward; the character for the verb "sees" features an eye walking on legs; "horse" depicts the animal with four legs. Unlike the written English sentence, the Chinese characters contain the idea of movement in each visual figure rather than distributing various functions among three alphabetic symbols. The man who observes the horse is linked to the animal not merely through grammatical relations (subject, verb, object) but by shared placement and physical properties; the eye literally *walks* toward the horse. Fenollosa summarizes his second example, "Sun Rises [in the] East," as "The sun . . . on one side, on the other the sign of the east, which is the sun entangled in the branches of a tree" (33). The middle sign, "rises," combines both: the sun rising above the horizon plus the trunk-line of the tree-sign. "East" ceases to be an abstract position on the compass but is concretized in an image of the sun seen through trees in the morning. Pound adapted this principle of layered images in the construction of much larger poetic units, juxtaposing one concrete image with another without transitions or connectives. Thus, the most characteristic feature of modernist poetry in English—an extended montage of disconnected elements—was in part derived from a misreading of Chinese written language in order to suit a visualist imperative.

Dirksen Bauman notes that Pound's experiments with the Chinese character hint at a "phantom limb phenomenon where writers have sensed language's severed visual-spatial mode and went groping after it" (316). What would happen, he continues, if the "deaf poet had been mythologized as the blind poet has been; would literature have developed differently"? Perhaps with this question in mind, Bauman challenged Peter Cook and Kenny Lerner, the Flying Words Project, to translate some of Fenollosa's phrases into American Sign Language, and the result is a sequence of transformations of the philologist's core phrases. Lerner and Cook's often droll response is perhaps not what Bauman had in mind when he suggested this translation project, but their performance highlights something important about the ways that signing poets resite or resituate poetry in the act of reciting it. At one level, Cook, who is deaf, attempts to respond as accurately as possible to the phrases that his hearing partner gives him, an intention signaled by his adoption of a Zenlike pose of concentration before beginning each translation. At another level, however, he extends the logic of Fenollosa's project by generating new phrases out of minimal examples in an increasingly chaotic semiotic package, all

the while using Lerner as the hearing straight man who assigns the translation tasks. From "sun tangled in branches of tree" or "man sees horse"
Cook signifies on the act of translating, taking on its darker associations
with *traduce* and *violate* by following out the surreal logic of each sign and
by performing his own variations on Lerner's words. If the point of Fenollosa's example is to unite subject and object through the visual image, then
that unity is vividly realized in a poet whose body is itself both the producer and text of his poem.

Take, for instance, the first example: "sun tangled in branches of tree":

> A tree in the early morning sun,
> As the sun nears the branches
> It burns down the whole tree,
> And the sun moves across the sky.[4]

In English, we hear the subordinate phrase "as the sun nears the branches"
as meaning that the sun is seen through leaves. Cook literalizes the phrase,
collapsing observer and object in the handshapes for SUN and TREE, both
of which feature the right arm raised vertically. Cook understands the English verb *nears* to mean that the tree literally approaches the sun, a proximity that Cook reinforces by allowing his right hand to sign TREE while
his left gradually brings the SUN sign closer and closer to the tree until the
tree is figuratively "burned down." Cook transfers the SUN sign to his right
hand and moves it to his right while the flickering embers of the TREE continue to burn in his left hand below.

When the same phrase is rendered a second time, the absurd logic
that links "tangled" with "burned down" goes through an even more extreme variation:

> Sun in early morning sun.
> As the sun approaches the sun
> The sun burns down the sun
> And the sun drifts across the sky.

Here the sign for TREE has been replaced (burned down?) by the sign for
the rising SUN, leading to the cosmic, comic collision of two suns. By map-

ping ASL signs onto Chinese ideograms, by combining handshapes for TREE and SUN, Cook is able to generate novel—if absurd—meanings while retaining the principle of homology and repetition that animates Fenollosa's essay.

In his second example, "man sees horse," Cook builds on the supposed difference between subject and direct object in English. In variation 1, the poem is straightforward: "walking person sees horse through fence." In variation 2 the seeing man becomes a "rubber necked man" whose head stretches through a fence to see the horse. In variation 4, a "rubber-eyed man" projects his eyes out of his head toward the horse, and his eyes then rebound back into the eye sockets. Here, instead of the mimetic economy that Pound celebrates in the Chinese character, Cook creates scenarios that focus on the destruction of horses, trees, sun, and man when language is removed from its voice and allowed to move through its own spatial logic. Furthermore, Cook produces rather unfaithful translations of Lerner's phrases as well, playing havoc with Pound's ideal of translation based on fidelity to an original. At every level, the values of economy and clarity reinforced by Pound are exploded and the image resited from the object onto the signifying body.

By speaking of signing poets *resiting* poetry I am relying on a pun that, like Jacques Derrida's neologism *différance* must be seen to be understood. In substituting an *a* for an *e* in the French word *différence,* Derrida signals language's unspoken difference from itself, the spatial differing and temporal deferring that are the basis of meaning-making. Similarly, in *Of Grammatology* Derrida deconstructs Ferdinand de Saussure's famous model of the sign (which, fortuitously for my purposes, utilizes both the image of a tree and a horse). In his schematic representation of the sign, Saussure shows how the relationship between the words "arbor" or "equos" and the material tree or horse is based on an arbitrary association between sign and referent (67). As in all oral languages; there is no necessary relationship between the phonemes that make up the word and the concept invoked. But as Derrida points out, Saussure assumes that the written sign is simply the outer representation of language's "internal" structure, a passive sign of a phonocentric intent. For Saussure, as for Plato, writing is secondary to its originary, oral form and as such is underwritten by a metaphysics of presence, a phonocentrism based on the

Logos or Word of God (Derrida 27–73). Unlike spoken language, writing—*écriture*—represents in its material form the difference from presence that is the basis of language. As Derrida concludes, "The play of difference, which, as Saussure reminded us, is the condition for the possibility and functioning of every sign, is in itself a silent play" (5).

Despite the rich implications of this "silent play" for the semiotics of signing, Derrida does not take sign language into account and thus fails to consider work like that of Peter Cook that would seem to complicate a phonocentric metaphysics. After all, if writing is not the material representation of a prior phonetic sign but "the condition for the possibility and functioning of every sign," then presumably manual signing would be a form of writing as well.[5] In ASL poetry, meaning is established through a body that is also a text; a tree can be literally tangled in a tree, thus challenging the interiority of the voice as something located within or prior to the body. By severing meaning from an ontologically grounded Logos and locating it on the expressive body, we may see "seeing" from an entirely different vantage.[6]

In the Name of the Father: Clayton Valli's "Snowflake" ↜

If ASL poetry asks us to reconsider the ocularcentric nature of modernist poetry, it also questions the "voice" upon which much modern poetic theory is based. Does the use of ASL mean that deaf poets have no purchase on the revived oral tradition that emerged during the 1960s and 1970s? Is there no reciting in ASL? Deaf scholars have pointed out the paradoxical fact that the closest analogue to ASL storytelling is the ancient oral tradition since both stress face-to-face contact between poet and audience.[7] Both rely on audience participation in knitting community together, and both stress qualities of variation, facial expression, and face-to-face exposure. Although, as Christopher Krentz points out, this conflation risks aligning ASL poetry with the oralist education encouraged by Alexander Graham Bell, it does point to the fuzzy boundaries between signed, spoken, and written poetries (52–53). For some Deaf activists, however, any rapprochement with the spoken is anathema. I have discussed the scandal of speech in signed poetry in chapter 3, but I want here to say something about the ability of ASL to represent the voice that has implications for a politics of Deaf community. In order to make this point I want to look at Clayton Valli's "Snowflake," a poem that may seem on the surface to have nothing to do with either the social or the spatial but which, in its manipulation of linguistic codes, ultimately speaks to the isolation of the deaf individual in audist culture.[8]

"Snowflake" is a small allegory about a deaf child of hearing parents, a story that parallels Valli's own upbringing in an oral household. The poem is divided into three segments. Part 1 describes a gray day when all of the leaves have fallen from the trees and the landscape is barren and empty. The fall of a single snowflake suddenly reminds the poet of a moment in the past, a memory of a small boy's face. That moment is described in part 2 as an interchange between the deaf boy and his hearing father. Part 3 returns to the present, the snow now covering the ground. A falling snowflake once again distracts the poet, but now it seems part of the white landscape rather than an isolate fleck. Parts 1 and 3 are in the present, serving as temporal bookends for part 2, the "social" portion of the poem that is set in the past. Although the entire poem is signed, Valli makes use of at least four modes of manual signing in order to display the various levels in which signed communication occurs. In the first case, the father brags to his friends in fluent English about his son's vocal skills. Valli signals the father's fluency in English by an expansive use of ASL that the child interprets as gibberish. Here, the representation of English fluency, seen from the standpoint of a deaf child, is a series of empty signs, the equivalent of "blah blah blah." Second, the father then turns to the child, switching to a more careful intonation, signaled in this case by a combination of signing, silent vocalization, and finger spelling. The father asks, in a slow, deliberate manner, "What is your name" and "How old are you"? The third mode is that of the child's attempts to respond orally to his father—"My name is . . ." and "I am five"—which are rendered in Signed Exact English (SEE), a form of signing that uses ASL signs but follows English word order and finger-spells English grammatical morphemes. The child never has a chance to finish his phrases because the father interrupts him to celebrate the son's verbal success. As the father changes modes to relate to his friends and then to his child, so Valli adjusts his representation of speech in each speech act situation. As the child adjusts his signifying function to accommodate English expectations, so Valli changes from ASL, to finger spelling, to SEE.

The fourth mode, the "snowflake" frame, contains or brackets the "speech" frame but also provides a poetic alternative to a discursive binary of speech/silence. Here Valli exploits the richness of ASL, utilizing extensive variations of handshape, body position, facial expression, and visual puns to create a wintery landscape as a metaphor for alienation. The use of repeated handshapes in various positions assists in creating rhythm, much as rhyme or alliteration links elements in traditional English verse. In describing the wintry landscape, for example, Valli uses the number 5 handshape (all five fingers spread out) as it appears in the sign for TREE (the right hand and arm placed vertically on top of the left hand horizontally extended in front of the chest, directed across the body). The TREE sign morphs into a swirling motion in front the face to suggest a tree full of leaves. This sign is followed by a rotating downward motion of the fiVE handshape in both hands to signify leaves falling. From the erect tree, to the tree full of leaves, to the tree bereft of leaves, a single handshape displays the transformation of a tree in winter.

In this section of the poem Valli deploys a familiar trope of romantic dejection in which the poet is alienated from the social world, unable to translate the natural landscape into his own condition. The world seems flat and gray; a cloud covers the sun, blending foreground and background into a blank emptiness. Then the poet observes a falling snowflake, a moment that begins a process of reflection upon a particular face and moment in the past that lifts the poet out of dejection and into time. This Coleridgian change from blank nature to memory, present to past, coincides with the child's verbal alienation from his father. But as in Coleridge or Wordsworth, the ability to remember and thus enter time permits a larger, more expansive view. The isolated snowflake and solitary deaf child of part 1 merge into a common landscape in part 3. The child *is* the father of the man, not by living beyond him (and the symbolic regime he represents) but by rearticulating childhood isolation in his own (signed) terms. Valli, the mature poet, depicts an earlier version of himself, marginalized in an oralist universe, who has now redefined childhood and audism by translating both into sign. The *site* of dejection is redeemed by the *sight* of a nature that the deaf child can now order and control.

Singing the Sign: Patrick Graybill, "Paradox" ✍

The oedipal trajectory of Valli's poem testifies to an important theme among deaf poets surrounding the issue of generation and language. Because most deaf persons live in families with members who are hearing, multiculturalism is a given and bilingualism a horizon. As the documentary *Sound and Fury* indicates, generational issues within Deaf culture are often linguistic: whether, in a household of hearing and deaf members, to raise a child in ASL or to reinforce oralism via cochlear implant or other medical intervention. Valli's poem quietly articulates tensions that exist between nonsigning, hearing parents and their deaf children. With the advent of new hearing technologies—cochlear implants, hearing aids— along with oral education and mainstreaming, the cultural heritage of Deaf World seems in jeopardy. Many ASL poems deal with generational tensions around language use, and in the case of Patrick Graybill's "Paradox," those tensions are figured through race and gender.

In "Paradox" Graybill describes a club or restaurant in which a black woman is singing a love song. As with the Valli example, the woman's song triggers a reflection on the poet's own relationship to his hearing parents. A rough paraphrase of the poem looks like this:

> A woman, who is black, sings a song. As the pianist plays the piano, she sings a song whose title is "My Man, Where Is the Man I Love?" White and black keys of the piano bounce up and down as her voice rises. There are women in the audience with men among them. All watch the singer as she cries out, "My man, where is the man I love?" The piano keys, black and white, come to a stop. In a white and black room, women rise and applaud the singer—men as well—applaud for a long time. The woman smiles, bows, walks over to someone seated. Her man! So that for her, the meaning of the song is just a song, nothing more.

> But deep inside myself, I am haunted by those words: "My man, where is the man I love?" My mother can hear and can sign. My father can hear but cannot sign. For me the story rings true throughout my life; "My man, where is the man I love?"

This seemingly simple tale contains a more complex story about how cultural differences are represented. The poem divides the world into racial and gendered categories. The woman is black; there are women *but also* men in the audience; the piano keys are black and white; the women applaud, *and so do the men;* the room is white and black. Such contrasts reinforce racial and gender differences at the same time that the repeated refrain reinforces a level of common ground. The black singer sings a love song for someone who is a projection of the song, not the man in the club where she sings. Graybill sings a song for his father who, like the addressee of the woman's song, is also not in the room. Despite differences of race, gender, and audiology, Graybill is able to empathize with a black hearing woman by resiting her desire onto his.

"Paradox" exposes the degree to which signing itself is a site of affective relations. The refrain, "Where is the man I love?" is heard differently by a poet for whom the interrogative in the title refers less to a place than a potentiality in language: "Where in language does the father whom I love live?" The black-and-white room where the song is heard, the black and white keys of the accompanying piano, the black and white features of the two singers, hearing and deaf, become contrastive features that heighten the common affective core between the two artists. The patterned repetitions of the poem serve to reinforce differences that the poem's coda disperses. The fact that the deaf listener cannot hear the song does not lessen his empathy with its emotive force, nor with its empathic implications, a fact vividly rendered by Graybill's ecstatic rendering of the song's refrain.

Resiting Poetry ⟆

Where is the politics of Deaf community in these very different examples? Peter Cook's reconfiguration of Chinese phrases, far from providing a satisfactory aesthetic closure, opens up the images to collision, violence, and semantic indeterminacy. While Valli's lyric draws upon a romantic trope of dejection, it represents that mode through an indictment of paternalist oralism, one made all the more poignant by the poet's identification of himself as the subject of the father's vocalization. Graybill draws on a black blues song to express his distance from his hearing, nonsigning father by identifying with a hearing black singer. These themes and strategies may not strike hearing persons as being particularly political, but for a bicultural d/Deaf audience, they embody a kind of double consciousness that interprets literary conventions through what I have been calling a deaf optic. Pound draws upon the Chinese ideogram to assert the primacy of visual images over the distancing effects of rhetoric. Peter Cook draws upon Pound's ocularcentric poetics to generate an imagism based on the signifying body and on the generative potential of handshapes to suggest new, unexpected meanings.

I might make one further observation about the term *siting* that goes beyond the spatial implications of sign language toward the social world in which ASL is used. I am referring here to the ways that d/Deaf poets are sited in social spaces of Deaf World: residential schools, deaf clubs, special ed classrooms, deaf rap and slam competitions, and, more recently, videotapes and DVDs. Certain cities—Rochester, Hartford, Philadelphia, Fremont, Baltimore, Washington, DC, have an almost mythic status within Deaf World equivalent to the great modernist metropoles of Paris, London, and Zurich. These places are identified not only with deaf schools but with the communities that form around them, the institutions and businesses that support these communities, the families that raise children—hearing and deaf—within them. Peter Cook's oralist education at Massachusetts's Clarke School, Clayton Valli's training at the Austine School for the Deaf, and Patrick Graybill's experiences at the Kansas School for the Deaf and Gallaudet University must be considered as foundational elements of their work, as significant to their creative life as Paris was to the expatriate generation of writers. The history of modern poetry is a material history of publishers, magazines, journals, and essays on the Chinese written character. Coffeehouses, bars, and salons become important adjuncts of literary professionalism, to be sure, but the fact of the book and its reception makes literary community largely a matter of print. For the Deaf poet, shared cultural traditions are sited around specific performances, no one of which is ever quite the same. Presence may be represented by the metaphor of a snowflake, but it can never be dissevered from an audience before which the figure is enacted.

So what is golf? I return to Simi Linton's initial question to ask, again, what is the field on which the game is played and how does that field include and exclude certain players? In the case of poetry, the game concerns language, and, as Wittgenstein observes, "What belongs to a language game is a whole culture" (8). Wittgenstein is discussing the situated nature of cultural values—the fact that aesthetic ideals of beauty are products of specific class and educational assumptions. Translating into our terms with ASL poetry, we might say that what belongs to the language game called poetry, at least within hearing society, is a set of self-evident values concerning poetry's association with the voice and sound. But an equally potent principle of poetry is its ability to challenge linguistic norms. As a genre, poetry is enriched most when its rules are broken, when its formulas and rhetorics are challenged. Ezra Pound had just such a challenge in mind when he advocated the "direct presentation of the thing" against the inflated rhetoric of Edwardian verse; the Chinese character became his alternative. Pound's and Williams's vaunting of the visual image and objectivist thing-in-itself invented the subsequent language games of modernism by erasing the word in pursuit of the world. The "whole culture" interpellated within the language game of modernism knows the score and reads the page.

For Peter Cook, Clayton Valli, and Patrick Graybill, Wittgenstein's phrase means something else. What belongs to the language game of ASL is a "whole culture" that lives in a colonial relation to the spoken word. Deaf poets' transformations of handshape, body position, diction, and register continue a modernist effort to defamiliarize language, to see differently. But they signify on sight as well, bringing into vivid presence the body and expressiveness that have been the dream of poetry since the Romantics. In an era in which the study of poetry in the academy has fallen on hard times, ASL performance offers an opportunity to revivify the art, not by adding increments to an existing canon but by rethinking the metaphors of vision and presence upon which poetry has been erected. When ASL poetry is brought into the poetry classroom—and into the ASL classroom as well—we may begin to understand rhyme anew when tree is tangled in tree.

Chapter 5

Missing Larry

The Poetics of Disability in Larry Eigner

how to dance
sitting down
    —CHARLES OLSON, "Tyrian Business"

Ramps ⌣

The year 2000 marked the tenth anniversary of the Americans with Disabilities Act, an event commemorated in June by a twenty-four-city relay
by disabled athletes and activists. The torch for this relay arrived in Southern California, carried by Sarah Will in a jet ski on Venice Beach. After
handing the torch to another disabled athlete, Will was lifted into her
wheelchair to join a trek down Venice Boulevard to the Western Center for
Independent Living.[1] Although some disability activists might criticize
the triumphalist character of this celebration—crippled athletes hitting
the beach in jet skis—the event's climax at an Independent Living center
was a fitting destination for persons who came out of various medical
closets in the 1960s and began living together in communal spaces and
public housing. The Center for Independent Living is, coincidentally, the
same venue that brought the poet Larry Eigner from his home in Swampscott, Massachusetts, in 1978 to live in Berkeley, California, where he spent
his last years.[2]

The passage of the ADA in 1990 capped three decades of activism by
persons who, for physical or psychological reasons, had been denied access to public buildings, insurance policies, housing, medical treatment,

signage, education, marriage, sexuality, and childbearing—not to mention legal representation and respect. Activism on their behalf began in social movements of the 1960s, but unlike antiwar, feminist, and civil rights struggles, the disability rights movement has not—until recently—received the same attention by historians of civil rights, This silence is odd since the disabled community cuts across all demographic, racial, and class lines and, potentially, includes everyone. It may be that the very pervasiveness of disability contributes to its marginal status as a rights-claiming category.

There are a number of reasons why the subject of disability is often omitted in the roster of 1960s social movements, although this absence is being corrected in recent books dealing with disability history.[3] Civil rights legislation of the 1950s and 1960s could invoke long traditions of advocacy going back to antebellum abolitionism; the antiwar movement grew out of pacifist and anti-imperialist politics of the nineteenth century; feminism grew out of suffragism and the labor movement. Disabled persons, however, were treated as medical "cases," best kept out of sight, their wheelchairs, braces, and oxygen tents sequestered in hospitals, clinics, and asylums. Individual disabilities were treated independently of one another, balkanized by separate regimes of treatment, therapy, and social service. Social support often came from charity movements and parental groups that reinforced a paternalist ethos of the disabled person as innocent victim or child rather than fully vested citizen. Nor was the disability community unified in its goals and social agendas. Persons with occasional or nonapparent disabilities may choose to pass in able-bodied culture and refuse the protections of social legislation; someone who loses sight late in life may lack the same institutional and cultural support as someone blind from birth; Deaf persons often do not want to be viewed as disabled, preferring to see themselves as a linguistic minority; persons with cognitive or developmental disabilities are often separated from those with physical impairments. Forging alliances among such disparate populations was, needless to say, difficult for early disability rights activists who sought coalitional formations across medical lines yet honored material differences among separate disabilities.

Beyond these factors, there were economic disincentives to recognizing disability as a civil right since redress required proactive investment in infrastructure modification, technologies, sign language interpreters,

transportation, and other accommodations. Providing ramps and elevators for wheelchairs, TDDs, and braille signage would cost businesses
money, and many legislators felt that federal funds should not be spent
when private philanthropy could serve the same function. As Lennard
Davis point out, both the political Left and Right perceived the disabled
body as "unproductive," which, in a world based upon instrumentality
and capitalization, was not a basis upon which class analysis or public policy could be forged ("Nation" 18). As I suggest in chapter 7, "universal design" means more than ramps for wheelchair users or "talking" traffic signals for blind and seeing impaired persons; it implies breaking the hold of
stigma in order to examine the ways in which a rhetoric of normalcy in-
fects social attitudes and thwarts the forming of community. Recently, one
of my colleagues who is active in the field of minority rights complained
about the university administration's insensitivity to diversity: "It was like
talking to a deaf person," he said, linking authorities who *won't* listen to
people who *can't.* The idea that the deaf are "dumb," in any sense of that
term, is precisely the stigma that needs to be erased if alliances between
traditional civil rights based on class, race, gender, and sexuality are to be
forged with disability.

Which is why a poetics—as much as a politics—of disability is important: because it theorizes the ways that poetry defamiliarizes not only
language but the body normalized *within* language. A poetics of disability
might unsettle the thematics of embodiment as it appeared in any number of literary and artistic movements of the 1960s. This same thematics
was shared with the New Left in its stress on the physical body as localized
site of the social. Whether in feminism's focus on reproductive rights,
youth culture's fetish of sexual liberation, cultural nationalist celebrations
of "race men," or the antiwar movement's politics of heroic resistance, the
healthy, preferably young body becomes a marker of political agency.
Within the world of art, this same emphasis on a normalized body
emerged through a set of imbricated metaphors—gesture, breath, orality,
performance, "leaping" poetry, "action" painting, projective verse, deep
image, happenings, spontaneous bop prosody—that organized what
Daniel Belgrad has called "the culture of spontaneity" in the 1960s. While
a poetics of embodiment foregrounds the body as source for artistic production, it nevertheless calls for some unmediated physical or mental core
unhampered by prostheses, breathing tubes, or electric scooters.

What would happen if we subjected a poetics of embodiment to the actual bodies and mental conditions of its authors? What would it mean to read the 1960s poetics of process and expression for its dependence on ableist models, while recognizing its celebration of idiosyncrasy and difference? By this optic, we might see Robert Lowell, Anne Sexton, and John Berryman not only as confessional poets but as persons who lived with depression or bipolar disorder, for whom personal testimony was accompanied by hospitalization, medicalization, and family trauma. What would it mean to think of Charles Olson's "breath" line as coming from someone with chronic emphysema exacerbated by heavy smoking? What if we added to Audre Lorde's multicultural description of herself as a Black, lesbian, mother, "sister outsider," a person with breast cancer (as she herself does in *The Cancer Journals*)? Robert Creeley's lines in "The Immoral Proposition," "to look at it is more / than it was," mean something very particular when we know that their author has only one eye (125). To what extent are Elizabeth Bishop's numerous references to suffocation and claustrophobia in her poems an outgrowth of a life with severe asthma? Robert Duncan's phrase "I see always the underside turning" may refer to his interest in theosophy and the occult, but it also derives from the poet's visual disorder, in which one eye sees the near and the other far.[4] Was William Carlos Williams's development of the triadic stepped foot in his later career a dimension of his prosody or a typographical response to speech disorders resulting from a series of strokes? It is worth remembering that the signature poem of the era was not only a poem about the madness of the best minds of the poet's generation, but about the carceral and therapeutic controls that defined those minds as mad, written by someone who was himself "expelled from the academies for crazy."[5] And if we include in our list the effects of alcoholism and substance abuse, a good deal of critical discussion of 1960s poetry could be enlisted around disability issues.

I am not suggesting that a focus on the disabled body is the only way to read postwar poetry, but it is worth noting that its poetics of embodiment brought a renewed focus on the vicissitudes of hand and eye, musculature and voice, as dimensions of the poetic. The salient feature of poetries generated out of Beat, Black Mountain, New York school, deep image, and other nonformalist poetries was a belief in the poem's registration of physiological and cognitive response, the line as "score for the voice," the poem as act or gesture.[6] Charles Olson's assertion that "Limits / are what any of us / are inside of" speaks as much for the creative potential of the disabled artist as it does for the American self-reliant hero of his *Maximus Poems* (17). Perhaps it would be more balanced to say that the self-evident status of a certain kind of body has often underwritten an expressivist poetics whose romantic origins can be traced to a tubercular Keats, syphilitic Shelley and Nietzsche, clubfooted Byron, and mad John Clare and Gérard de Nerval.

Missing Larry ⮌

My title refers to Larry Eigner, a significant figure in the New American Poetry, who is missing in a number of senses. On a personal level, I miss Larry, who died in February 1996 as a poet whose curiosity and attentiveness remain a model of poetic integrity. Although his movements were extremely restricted due to cerebral palsy contracted at birth, he was by no means "missing" from the poetry world, particularly after his move to Berkeley. Thanks to the efforts of Bob Grenier, Kathleen Frumkin, and Jack Foley, Larry was present at many readings, talks, and parties throughout the 1980s. Nor, as those who knew him can attest, was he a reticent presence at such events. He was a central influence on the emerging "Language writing" movement of the mid-1970s, publishing in their magazines (*L=A=N=G=U=A=G=E, Bezoar, This, Hills*) and participating in their talk and reading series. His emphasis on clear, direct presentation of moment-to-moment perceptions also linked him to the older objectivists (George Oppen, Carl Rakosi, Charles Reznikoff, and Louis Zukofsky) as well as poets of his own generation living in the San Francisco Bay region such as Robert Duncan and Michael McClure.

A second dimension to my title refers to the Eigner missing from discussions of postwar poetry. Although he was centrally identified with the Black Mountain movement and corresponded with Olson, Creeley, Duncan, Corman, and others, he is seldom mentioned in synoptic studies (including my own work) of that generation. What few critical accounts exist of his work come from poets. Robert Duncan, Denise Levertov, Clark Coolidge, Cid Corman, Charles Bernstein, Robert Hass, Ron Silliman, Barrett Watten have all written appreciations of his work, but he has had little response from the critics.[7] And although he was aligned with Language writing later in his life, his name seldom appears in books or articles about that movement.[8] Perhaps most surprisingly, given his centrality in the New American Poetry, he is seldom included in discussions of disability arts, with the exception of an appearance in Kenny Fries' anthology of disability writing, *Staring Back*.[9]

This brings me to the tertiary level of my title—the absence of cerebral palsy in discussions of Eigner's poetry. In what little critical treatment of his work exists, the fact of his physical condition is seldom mentioned. The lack of reference to cerebral palsy leads me to ask how one might theorize disability where least apparent: how to retrieve from recalcitrant silences, markers of a neurological condition that mediated all aspects of Eigner's life.[10] In the process, we might discover ways of retrieving other social markers—of race, sexuality, class—where not immediately apparent. Eigner by no means adhered to New Critical warnings about the biographical fallacy—the idea that poems should finesse biographical or historical contexts through formal, rhetorical means. At the same time, he seldom foregrounded his mediated physical condition—his daily regimes of physical exercise, his limited mobility, his slurred speech—preferring to record real-time perception and observation. In order to retrieve disability from this lacuna we need to "crip" cultural forms, not simply to find disability references but to see the ways Eigner's work unseats normalizing discourses of embodiment. Cripping Larry Eigner allows us to read the body of his work in terms of his "different" body and to understand how the silences surrounding his poetry are, in some way, a dimension of—perhaps a refusal of—that embodiment.

To confront this issue, I have appropriated Barrett Watten's important essay "Missing 'X,'" which locates the salient features of Eigner's writing in its suppression of predication and syntactic closure. According to Watten, the most characteristic feature of Eigner's poetry is its truncation or effacement of rhetorical connectives, creating a "predicate for which the act of reference is located outside of or is generalized by the entire poem" (178). One could supply an *X* for elements outside the poem that are nevertheless implicit in the phrase-to-phrase, stanza-to-stanza movement. Hence, to take Watten's example, Eigner's lines "Imagination heavy with / worn power" could be rewritten as "an element of the world is 'Imagination heavy with /worn power.'" The couplet "the wind tugging / leaves" could be rewritten as "an element of this poem is 'the wind tugging / leaves.'" The suppression of subjects and predicates allows Eigner's noun phrases to function independently of any overarching narrative, creating unexpected links and suturing discontinuous phrases. To some extent, Eigner's use of abbreviated phrases resembles the practice of Language writers—including Watten—who restrict the logical and rhetorical completion of a period, leaving shards to be recombined in new structures.

The implications of Watten's argument are significant for differentiating Eigner's poetry from that of more traditional poets for whom metaphor often contextualizes the outside within the poem. For someone like Hart Crane, as Watten observes, predication is propositional; all grammatical elements work to render an idealized object. An object (Crane's "Royal Palm" is his example) may be invoked by discontinuous means; nevertheless, it organizes the processes of predication and metaphorization. All figures, however oblique, point toward a single focal point. Eigner, on the other hand, creates a mobile grammatical structure in which subjects and predicates occupy multiple positions. "In Eigner an absolute object is not referred to in the poem. Rather the entire idiom is predicated on the lack of such reference" (179). But what is the nature of this "outside" that serves as an absent cause for partial phrases? What are the implications for the disabled poet when we base predication on "lack"? Is the mobility of noun phrases strictly a function of indeterminate syntax, or a register of alternative modes of mobility and cognition in a world based on performance? The danger of providing concrete answers to these questions is that they make Eigner's poetry a compensatory response for physical limits rather than a critical engagement with them. Conscious of this danger, I want to extend Watten's useful speculations about predication to describe the ways that the "missing X" could also refer to an unstated physical condition that organizes all responses to a present world. And since that world is defined by compulsory able-bodiedness, *not* referring to its coherence and unity may indicate a nascent critique.

Page / Room / Weather ⌐

In order to discuss Eigner's poetry in terms of disability we must first honor his own reticence on the subject. Throughout his memoirs, interviews, and poetry, the subject of his cerebral palsy seldom appears. In his author's biography at the end of Donald Allen's anthology *The New American Poetry,* Eigner describes himself as a "shut-in partly" (436). Bob Grenier observes that "Larry's work does not *derive* from his palsy," but on the other hand, his poetry cannot help but be affected by it. In order to discover disability where it is not present, it is first necessary to find where it is—in Eigner's numerous prose writings, memoirs, and stories. Consider the following passage from his 1969 memoir, "What a Time, Distance":

> Cigarette cigar signs stores mostly Variety groceries and how many things candy a little not much good might very well be a good deal everything smelled bread was designed with packaged loaf fresh and down the street daily paper words flashes and then sentence dateline dispatches . . . (*Selected Poems* 114)

Here, Eigner remembers childhood experiences in a variety store, the sights and smells of products and signage rendered in quick succession. One might imagine such passages divided into lines and splayed out over a page, but these memories are constantly mediated by conditions of restricted motion, regimes of physiotherapy and exercise, which frame his access to such "variety":

> Over the toilet rim in the bathroom at home into the bowl his weemer between large knuckles, cigarette shifted to mouth preparatory or in other of grandfather's hands. Coffee label. Good to the last drop. Waste not want not. To go as long as you could manage it. Bread is the staff of life, Grampa said many times buttering it at the beginning of dinner. Relax, try how get to fling ahead legs loosened quick as anything in being walked to different rooms the times he wasn't creeping to do it yourself as soon as possible, idea to make no trouble or spoil things but live when somebody agreed to a walk as he ought to have, sort of homework from the therapy exercising not to sit back need to start all over to come from behind. Thimble yarn darn stocking waterglass stretch wrongside patch, cocoon tobacco cellophane bullet wake finger ring. (*Selected Poems* 115)

A series of Joycean associations mark this passage—from peeing, with his grandfather's help, to a coffee label and its ad ("Good to the last drop"), to depression-era adages about thrift ("Waste not want not") and health ("Bread is the staff of life"). These axioms rhyme with internalized parental imperatives regarding physical control ("Relax") and self-motivation ("do it yourself"), which for the young boy with motor impairment mark his distance from an able-bodied world. Those difficulties are rendered syntactically in the phrase "try how get to fling ahead legs loosened quick as anything," which may provide some verbal equivalent of the child's anxiety over muscular control.[11] Adult advice to "make no trouble or spoil things but live when somebody agree[s] to a walk," express a world of agency where everything from urinating to walking requires assistance.

This brief passage could serve as the "missing X" for many poems in which reference to physical limits has been evacuated, leaving only the "variety" of the Variety store on the page. In his prose, Eigner merges sensuous associations with things seen and felt ("thimble yarn darn stocking") with physical contexts of their apprehension. In his poetry, specific references to those contexts drops away, leaving acts of attention and cognition paramount. Those acts are deployed through three interrelated spaces: the page on which he worked, the room in which he lived, the weather or landscape he saw from that room. I would like to look for Larry in these three frames.

Eigner's is decisively a poetry of the page, a field of intense activity produced entirely with his right index finger, the one digit over which he had some control. The page—specifically the 8½ by 11 typewriter page—is the measure of the poem, determining its lineation, length, and typographic organization.[12] Although a few poems run on for several pages, often as not Eigner continues the poem as a second column on the same page.[13] Nor is the machine by which he produced those pages insignificant. Because Eigner needed to lean on the keys and peer closely at the sheet of paper, he could not use an electric typewriter and thus worked with a succession of Royal or Remington portables that permitted him a degree of flexibility in composition. The manual typewriter also allowed him to release the platen occasionally and adjust the spacing between words or lines, jamming letters or punctuation together or running one line onto the next. Eigner's careful spacing of letters and words, his indentations and double columns, could be seen as typographic idiosyncrasy, a variation on Charles Olson's "field" poetics, but they are also cognitive maps of his internally distanced relation to space. In a video of Eigner's funeral made by Cloud House productions, the filmmaker, Kush, returns to Eigner's house following the gravesite ceremony, and trains his camera on Eigner's typewriter for several minutes, a cenotaph for the poet's living remains.

We can see the characteristic qualities of Eigner's page in a section from *air the trees* (figure 6). The page is divided into three areas, a long, short-lined poem that fills the right half of the page, a short epigram to its left, and a longer poem—perhaps a continuation of the second—at the bottom left. Each of the three elements drifts gradually from left to right, reflecting Eigner's characteristic carriage shift, one that never quite seems to reach the left margin. While it would be impossible to verify that this rightward drifting lineation was a result of his physical difficulty in shifting the carriage, it was certainly the case that typing, for Eigner, required a considerable effort. Thus the epigrammatic tercet at the left, "slow is / the / poem," may describe considerably more than a Chaucerian resignation ("The lyf so short, the craft so long to lerne") and testify to the sheer physical difficulty of making a mark on a page.[14] Acts such as hitting the space bar, putting a new sheet of paper into the typewriter, or moving the carriage for a new line are no small features in creating the measure of Eigner's line.

The poem in question—or perhaps three poems—seems to concern a seascape with birds, whales, clouds, and islands. At the center of the longer section is a reflection on the poet's reflexive interest in the shifting movements within this landscape:

    heat

        past sunshine

           vibrations of air
                spiders, then birds, settle

        reflexive
           man
           bringing what he can

        interest

Small, flightless birds
the voice   far   tinkling bells

museum

of sorts,   the rats destroyed

moving ashore, M i d w a y

slow is   flat wall of the sea
t h e
poem   and sky

each island
rose

farther than any whale

fins

breathing above the waves
the mirrors

heat

past sunshine

vibrations of air
spiders, then birds, settle

reflexive
man
menageries   bringing what he can
from the bottom
interest
rock crumbles to earth
under rain   in
the seas
the quickening run-though
clouds mulct the moon
flats   one thing at a time

the whale is still hunted   tides, a large motion
in certain parts
small waves give boats
prodigal
the deep light

Fig. 6. "Small, flightless birds" from *air the trees* by Larry Eigner.
(Reprinted by permission of the estate of Larry Eigner.)

> in
>
> the quickening run-though
>
> one thing at a time
>
> tides, a large motion
>
> small waves give boats
>
> (*air* 25)

The phrase "quickening run-though" appears to be a typo for "run-through," in which case the poem chronicles its somewhat tentative, incomplete nature, as though Eigner is trying to approximate multiple simultaneous perceptions in a linear form. The poem *does* seem to be about a "reflexive / man / bringing what he can" to the diversity of movements suggested by this watery landscape. As in Wallace Stevens's "Sea Surface Full of Clouds," with its five balanced variations on the phrase "that November off Tehuantepec," Eigner wants to render a seascape that, by its very nature, cannot be fixed: "tides, a large motion // small waves give boats." The couplet compacts the "large" motion of tides and their local effects on "small waves" and "boats," and these contrasts are further enhanced by the lines to the left of these:

> rock crumbles to earth
> under rain
> the seas
>
> clouds mulct the moon
> flats
>
> the whale is still hunted
> in certain parts
>
> prodigal
> the deep light

The poet's "reflexive" interest in things leads to reflections on the creation of geological forms through the interaction of rock and water. The whale, "prodigal / the deep light," stands as the talismanic figure for the poem's contrasts—large yet human, mammal yet stonelike, deep yet surfacing, inert yet "prodigal." Eigner's steady attention to phrasing and evenly patterned syllables ("the voice far tinkling bells," "small waves give boats") shows an intense concentration on small verbal elements, yet his focus is always on the creation and destruction of large forces. The interplay of three separate elements on the page permits each to join with the others so that, for example, the reference to islands rising like whales in the longer poem seems to continue in the reference to "menageries / from the bottom" in the third.

I have chosen an example that does not thematize disability in order to suggest how the material limits of the poet's physical act of writing govern the creation of rhythm. If the poem is "slow," as he says, it is not for lack of interest or attention. Rather, that "slowness" permits a degree of discrimination and attention; the space of the poem is, in Eigner's case, less a score for the voice than a map of intensities whose subject is "a large motion" of global, geological forces.

The vantage from which he creates this page and watches the world is his room. The best description of his Swampscott room is in the author's biography at the back of *Windows / Walls / Yard / Ways*, which was probably written by Eigner, but utilizing a third-person perspective. In it he describes

> a 2-windowed bedroom (summer heat, winter cold, and snow, wind, springtime, Fall) overlooking backyard and porch with clothesreel in a closed-in while big enough neighborhood (sidestreet and 2 dead-end sidestreets, a path through woods, shortcut to the beach before the easterly one nearer the shore ended, after its joint with Eigner's street at the foot of the hill much steeper than the one going down from the town's main road. (195)

When he moved to Berkeley, that room, as the PBS *United States of Poetry* documentary segment on him indicates, is crammed with pages, each filed in dated folders and placed in shelves at wheelchair height. Like Emily Dickinson, Eigner's "endless / Room at the center" plays a significant role in determining the content of the poems (*Selected Poems* xiii). Until 1978, when he moved to California, Eigner spent most of his time in a porch at the front of his parents's home in Swampscott, Massachusetts, from which vantage he observed the birds, trees, passing cars, clouds, storms, and sunlight that populate his verse.

> squirrels everywhere all
>> of
>>
>> a
>>
>> sudden
>
>> *(Things Stirring 59)*

> what birds say   comes in
>> all the windows
>
>> no end of wires through trees
>
>> *(Things Stirring 36)*

The haiku-like spareness of such lines suggests an imagist emphasis on objects, but it becomes clear that Eigner's room is porous. He may hear birds through the windows, but he observes that they sit on the same wires that penetrate the house with news from elsewhere. What might appear as a limited perspective is instead figured by him as "inward performance," the active measurement of spaces and distances by an unusually sensuous, alert mind:

> The midnight birds remind me of day
> though they are
>
>> out in the night
> beyond the curtain I can't see
>
> Somehow bedrooms don't carry
> tradition   I
> and the boxed radio
> is off. But what am I reading
>
> inward performance

> Has relevance. Allows me to hear
> while something speaks. As for the bed
> straightened by visible hands
> only it is huge
> when I feel   down in darkness
>
> > (*Selected Poems* 4)

Lying in bed at midnight, listening to birds outside, the poet feels like a radio, an instrument that although turned off continues to receive messages. The birds beyond his room, the tradition beyond the bedroom, "visible hands" that straighten the bed—these are forms of agency that seem "huge" and threatening. Yet against these "outward" forces, "inward performance" (of which the poem is a record) sustains his nocturnal revery. The awkward phrase, "Somehow bedrooms don't carry / tradition" can be seen as a rueful recognition of the poet's confined position. In a world where individual talent is measured against a heroic tradition, one realized in domestic spaces like bedrooms may seem insignificant. Opposed to outward measures of cultural and social value rests the "inward" ability to imagine absent birds as present, night birds in day.

To some extent, the "boxed radio" provides a countertradition for Eigner to that of Eliot or Pound, bringing a world of music and news into his room. The radio provided Eigner with a fruitful early poetic education when he discovered Cid Corman's radio show in 1949 that exposed him to many of the poets with whom he would later be associated. "Radio and TV have been audio-visual prosthesis," he says in a felicitous merging of media with the disabled body (*areas* 163). But the intrusion of the news also brings with it a world increasingly administered by the media:

> the more read   more
>
> >   jump
>
> > at the firecrackers
>
> > > after what   knowledge
>
> > jets   blades
> >   these days

n b c
   from above

      there's no bird like a bell

the road of life
   is it still going the

      isle
         is full the
    pony express?

      people like radios
      radios as people

he claps   she swings

    they're passing somewhere

        between bursts

                (*Things Stirring* 98)

For the person with limited mobility, this poem is strikingly rich in movement. Eigner here experiences the Vietnam War vicariously through its
displacement in July 4 celebrations (the title is "4th 4th"). He compares
himself to Caliban in *The Tempest,* alarmed at Prospero's magical "isle /
. . . full [of noises]." Those noises include the sound of firecrackers in the
neighborhood that lead him to think of T. S. Eliot's "Gerontion" ("After
what knowledge / what forgiveness") and then militarism ("jets blades /
these days") and their appearance in the media ("nbc / from above"). Although the radio provides Eigner with knowledge of the violent outer
world, it reminds him of how much people resemble their radios, how
much "nbc / from above" determines what knowledge can be. If, as I have
surmised, he is playing a subaltern Caliban to Prospero's NBC, his connection to birds, clouds, and nature is potentially subversive. This would
seem to be the significance of the final lines, in which he hears a couple
outside: "he claps / she swings / they're passing somewhere / between
bursts." Here, "bursts" extends reference to firecrackers and distant war-

fare in Southeast Asia, but the sounds also provide a rhythmic—and perhaps redemptive—contrast to the news. Perhaps they express a positive answer to the question raised midway through the poem: "the road of life / is it still going . . ."

Once again, these examples do not address cerebral palsy directly; but they embody its effects on the poet as he registers the world from a stationary vantage. So attentive is Eigner to the processes of measuring thought and attention that the subject often dissolves into its acts of perception and cognition. This gives the work an oddly unstable feel as lines shift from one location to another, never pausing to conceptualize a scene but allowing, rather, the play of attentions to govern movement. What might be regarded as a form of impersonality turns out to be an immersion of the subject into his perceptual acts:

back to it

The good things go by so softly
Themselves it is our strengths
that run wild

The good and the strong, dissipant,
      an ob-jective joy
            sky
is empty   There are clouds
there must be sound
there

   the horizons are nothing

                  the rain sometimes is not
                  negligible

        out on the sky
            the other direction
    growing until it is nothing

there are mirages and numberless deserts

      inside the other house

lines, broken curbs

         travel and distance
proportion themselves

    we must be animate,   and   walk
turn, abruptly

    the lines are irregular

                             (*Selected Poems* 24)

These lines *are* irregular, carving the page in variable indentations and spacings. The couplet "the rain sometimes is not / negligible" sits at the right gutter, at the edge of the poem, its double negative animating the contrast between a sky that is both "empty" and full of clouds. Moreover, the poem shifts rapidly between reflective ("it is our strengths / that run wild") and descriptive ("sky / is empty") observations. By juxtaposing these two levels, subjective and objective, without transition, the poem maps a "dissipant . . . joy."

The irregularity of these lines carries more than prosodic implications. For Eigner in his closed-in porch, the issue of access is a problem and a way of being. For him, "travel and distance" *do* proportion themselves, relative to physical ability. The imperative to "be animate, and walk / turn, abruptly" can only be performed on the page; as a physical possibility, such imperatives must be measured in terms of "lines, broken curbs." One of the key provisions of the ADA was the erecting of curb cuts for wheelchair users, and although Eigner could not, in the late 1950s when the poem was written, imagine such accommodation, he is speaking of irregular surfaces within the poem as a prosodic principle, and in the world, as a physical set of limitations. That is, Eigner measures an objective world full of "lines" and "broken curbs" as one which he must negotiate with difficulty.

"I Can't Believe I'm Here" ⌣

Such negotiations of textual and physical barriers may, as I have indicated, manifest themselves on a page, but they no less dramatize senses of historical otherness that Eigner felt keenly. The claims of presence that animate many of his poems are often filtered through secondary voices—radio news commentators, public officials, friends and correspondents—that ventriloquize his participation. The plural pronoun above who announces "we must be animate" is as much the voice of social mobility and ableism as it is a measure of Eigner's "irregular" status within such a frame. In the following example, the "I" who announces "I can't believe I'm here" is not the poet who celebrates survival out of physical infirmity but the survivor of a Nazi death camp interviewed in Claude Lanzmann's film *Shoah,* who, in revisiting the Polish camp of Chelmo, marks his disbelief at being able to return:

> skulls piled along the wall
>
> I can't believe I'm here
>
> yes, this is the place
>
> over here were the ovens
>
> trees (pointing)
>
> planted to hide the graves
>
> at first they just burned the bodies
>
> flame up in the sky
>   ("Dance" [n.p.])

These lines are the opening to a remarkable sheaf of poems that Eigner collected for a project (never completed) on the subject of "Dance" (cf. figure 7a). The chapbook was to be part of a second series of responses to Charles Olson's "Plan for the Curriculum of the Soul," a project announced in the late 1960s by Olson, for which various poets were assigned topics.[15] Eigner's selection, "Dance," might seem an unlikely choice until one understands that for him, dance is a way of talking about movement within severely restricted limits—alternative choreographies that defamiliarize normal movement. And for Eigner as a Jew, such restriction implies the difficulty of movement within a moment of historical erasure. The synthesis of two discourses—of disability and race—come together in a poem written, on the same page to the left of the poem above:

> They made him sing along the river
>   the beautiful the beautiful river
>   (and race with ankles tied)
>   —he was agile
>
>   while people were dying
>   (incinerating
>   he had to
>   choose life
>   age 13 and a half
>   so he's one of the two survivors
>
>   out of 300,000

Here is the most disturbed image of dance imaginable: a Jewish boy is forced to run with bound ankles for the amusement of his Nazi captors, the nearby crematoria reminding him of what might befall him. "[He] was agile," the commentator asserts, although the movement must also have been ungainly and awkward. One of the villagers remembered him as having a "lovely singing voice," and another explained that the German captors "made him sing on the river. He was a toy to amuse them. He had to do it. He sang, but his heart wept" (Lanzmann 6). These remarks are transformed by Eigner into a reference to African American spirituals ("the beautiful, the beautiful river") that links the condition of Holocaust child to black American, Jewish poet to Auschwitz survivor, Jewish survivor to crippled poet.

The epigraph to this page is from "The Dance" section of Hart Crane's *The Bridge:* "The long moan of a dance is in the sky," but given the context in Eigner's poem, this moan could also be the smoke from the crematoria (73). Eigner thought of titling his series "Gyre / (scope) / loop the / loop,"

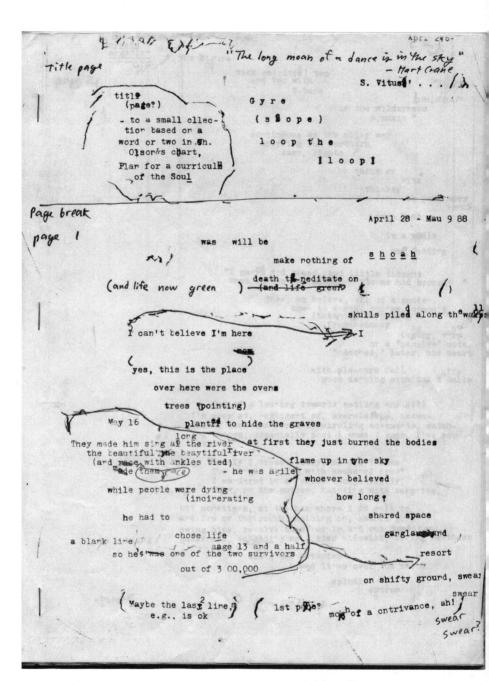

Fig. 7a. "Gyre / (scope) / loop the / loop," from *Dance* by Larry Eigner (unpublished MS). (Reprinted by permission of the Estate of Larry Eigner.)

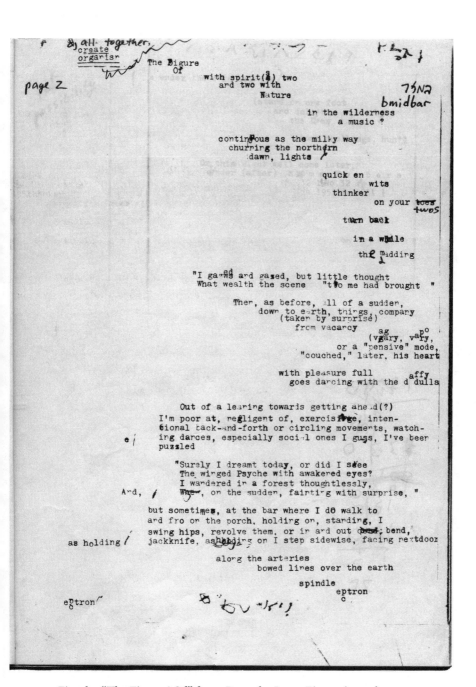

Fig. 7b. "The Figure / Of" from *Dance* by Larry Eigner (unpublished MS). (Reprinted by permission of the Estate of Larry Eigner.)

as if to condense the metaphors of stability (gyroscope), perception ("scope"), historical cyclicity (Yeats's gyres), and vertiginous movement ("loop the / loop") in one figure. It is an ideogram that merges Eigner's primary concerns with perception and place, but sets them against the backdrop of historical vertigo, the rightward shifting margin marking the stumbling movement of movements under duress. The incredulous testimony of survival ("I can't believe I'm here") is measured against an act of physical awkwardness that resembles a dance of death, not unlike the coffle songs and shuffle dances developed by black slaves in the antebellum South. Such powerful mergings of physical grace with carceral control turns "Dance" into a personal signature for Eigner's proprioceptive position.

Eigner's ventriloquized testimony at being "here" in the shadow of the Holocaust is measured against his own attempts at dance, described in a subsequent section of the poem that invokes, as well, Wordsworth's "I Wandered lonely as a Cloud" and Keats's "Ode to Psyche" (figure 7b). From Wordsworth's lyrical invocation of a "jocund company" of dancing flowers and Keats's invocation of seeing the "winged Psyche with awakened eyes," Eigner insinuates his own daily physical exercises:

> Out of a leaning towards getting ahead (?)
> I'm poor at, negligent of, exercise, inten-
> tional back-and-forth or circling movements, watch-
> ing dances, especially social ones I guess, I've been
> puzzled . . .
> . . . .
> but sometimes, at the bar where I do walk to
> and fro on the porch. holding on, standing, I
> swing hips, revolve them, or in and out, bend,
> as holding / jacknife, as holding on I step sidewise, facing nextdoor
>
> along the arteries
> bowed lines over the earth
> spindle

The transition from Auschwitz and the young Jew's coerced, awkward dance to Wordsworth's Lake Country may seem an impossible leap, but the connection seems to be made through the poet's awareness of his own bodily movements. As if to mimic the play of poetic line and dance he segues into an iambic cadence ("but sometimes, at the bar where I do walk") and sees himself "at the bar" like a ballet dancer practicing plié. By linking his physical exercises to romantic versions of transcendence in Wordsworth or Keats, Eigner takes the subject of dance into his own territory. His enjambments and irregular meters contrast to the steady iambs in the romantic poets, yet his lines pace out an equivalent rhythm to his own motions. In his final image, the various representations of dance—those of his own and of romantic poets—coincide in a kind of cosmic merging "along the arteries / bowed lines over the earth // spindle."

Nothing about Us without Us ⌇

As a cripple, I swagger.
—NANCY MAIRS

Discussing poems like "back to it" and "Dance" in terms of physical access or physical limitations poses an interpretive dilemma: how to avoid reducing the poem to an allegory of disability while respecting the complex social valences of terms like "strength," "travel," and "animate." Are the "good things" that go by "softly" good because they are unobtrusive and thus invisible—the ableist position—or because there is a physically mediated perspective that registers their passing? Because Eigner seldom uses the first-person pronoun except when quoting someone else, we cannot easily identify his attitudes about disability or social ostracism. Yet there are moments when the "I" in quotation marks seems to meet the ontological I, and we hear the poet speak in propria persona:

> I have felt it as they've said
> there is nothing to say
>
> there is everything to speak of
> but the words are words
>
> When you speak that is a sound
> what have you done, when you have spoken
>
> of nothing

or something I will remember

After trying my animal noise
i break out with a man's cry

(*Selected Poems* 79)

Were this a poem by Robert Creeley, such lines could be describing the mediating force of language in claiming identity: "As soon as / I speak, I / speaks" (294). In Eigner's case, we must include in the poem's deixis the opprobrium by which the disabled person is interpellated in society. "I have felt it as they've said" may include feelings inflicted upon one whose own speech may appear to others as an "animal noise." Terms for agency ("I will remember," "i break out with a man's cry") must be framed by the difficulty of utterance when there is, to all intents, no interlocutor.

I began this chapter by wondering how to represent disability where it is missing, both in critical discourse and in the poet's own writing. In the 1950s and 1960s, when Eigner was establishing his literary identity, and despite increasing support for social and cultural difference, people with visible disabilities like cerebral palsy, polio, MS and Down syndrome were still considered wards of a welfare state, "shut-ins," poster children for charity telethons. People with disabilities were in many respects invisible, within both the public sphere and emergent social movements. They inhabited medical closets that could be cautiously opened for purposes of sympathy or compassion and as quickly closed again. To be disabled was to be one of Jerry's kids.[16]

During this period there were few activists like Nancy Mairs who could emerge from the disabled closet and use the term "cripple" with arrogance and pride:

> Perhaps I want them to wince. I want them to see me as a tough customer, one to whom the fates / gods / viruses have not been kind, but who can face the brutal truth of her existence squarely. As a cripple, I swagger. (9)

Mairs writes her coming-out narrative as a person with multiple sclerosis for whom there is no Stonewall or March on Washington to galvanize action. For Larry Eigner in the 1960s, his parent's home in Swampscott was both a safe haven and a closet, in Eve Sedgwick's sense, a place of refuge but also a speech act, a place of inward performance but also performativity. The missing X in Eigner's poems is, to adapt Sedgwick, "not a particular silence, but a silence that accrues particularity by fits and starts, in relation to the discourse that surrounds and differentially constitutes it" (3). That discourse, in the 1960s, is called ableism, and not to speak its sentences is to stutter or mumble, to divert attention from the normalized body outward onto birds, sky and weather. Such a world could never sustain itself as outer or other but was constantly being refigured and remapped through Eigner's difficult syntax and variable lineation. This was Eigner's letter to the world, not an X but a lowercase i that says, "After trying my animal noise / i break out with a man's cry."

Chapter 6

Nostalgia for Light

Being Blind at the Museum

So what is a gaze? It is perhaps the sum of all our dreams
in which we forget the nightmare, when we can look in a
different way.
— EVGEN BAVCAR

Blind at the Museum ∽

In the opening of the Proteus chapter of *Ulysses* Stephen Dedalus wanders
on Sandymount Strand, questioning the "ineluctable modality of the visible" by asking if the world disappears when he cannot see it. He tests his
ruminations by closing his eyes. What he discovers is not the absence of
space but an acute awareness of time, registered through the sound of his
own footsteps clattering over the cobbles. What he loses of space he re-
gains as duration. Then he opens his eyes: "See now. There all the time
without you: and ever shall be, world without end" (31). Like Dr. Johnson,
Stephen repudiates idealism by knocking his sconce against the rock of reality. He does so by trying on blindness to discover being in time—Aristotle's *nacheinander*—a reconciliation he desperately needs if he is to move
beyond his own solipsism and the narrow sensationalist categories he has
inherited from eighteenth-century aesthetics. For the increasingly blind
James Joyce, Stephen's experiment in not-seeing was a marker of his tenuous relationship to that "ineluctable modality of the visible" upon which
so much modernist art is based. If we forget Joyce's blindness in reading
Ulysses, it is due in part to his success in creating the aesthetic terms by

which modernist works—including his novel—sought to transcend the conditions of their imagining. If we remember Joyce's blindness, we reenter modernism through a glass darkly.

Stephen Dedalus's experiment could be seen as a model for more recent attempts to rethink the museum—and by extension, the aesthetic— as a critical vehicle for exploring the visual as a cultural product. Much postwar art has utilized the installation space to challenge modernist ocularity by breaking down the gallery walls, digging up the floor, introducing performance and dance, creating new acoustic spaces out of sound and text, and perhaps most significantly by moving outside the museum walls to sites and spaces in the larger public arena. A good deal of this effort has been inspired by Marcel Duchamp, who in late works like *Etant Données* brings the viewer (figuratively and literally) to the keyhole to peer at a naked figure on the other side and thus experience aesthetic viewing as a kind of prurience. His attack on the retinal in art raises the question of the work's institutional status, its participation in scopic regimes reinforced by museums, galleries, architecture, patronage, and art historical discourse. From *Nude Descending the Staircase* through the "Large Glass" to the readymades and chess games, Duchamp's example as an artist was to rethink the retinal basis of art through the very art historical means that foregrounds the eye as self-evident arbiter of value.

To imagine a "Museum Without Walls," as Andre Malraux, called it, is to recognize the museum as a historically and culturally limited concept, something defined by an age of collecting, consumption, and categorization. What would it mean to reenter the museum's walls with a guide dog or white cane? A number of recent exhibitions and colloquia have focused on blindness and the museum, foregrounding the work of blind artists and proposing new curatorial and docent implications of access for sight-impaired visitors.[1] One common theme of these events is that the blind have a great deal to teach the sighted not only about blindness but about seeing and about the assumptions that sighted persons bring to the larger cultural field. As Georgina Kleege said in one such colloquium, "[To most people] the very topic of this symposium ["Blind at the Museum"] may seem the punch line to a tasteless joke ... 'that makes about as much sense as a blind person at an art museum'" ("What We Talk About" 1). By reinterpreting the museum through blindness we may rethink its commitment to visibility from the standpoint of access to the buildings, galleries, and institutional venues that produce aesthetic pleasure for sighted as well as nonsighted visitors.

In some respects, classical aesthetics has always been about access, a "prosthesis to reason," as Terry Eagleton phrases it, by which the materiality of the body can be aligned with lofty rationality (16). Kant's idea that the beautiful object must inspire similar feelings in everyone assumes that everyone occupies the same natural (sighted) standpoint. For Kant aesthetic judgments do not depend on pure sensation (what he calls "agreeableness") nor rational, cognitive choices but, rather, on disinterested feelings that are validated when they elicit reciprocal response in others. Although Kant's idea of aesthetic judgment is class-specific and presumes a form of moneyed, educated privilege, it promises a form of intersubjectivity and community outside of institutional venues. Given this, what if we shift the emphasis from the private appreciation of a beautiful object to the social consent it produces? What if we turned our attention from the insular act of perception to the constituencies enlisted in its validation?

This is what happens when disability is brought into the aesthetic arena. The hypothetical "normal" body and sensoriums that underwrite aesthetic distance are challenged when the observer is in a wheelchair or uses sign language or holds a white cane. Disinterested contemplation means something different for the blind museum visitor denied the ability to touch the surfaces of sculpture or the deaf viewer who enters a sound-based installation. Equally, criteria of formal coherence are altered dramatically when we subject them to classical models of bodily perfection. Performance artists have made this aesthetics the subject of their work by placing their bodies—and their wheelchairs, prostheses, hearing aids—in the foreground. I have already described Mary Duffy's "tableau vivant" performances in which the armless artist appears nude in the posture of classical sculptures, delivering monologues on the gendered conditions by which female beauty is assessed. Lynn Manning, who lost his sight as a result of a gunshot wound, creates elaborate autobiographical performances using multiple personae that embody social attitudes connecting race, blindness, and masculinity. William Pope's "Crawl" pieces involve the African American artist crawling long distances on his hands and knees along public thoroughfares, illustrating problems of public access that link poor, minority, and disability communities. Although he is not visibly disabled himself, Pope constructs his art out of the obstacles faced by nonnormative (racialized, sexed, disabled) bodies in instrumentalized environments.

In one of his performances, Pope walks naked up a shallow river, carrying a mirror on his back—a complex metaphor for mimesis in racialized America. It is a salient commentary on the meaning of nature when the vehicle by which it is reflected is borne on a black body. Pope's performance emphasizes the extent to which American exceptionalist myths of uncorrupted nature and wilderness were historically dependent on a racialized other—his labor, progeny, and material worth. Pope's mirror is a resonant metaphor for the role of mediated visibility especially appropriate to the work of blind visual artists.[2] As I hope to suggest, the ocularcentric focus of modern art is dramatically contested when we consider the work of blind photographers such as Evgen Bavcar, Flo Fox, Paco Grande, John Dugdale, Kurt Weston, Pedro Hidalgo, Alice Wingwall, and the mixed-media work of Ryan Knighton, who resite the visual through the technological means by which modernist ocularity was created. In their work the meaning of the photograph is diverted from the developed print to the discursive processes that precede and accompany the clicking of the shutter. In each of these cases, the great theme of modernist defamiliarization is revived to ask for whom the familiar is familiar, and by what presumption of access is it made strange?

These discursive processes are, of course, historically contingent, and any attempt to understand the meaning of blindness must account for the etiology and social meanings of sightedness. In the case of Derek Jarman's last film, *Blue* (1993), the background must include the blindness caused by complications associated with AIDS that claimed his life in 1994. *Blue* is a film whose visual component consists of a blue screen sustained for seventy minutes, while a sound track presents readings from Jarman's journals and poems along with a score composed by Simon Turner. By eliminating images from film, Jarman places the audience in his own sightless condition, one in which the visual is articulated through an acoustic environment. At the same time, the filmmaker's refusal of images provides a corrective to the standard representation of AIDS, during the 1980s: the figure of a gaunt, skeletal gay man.[3] In this gesture, Jarman repudiates a culture of spectacle—and the bodies on which it relies—and replaces it with one of pure potential, even transcendence—that he associates with the blue of Yves Klein's monochromes.

The issues raised by the blind photographer and filmmaker involve questions of legitimation in a world no longer validated by retinal terms. This is the subject of Jocelyn Moorehouse's 1991 movie *Proof,* in which the blind photographer Martin (Hugo Weaving) takes pictures of the world around him and then enlists others to describe what they see. For Martin, the photograph is not an auratic object destined for the museum gallery but the site of a complex feedback system in which an imagined world may be corrected and verified against an oral report. In this film, photography is less about the object printed in the darkroom than the conversations Martin has with others who serve as prostheses for his aesthetic project. Although he relies on associates to tell him what they see in his photographs, he seldom trusts their testimony. When his newfound friend Andy (Russell Crowe) begins to leave out incriminating information from his descriptions of certain photographs, the function of validation is undermined, and the proof—photographic and social—is ruptured irrevocably. Complicating Martin's life is the fact that his housekeeper, Celia (Genevieve Picot), is in love with him even though he does not reciprocate her interest. She, too, is a photographer, who covers her walls with enlarged photographs of Martin. When Andy comes on the scene, she turns her attentions to him, creating a fissure in the somewhat sadomasochistic ménage that she and Martin have created. At one point Martin unknowingly photographs a scene in a park in which Andy (who was supposed to be somewhere else) is accidentally caught by the camera lens. When Martin discovers that his friend was present in this scene, his fragile trust in his friend deteriorates.

What might have seemed like an account of art's overcoming of disability becomes a subtle critique of what happens when an obsession with validation usurps human contact. At the same time, *Proof* raises the question of its own specularity by creating a protagonist whose gaze is directly linked to a technological process. Even though we may know what Martin doesn't about his surroundings, as a blind photographer, he knows better than anyone—to his endless dismay—about the limits of what constitutes proof for sighted people. Thus in *Proof* the making of images recursively questions the ability of language to establish and contain a world.

Desiring Images: Evgen Bavcar ↩

I photograph what I imagine—like Don Quijote.
—EVGEN BAVCAR

Proof raises the question of whether photography is primarily about the
phenomenal world or about the knowledge that phenomena verify. For
Martin, the tenuous community he forms with his interlocutors constitutes his world, one formed around images he makes but cannot see. The
issue of validation becomes key in the work of Slovenian photographer
Evgen Bavcar (E-oo-gen Ba-oo-char), who lost his sight in childhood and
whose art offers a complex riposte to the retinal definition of photography. Bavcar's photographs depend on the creation of a highly specific
mnemonic world dedicated to the memory of light. Although his images
are intensely private and personal, their conception is dialogical and collaborative. He takes photographs with the help of assistants whose descriptions of a scene help determine the placement of the camera, opening of aperture, and development of the final print. "I submit [my
photographs] to the eyes of others, giving them the privilege of narrating
them to me, in order for them to exist" ("Images of Elsewhere" n.p.). A
vivid instance of this dialogical quality of photography can be seen in the
fact that when shooting human subjects, Bavcar places the camera lens
not at the level of his eye but of his mouth as though to establish his relationship to his subject as a kind of conversation. The intensity of light is
measured by a "talking" light meter that registers gradations of light by
sound. And although autofocus helps adjust for space, he uses his hands
and body to measure distance. His hands often appear in the photographs
to mark his proximity to his subject but also to sign his physical presence
as creator. "The rest," as he says, "is achieved by the desire for images that
inhabits me" (qtd. in Bavcar, "Mirror").[4]
      That desire is dominated by recurring images from the period before
he lost his sight at age twelve. The photograph as embodiment of desire is
realized in his emphasis on memory and dream images in which objects,
buildings, and figures seem detached from their backgrounds, isolated
against a neutral black backdrop. Many of his photographs are taken at
night; objects or buildings are lit by flashlights or other focused light
sources that isolate the subject and give it a luminous, otherworldly qual-

ity. Through the use of long—often very long—exposures in his black-and-white photos, Bavcar gains a great amount of detail, but by moving objects in the visual field, certain elements are blurred. The effect is that of waving a flashlight in the dark so that the light leaves a trace of its trajectory in space. The combination of objects in tight focus, surrounded by blurred outlines, creates an unsettling oscillation between presence and absence, stasis and movement.

In the series from which I have derived my title, "Nostalgie de la lumière," Bavcar imposes cutouts of swallows—his signature bird—against trees, gates, bicycles, and childhood photographs. In one, the swallows surround a bicycle that stands out against a black background (fig. 8).[5] The bicycle seems etched in light—as though the photographer has traced its outline to both heighten its isolated quality and dematerialize its solidity. The bicycle is surrounded by luminous cutouts of swallows held by disembodied hands that fill in the black space above the bicycle or else intrude through the spokes below. While bicycle and birds promise flight and freedom, their potential for movement is undermined by the absence of a rider and by the ghostly hands that hold the cutouts. The swallows become static design features rather than mimetic representations, their schematic shapes caught in a direct, frontal light as though suddenly arrested by swerving headlights only to disappear again into the darkness. As an autobiographical image, the bicycle represents the barriers between his sight and blindness, between a moment when the artist could see swallows flying through his family barn in Slovenia and their schematic representation in his memory.

A second photograph from the same series continues the swallow motif, this time as a lattice of birds covering a rustic metal gate (fig. 9). The photograph is shot from a low angle—a child's perspective perhaps—bounded on right and left sides by brightly lit ornate twin columns that support the gate. The gate is closed, and shrubbery appears to be growing at its base, suggesting that it has not been opened in a long time. As a metaphor for lost youth and sight, the photograph depicts a barred access to some obscure space beyond, but the balanced composition of the photo, the uneven placement of the swallows throughout the gate, and the strong frontal light create a composition that is less about loss of youth than about the uncanny nature of its return. The photograph depicts a "real" place in Bavcar's childhood as well as a dreamspace etched in high-

Fig. 8. *Bicycle and Swallows* by Evgan Bavcar (*Le voyeur absolu* 55).
(Reprinted by permission of the photographer, Evgen Bavcar.)

contrast lights and darks. The schematic outlines of the swallows and the
hands that hold them do not pretend to imitate actual birds but mark
their presence as mnemonic placeholders.

When I referred to the way that light touches or outlines an object in
Bavcar's work, I was thinking of how often his hands intrude into his photographs. In one image, the artist's hand touches a stone at the ruins of
Pompeii, linking the present act of photography with ancient disruptions,
personal and geological, that constitute cultural memory (fig. 10). In his
portraits of nudes, hands touch the body of the model, often wrapping
her in an ethereal cocoon of hands. At one level the appearance of hands
instantiates his stated pleasure in being able to touch sculpture at a museum: "La sculpture . . . me procure un sentiment esthétique immédiat,
dans la mesure où l'on m'autorise à toucher les statues, ce qui n'est pas
toujours le cas" (Sculpture gives me an immediate aesthetic feeling, insofar as I am authorized to touch the statues, something that is not always
the case [*Le voyeur absolu* 15]). At another level the presence of his hand is

Fig. 9. *Gate and Swallows* by Evgan Bavcar (*Le voyeur absolu* 31).
(Reprinted by permission of the photographer, Evgen Bavcar.)

a kind of signature or mark by which he insinuates himself into and onto the subject of his image. He is not alone among blind photographers in this practice. Several of Alice Wingwall's photographs of architectural sites feature her hand emerging from the lower portion of the photo to gesture toward her subject, and John Dugdale has created a series of images with raised, textured surfaces that can be touched. The reference to hands and touch seems to verify Joseph Grigely's remark quoted in an earlier epigraph: for nonsighted people touch is a form of seeing.

The visual rhetoric of touch, whether erotic or aesthetic, is elaborately developed in two photographs based on Michelangelo's sculpture *Aurora*, located above the tomb of Lorenzo de Medici in Florence. In *A Close Up View* (fig. 11) the photographer's hand extends from the lower left corner of the photograph to touch the face of an awakening Dawn. Because the figure's eyes are open, the gesture is an iconic moment of the blind hand touching the inauguration of light. We can understand his gesture as a practical one as he measures the distance of the camera from his subject.

Fig. 10. *The Hand on the Stone, Pompeii* by Evgan Bavcar ("Mirror of Dreams"). (Reprinted by permission of the photographer, Evgen Bavcar.)

But we can also understand it as marking his mediated relationship to light, thematized in the figure of Aurora. Furthermore, Bavcar has chosen a particularly complex piece of sculpture to touch, a memento mori embodied in a figure that represents awakening and the emergence of light. But the sculpture is complex in another sense, for in order for Bavcar to lay his hands on its surface, he must reach an object that is ten feet above the floor of the Medici Chapel, indicating both an intellectual and physical difficulty of achieving contact. By framing what would be an awkward perspective for any viewer, Bavcar erases the realistic location of sculpture in space and resituates it in terms of the photograph itself.

A companion photograph to the first *Aurora (Work by Michelangelo with Autograph)* features the sculpture from a slightly greater distance, using even more dramatic chiaroscuro (fig. 12). This time the intruding hand is replaced by a fragment of writing in white superimposed over the sculpture on the left side of the photograph. The text is in script, suggest-

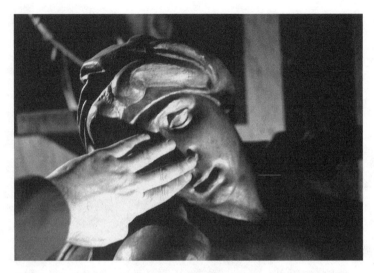

Fig. 11. *A Close Up View* by Evgan Bavcar ("Mirror of Dreams"). (Reprinted by permission of the photographer, Evgen Bavcar.)

Fig. 12. *Work by Michelangelo with Autograph* by Evgan Bavcar ("Mirror of Dreams"). (Reprinted by permission of the photographer, Evgen Bavcar.)

ing once again the hand of the artist writing directly on the photograph. The effect is to create depth to the photo—as though Michelangelo's reclining figure were being seen through a window on which a text is inscribed. But the writing is luminous, created out of the same light that illuminates *Aurora*'s left hand, which is now visible on the right of the photograph. The high-contrast lighting places Aurora in an intermediate landscape, between darkness and dawn, sculpted marble and written text.

In his *Memoirs of the Blind*, Jacques Derrida links the three terms I have been discussing—writing, drawing, and blindness—in a philosophical meditation on artists' depictions of the blind. He suggests that representations of the blind person's outstretched hand in a drawing embodies the structural role of blindness at the heart of draftsmanship. The artist in representing the blind represents himself in the act of feeling his way toward articulation and design. In such drawings "A hand of the blind ventures forth alone or disconnected in a poorly delimited space; it feels its way, it gropes, it caresses as much as it inscribes" (3). This, Derrida feels, can be compared to what happens when one writes without looking at the page, the author creating notations in an obscurity, a text reserved not for reading but for memory. The groping hand is the sign of both artist and writer working *toward*, rather than *from*, knowledge. To represent the blind person's hand is to draw attention to the hand that holds the stylus or pen. What Derrida treats metaphorically as the sighted artist's relationship to his blind subject, Bavcar treats literally as the hand of the blind artist moving into or across his own photograph, breaking the frame of the image by touching the object.

As in the Michelangelo portraits, Bavcar often "draws" on the surface of the photograph, either by superimposing text or by creating elaborate scribbles by a focused light source. In one, a Paris street scene features a series of cartoon Eiffel Towers jauntily dancing in air like ghostly wraiths from a nineteenth-century phantastikon (fig. 13). In another from the same series a blurry image of Notre Dame at night is flanked on the lower half of the photograph by a mixture of blurred light squiggles and superimposed writing, as though to literalize the idea of Paris as "the city of light."[6] And in other photographs, Bavcar outlines or frames objects in light, roughly tracing outlines and surfaces. A self-portrait shows the photographer sitting on a high stool, holding a car tire and wearing a black borsalino hat. Surrounding his body, hat, and tire is a continuous stream

Fig. 13. *Les Images de Paris (Eiffel Towers)* by Evgan Bavcar (*Le voyeur absolu* 48). (Reprinted by permission of the photographer, Evgen Bavcar.)

of white light that provides a kind of dazzling, scribbled outline in contrast to the inert figure. A reclining nude is caught in a strong focal light upon which is superimposed a dense calligraphy of squiggles and arcs. These acts of light-writing display the artist's (or perhaps his assistant's) hand, sometimes literally, in marking the surface of the print, but because writing is done with a moving light source, the static image is distorted and the photographs achieve a painterly texture.

Bavcar's portraits of nudes bring together the various strands that I have mentioned—light, touch, writing—and connect them with an Eros that is both tender and unsettling. In these portraits, women are photographed in a darkened room, reclining or sitting on a white sheet or drape and lit by a frontal light that neither flatters nor softens the body. In most of the photographs, the models look away from the camera, their expressions neutral, self-absorbed, and blank. Bavcar's characteristic calligraphic light often outlines the body and blurs the boundaries between photograph and subject. Bavcar's characteristic intruding hands frame

Fig. 14. *Vue tactile* by Evgan Bavcar (*Le voyeur absolu* 108).
(Reprinted by permission of the photographer, Evgen Bavcar.)

and touch the bodies, but because the hands are superimposed through double exposure, touch is mediated by the photographic process itself (fig. 14). In one case, the hand on the woman's body is replaced by braille dots that spell the German word for "desire" *(sehnsucht),* thus substituting for the artist's touch a language *of touch* printed directly on the body (fig. 15). The black braille dots join the photographer's blindness to the language of touch by which he represents light and sight—and thus desire.

It could be argued that despite Bavcar's complex relationship to the photographic medium, he nevertheless produces objects that may be placed quite easily alongside classic work of modernist photography— from Man Ray and Albert Stieglitz to Cindy Sherman and Sophie Calle. It is all very well to describe his photographic process as challenging mimetic criteria by introducing dream materials, but this doesn't change the ocular nature of the object on the wall. This is why the museum or gallery that displays his work is so important in establishing the photograph's larger meaning by framing and historicizing the multiple sites in

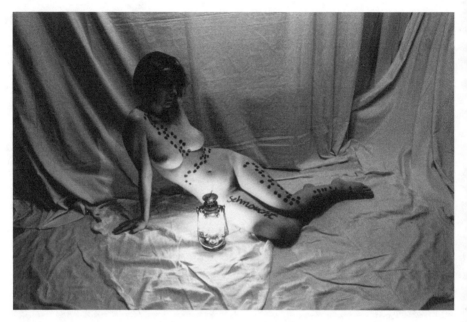

Fig. 15. *Caresses de la lumière* by Evgan Bavcar (*Le voyeur absolu*
107). (Reprinted by permission of the photographer, Evgen Bavcar.)

which the photographer's gaze exists—from the conversations he establishes with his assistants to his various writings, philosophical essays, and
pedagogy and finally to the docent presentation in the gallery space. Bavcar's photographs, in a sense, do not exist on the wall—even though he
has been widely exhibited in Europe and North America—but rather in
the recursive relationship created between interlocutor and artist. As he
says, "My gaze exists only through the simulacrum of the photo that has
been seen by someone else. That gaze makes me happy and induces the
images to come to life inside me" ("Mirror of Dreams").

Bavcar's photography is haunted by the past. His resolutely monochromatic black-and-white palette constitutes a field of nostalgia, a
farewell to a world of images: "je garde le souvenir trés vif de ces moments
d'adieux au monde visible. Mais la monochromie a envahi mon existence,
et je dois faire un effort pour conserver la palette des nuances, pour que le
monde échappe à la monotonie et à la transparence (But monochromy in-
vaded my life, and I must make an effort to retain the palette of subtle

shades so that the world escapes monochromy and transparency [*Le voyeur absolu* 10]). In constructing a mnemonic landscape he can address sculpture, faces, bicycles, swallows through the "voice" of his lens and touch them through the "hand" of his camera. Because Bavcar lost his sight over time and at a young age (he began to lose his sight at age eleven) the issues of memory and desire are central to his work, but there is, as I have said, a dialogic quality to the photographs that insists on their collaborative origins and their transformative potential for the sighted viewer. Bavcar understands the productive contradiction associated with a blind photographer by wearing, on his lapel, a discreet mirror, as though to force anyone who would see in him only a blind man to reflect on the structural blindness at the heart of the gaze.[7] In a sense, his photographs hold that tiny mirror up to a nature, retaining in its circle the desire of sighted persons to see themselves reflected in the art they value. The camera may capture the world for the photographer who can look through the lens, but in the hands of the blind photographer it serves as a third eye that can see, as Bavcar says, "another light behind the black square of Malevich."

Into the Blue: Derek Jarman's *Pharmakon* ◡

There are gold flecks in the lapis.
—DEREK JARMAN, *Chroma*

The attempt to recuperate lost images inspires Bavcar's work, producing photographs that exist in the interstices of sight and memory. To some extent he revives some of the uncanny qualities with which early visual technologies were invested—from the phantastikons and ghost shows of Victorian parlors to the panoramas and early moving pictures of the late nineteenth and early twentieth centuries. In early photographic experiment the boundary between technology and epiphenomena was blurred and the criteria of verisimilitude sacrificed to expressive and symbolic features. For the painter and filmmaker Derek Jarman, who lost his sight due to complications from AIDS, it is the inadequacy of images to the worldwide pandemic that motivates his last film. *Blue* is a seventy-minute film whose visual track consists of a video-generated blue field, identical to the one produced by turning off the video recorder while leaving the television on its auxiliary channel. Superimposed on the blue field is a sound track featuring Jarman and other friends reading from the director's notebooks and writings.

If the black square of Malevich inspires Bavcar's photographs, the blue monochromatic paintings of Yves Klein serve a similar function in *Blue*. Jarman had been interested in making a film about Klein since 1987, first as a documentary and later as a minimalist film based on Klein's paintings. The inspiration for a "blue" film (Jarman often exploits the sexual double entendre) derives, in part, from Klein's monochrome paintings in IKB (International Klein Blue) begun in 1955. Klein's obsession with ultramarine pigment was based, to some extent, on the painter's interest in Rosicrucian color theory, but it was no less a fixation on the sheer materiality of pigment in its raw, unmixed state, unaffected by line or design. As Peter Wollen says, the effect of Klein's work is "to preserve the granularity of the pigment and to seal it so that a thickness of pure pigment can be hung vertically on the wall, like an upended tray" (117). For Klein, color is not something applied to a figure; it becomes the subject of the painting itself. "I refuse to make a spectacle of my painting!" Klein says; "I refuse to compare and bring together one strong element or another, and then weaker ones, in order to highlight them" (76).

Jarman's films and paintings had always displayed a keen sensitivity to opulent color, as evident in *Caravaggio* or *Edward II,* and his long fascination with Klein's monochromatic paintings led to several experiments with the idea of a movie without images. On one level, the imageless film was a way of contesting the fetish of images in everyday life—in advertising, media, television—a theme that animates much of Jarman's writings. But when he began to lose his sight as a consequence of cytomegalovirus (CMV), which affects persons in the later stages of AIDS, Jarman was able to fuse autobiographical and political elements in a film that implicates the viewer as well.[8] Like Bavcar, Jarman holds up a kind of mirror, but it is one that forces us to experience the artist's blindness and, at the same time, reevaluate the desire for images that animates the scopic character of cinema. In this sense, Jarman replicates Stephen Dedalus's self-blinding on Sandymount Strand, but through the aesthetic field of Klein's color theory and the political field of AIDS activism.

These strange bedfellows—the aesthetic and the political—are joined in the film's insistence on blue as a figure for transcendence and charity that Jarman associates with the blue of the Virgin's cloak in Renaissance painting. Yet if blue is a remedy, it is also partly a poison, as Caravaggio says in Jarman's movie about the painter (qtd. in Pencak 157). According to Plato, in Derrida's reading of the *Phaedrus*, the *pharmakon* of writing is described as an aid to memory—a remedy against forgetting—yet it limits our ability to practice our memory through dialectics. The permanence it proffers through script is denied by its distance from originary speech. The Greek word *pharmakon* contains both terms—remedy and poison— in its etymology, providing Derrida with a felicitous term for writing's duplicit character as carrier as well as displacement of truth. Applied to Jarman's film, the monochromatic blue implies purity, infinitude, and transcendence, but it is also associated with the loss of sight and what in the film he calls the "blue funk" that results. As the voice-over explains, the drugs that Jarman takes to sustain his life also produce side effects that make life unendurable. Blue as *pharmakon* combines a Whitmanian optimism and comradeship—"the terrestrial paradise"—with the memory of lost comrades due to AIDS:

> Blue is the universal love in which man bathes—it is the terrestrial paradise.
>
> I'm walking along the beach in a howling gale—
> Another year is passing
> In the roaring waters
> I hear the voices of dead friends
> Love is life that lasts forever.
> My heart's memory turns to you
> David.   Howard.   Graham.   Terry.   Paul . . .
>
> (5)

As I said in my introduction to this chapter, attempts to represent AIDS in the early stages of the pandemic often featured the image of a gaunt gay man, his skin wasted, his eyes sunken in hollow sockets. Whether in programs like CBS's *Sixty Minutes* in its segment "AIDS Hits Home" or in the photographs of Nicholas Nixon or Rosalind Solomon, attempts to "put a face" to individuals with AIDS invariably tended to focus on their isolation and misery.[9] The camera that probes the domestic and medical spaces of persons with AIDS intrudes on and violates privacy, satisfying a certain prurient curiosity among the well. Protests by ACT UP against the 1988 Museum of Modern Art exhibition of Nicholas Nixon's photographs argued that such images present a distorted view of AIDS and do not imagine people living and coping with the syndrome. Flyers distributed by ACT UP in front of the museum read, "No More Pictures Without Context," and concluded, "Stop Looking at Us; Start Listening to Us." As Douglas Crimp and Paula Treichler point out, such appeals were addressed to heterosexuals whose interest in people dying with AIDS may have been motivated less by sympathy than by the threat of AIDS to the straight population. Jarman's film literalizes this slogan by refusing the visual aspect of cinema and forcing viewers to "listen."

Although Jarman contests the spectacle of AIDS in the media, he is not comfortable with attempts to soften its devastating effects:

> I shall not win the battle against the virus—in spite of the slogans like "Living with AIDS." The virus was appropriated by the well—so we have to live with AIDS while they spread the quilt for the moths of Ithaca across the wine dark sea.
>
> Awareness is heightened by this, but something else is lost. A sense of reality drowned in theatre.
>
> Thinking blind, becoming blind. (*Blue* 9)

How, then, to represent AIDS without supplying yet another image? Jarman recognizes that AIDS is an "epidemic of signification," as Treichler calls it, as much as one of microbes and T cells. Stitching an AIDS quilt or relying on bromides such as "living with AIDS" may raise awareness among the "well," but they are inadequate to the painful reality of the disease, the excruciating pain of drug therapies, the loss of friends and lovers. What is necessary is a new epistemology—"Thinking blind, becoming blind"—that the film produces through its repudiation of images and its voice-over's pragmatic stance:

> Fate is the strongest
> Fate Fated Fatal
> I resign myself to Fate

Blind Fate
The drip stings
A lump swells up in my arm
Out comes the drip
An electric shock sparks up my arm
How can I walk away with a drip attached to me?
How am I going to walk away from this?

(9–10)

No triumphalist victory here. The intravenous drip that dispenses DHPG, a life-sustaining drug, also corrects Buddhist quietism: "The Gautama Buddha instructs me to walk away from illness. / But he wasn't attached to a drip" (9). Jarman's rueful humor throughout the film is itself a remedy against the rhetoric of fate.

The monochromatic blue field is only one half of the film; the other is a voice-over that occupies a curious diegetic function. In a film without images, the sound track is always extradiegetic, but since there are no pictures to which the voices could refer, the sound track *becomes* the picture. As an allegory of AIDS, Jarman's strategy embodies the condition of gay men in the 1980s whose bodies were figured as representing the disease yet whose identities and voices were often silenced in public debate. The popular representation of AIDS became the body of a gay man. *Blue* supplies a voice, consisting of Jarman and colleagues (Tilda Swanson, John Quentin, Nigel Terry) reading from the director's journals and writings, accompanied by Simon Turner's score.[10] This narrative superimposed on a blue screen permits the director to create, as Tim Lawrence says, "an autobiographical film about AIDS without filming himself" (249). On the one hand, this strategy universalizes the AIDS experience by removing it from an individual face; at the same time, it particularizes the experience of one person by focusing on his daily regimens of medications, doctors' examinations, and the sheer boredom of waiting. Juxtaposed to the intensely personal, medicalized experience of AIDS, Jarman refers to more global issues—the war in the former Yugoslavia, attacks on homosexuality, and new reports on safe sex. These interlocking strands of personal and public histories track the movement of Jarman's disease, from its diagnosis in 1986 to its later stages and blindness.

Embedded within the text is an allegory of hope, figured through a boy, associated with blue, whose birth opens the film:

You say to the boy open your eyes
When he opens his eyes and sees the light
You make him cry out. Saying
O Blue come forth
O Blue arise
O Blue ascend
O Blue come in

(3)

This invocation is followed by the grim quotidian, both global and personal

I am sitting with some friends in this cafe drinking coffee served by young refugees from Bosnia. The war rages across the newspapers and through the ruined streets of Sarajevo.

Tania said "Your clothes are on back to front and inside out." Since there were only two of us here I took them off and put them right then and there. I am always here before the doors open

What need of so much news from abroad while all that concerns either life or death is all transacting and at work within me.

I step off the kerb and a cyclist nearly knocks me down. Flying in from the dark he nearly parted my hair.

I step into a blue funk. (3)

The conflict in the Balkans is brought home by the refugees who serve him coffee. His increasing sight-impairment leads to difficulties in dressing or stepping off a curb. The bad news from abroad and the bad news in his own body thrust him into a "blue funk." Later, at St. Bartholomew's Hospital, his doctor dilates his eyes with belladonna while flashing a light into his eyes:

Look left
Look down
Look up
Look right

Blue flashes in my eyes.

(4)

The sudden blue flash of light that momentarily blinds him is, of course, a metonymy for the blue void that will ultimately claims his life. But this gives way to a series of associations with blue that remind him of "delphinium days" of earlier life: "Blue Bottle buzzing," "sky blue butterfly," "blue heat haze," "Blue of my heart / Blue of my dreams" (4). This battle between Proustian moments of blue in the past and the current moment of pain is figured as a battle between the prelapsarian Blue Boy and a reptilian evil that he calls "yellowbelly,"

> whose fetid breath scorches the trees yellow with ague . . . Evil swims in the yellow bile. Yellowbelly's snake eyes poison. He crawls over Eve's rotting apple wasp-like. Quick as a flash he stings Blue in the mouth—"Aaaugh!"—his hellish legions buzz and chuckle in the mustard gas. They'll piss all over you. Sharp nicotine-stained fangs bared. Blue transformed into an insectocutor, his Blue aura frying the foes. (17)

This hellish scene describes a change in the script from the redemptive associations of blue with the cult of innocence and the blue of redemption into the agon of deterioration, the body feeding upon itself.

From this point on, the film text becomes increasingly devoted to Jarman's experiences in hospital and his declining health:

> It started with sweats in the night and swollen glands. Then the black cancers spread across their faces—as they fought for breath TB and pneumonia hammered at the lungs, and Toxo at the brain. Reflexes scrambled—sweat poured through hair matted lie lianas in the tropical forest. Voices slurred—and then were lost forever. My pen chased this story across the page tossed this way and that in the storm. (8)

While being dripped with DHPG, for which Jarman comes to the hospital every day, he reads the drug's side effects, which include "increased risk of infection, low platelet count that increase the risk of bleeding, low red blood cell count (anaemia), fever, rash, abnormal liver function, chills" and dozens more (18–19). At the end of this list, Jarman reads the formulaic language on the wall of the doctor's office: "If you are concerned about any of the above side-effects or if you would like any further information, please ask your doctor" (19).

As the film comes to its conclusion, the optimism of blue transcendence is replaced by a cynicism registered by this voice of medicalized caution. Jarman indicts the charity of those who benefit from solicitude and attacks the apathy from within the Thatcher government: "Charity has allowed the uncaring to appear to care and is terrible for those dependent on it. It has become big business as the government shirks its responsibilities in these uncaring times" (21). Against such paternalistic solicitude, Jarman poses a queer riposte:

I am a mannish
Muff diving
Size queen
With bad attitude
An arse licking
Psychofag
Molesting the flies of privacy
Balling lesbian boys
A perverted heterodemon
Crossing purpose with death

I am a cock sucking
Straight acting
Lesbian man
With ball crushing bad manners
Laddish nymphomaniac politics
Spunky sexist desires
Of incestuous inversion and
Incorrect terminology
I am a Not Gay

(21–22)

There, Jarman seems to say; I've said it! I've assumed all of the possible forms of perversion and panic the straight world fears. This shout of anger is an attack on forms of solicitude that validate the bearer but eliminate the subject. "How are we perceived," Jarman queries, "if we are to be perceived at all? For the most part we are invisible" (12). The invisibility of gay persons as individuals during the early AIDS period is precisely what the static blue screen seems to embody.

The end of the text brings together the two contrasting forces of the movie—comic and tragic, quotidian and eternal, remedy and poison: "I caught myself looking at shoes in a shop window. I thought of going in and buying a pair, but stopped myself. The shoes I am wearing at the moment should be sufficient to walk me out of life" (28). This rueful recognition of last things produces a concluding lyric that invokes a mythic world of "azure seas" and "coral harbours" within which "Lost Boys / Sleep forever / In a dear embrace / Salt lips touching / In submarine gardens" (29). The combination of Peter Pan (Lost Boys) and *The Tempest* (submarine gardens) brings Jarman to an elegiac tribute, whether for himself or others who have died of AIDS. Speaking as much of the Blue Boy in the poem's opening as to his own imagined end, he concludes: "I place a delphinium, Blue, upon your grave" (30). The grave on which he places the flower is his own, and the flower itself is *Blue,* a movie that one literally never "sees." And in a paradox at the heart of the movie, by not seeing we are instructed how to see anew.

Behind the Black Square ✍

I began by speaking of modernism's reliance on the visual, on an aesthetics of perspectivalism, photographic realism, and phenomenological verification of the sort that troubles Stephen Dedalus's walk on Sandymount Strand. One might say that it was technologies like photography and film that gave rise to this ocularcentrism and, at the same time, marked its greatest challenge. For Walter Benjamin, photography destroys the auratic character of the unique artwork, creating the possibility of infinite replication and redundancy. In a less sympathetic vein, Heidegger despairs that our "hearing and seeing are perishing through radio and film

under the rule of technology" (48). For Max Horkheimer, new technologies of reproduction cause individuals to become "blinder, more hard of
hearing, less responsive" (qtd. in Levin 3). Reading such accounts, one begins to understand how easily the discourses of ocularity and audism are
elided with a discourse of ableism; blindness equals obtuseness; deafness
equals dumbness. If humans are losing access to authentic being, technology must be to blame, and disability becomes the enabling metaphor. The
loss of aura to technology is a major trope of modernism, but its strong
corollary is the recovery of the world through estrangement and defamiliarization. Blind artists from Joyce to Evgen Bavcar and Derek Jarman
draw the blind on the blind, framing the optical character of art, not to reinforce the imperative of sight but to resite seeing as a discursive construct, embedded in debates about what it means to live in the modern
world.

The phrase "discursive construct" often falls too easily on the tongue
these days. As Ian Hacking has pointed out, claims for social construction
have included everything from authorship and emotion to vital statistics,
Zulu nationalism and women refugees (1–2). While social constructionism recognizes the historical and ideological forces in which categories are
created, it tends to neutralize those forces, denying (or relativizing)
specific social formations in which identities are created. It is little com-
fort to persons in the late stages of AIDS to know that sight is a discursive
construct or that disease is the relatively recent product of a panoptical
imperative. It is worth finding some balance between these seemingly
ireconcilable binaries of social construction and identity politics to recognize the links between infectious disease and social stigma. I would place
more emphasis on the "discursive" side of the phrase because it is in material forms of representation (aesthetic theories, photographic conventions, gaze theory, religious attitudes, national health policy) that identities become sedimented. Jarman's catalog of queer stereotypes ("I am a
mannish / Muff diving /Size queen . . .") is a frontal response to moral ma-
jorities worldwide who use such categories to reinforce heteronormalcy.
In its operatic extravagance, Jarman's litany destroys any unitary "gay"
identity under which social opprobrium may be marshaled. His final
claim—"I am a Not Gay"—is perhaps the queerest threat of all because it
imagines an identity based around a negation. If a self-identified gay man
is a "Not Gay," does that make him heterosexual, or does it open the ques-

tion of sexuality to multiple forms for which there are no positive terms? The fact that AIDS today is found increasingly among heterosexual women and children complicates the attempt to define the syndrome as gay-related. In like fashion, blindness caused by AIDS has its own historical specificity. It is not the same blindness experienced by Bavcar (a childhood accident) or the painter Andy Potok (retinitis pigmentosa) or, for that matter, Oedipus (self-inflicted mutilation). Such distinctions need to be maintained, even as alliances within the blind community need to be forged. Although the effects of AIDS may be loss of sight, its etiology rests in social discourses around sexuality, immigration, race, and class.

Georgina Kleege begins her memoir *Sight Unseen* by saying, "Writing this book made me blind" (1). As she points out, writing the book itself did not destroy her eyesight (she has been sight impaired since eleven), but through its writing she gained an increased knowledge of what it *means* to be blind in an ocularcentric world: "I find it easy to imagine what it's like to be sighted. I had to write this book to learn what it means to be blind" (3). To this extent, blindness—like other social categories—is constituted within discursive regimes. In a like manner, being blind at the museum or walking with eyes closed on Sandymount Strand offers, for a sighted witness, a way to learn what it means to be sighted—with all of the metaphysical assumptions that the ocular metaphor implies. *I see what you're saying. I must have been blind not to see the implications. I've lost sight of the goal.* The work of blind artists lays bare the device of such ocular metaphors, giving blind and sighted visitors to the museum new ways to touch cultural forms and new rhetorics through which to see an image.[11]

Chapter 7

Universal Design

*The Work of Disability in an
Age of Globalization*

Today, something we do will touch your life.
—Union Carbide ad

Global Bodies ⌇

In the lobby of the World Bank in Washington, DC, is a statue of an aged blind man being led by a young boy, a memorial to the eradication of *onchocerciasis* or "river blindness" in Africa (Stiglitz 23) The statue's placement in a building synonymous with global economics may embody the bank's mandate to achieve "a world without poverty," as its motto implies, but it also reminds us of the ways that blindness has been used as a sign of weakness and dependency. In such metaphors, it is tempting to notice only the vehicle—poverty—without attending to the blind person who is its tenor, a diversion of emphasis that is all too common in the rhetoric of globalization.[1] That rhetoric is suffused with references to physical impairment—countries suffering from *crippling* debt; national leaders who are *deaf* to the needs of their people; poverty as a *cancer* spreading throughout a region. And while economic globalization claims to solve problems of world health, it often disables the very people it seeks to help by keeping countries in perpetual debt to structural adjustment programs, eliminating environmental protections, privatizing health care, and limiting access to generic medicines. Institutions like the World Bank or the International Monetary Fund often see themselves as free-market doctors who inject much-needed capital into failing economies, serving sick patients in need of private sector transfusions. But by making health care dependent on market reforms and private sector growth, those transfusions often turn out to prolong rather than cure the disease.

My title refers to the architectural design spurred by the passage of the Americans with Disabilities Act that provides access to the built environment for all people, disabled or not. Curb cuts, readable signage, wheelchair-accessible bathrooms, and ramps are the hallmarks of universal design, but the phrase takes on more insidious implications in a globalized environment. Structural adjustment policies (SAPs) instituted during the worldwide debt crises of the 1970s and 1980s may have protected global finance from default by allowing debtor nations to continue making interest payments on foreign loans, but they often did so at the expense of social programs, education, and health care in countries that had incurred such debts.[2] These countries, many of them former colonies liberated after World War II, became economically recolonized through dependence on the financial controls of the IMF, World Bank, and GATT (General Agreement on Tariffs and Trade).[3] Universal design, in this context, refers to the global aspirations of wealthy countries in configuring development around growth rather than social improvement. For disabled persons in the global community universal design is a mixed blessing. The increased access promised by the internationalization of social services, medicine, and technology is thwarted by narrowing the meaning of access to new markets and economic opportunities.

My subtitle poses a response to the conundrum of universal design by suggesting that disability, regarded not as a medical condition but a social and ideological category, unsettles a global panacea for health and human welfare. By adapting Walter Benjamin's title, "The Work of Art in the Age of Mechanical Reproduction," to my own, I want to indicate that just as modern modes of reproduction such as photography and film transformed the auratic character of the artwork in modernism, so disability defamiliarizes the seemingly inexorable pattern of capital movement, information exchange, and market integration by which globalization is known. Furthermore, disability troubles modernity's ideal of a perfectible, rationalized, and productive body as it was formulated through eugenics, comparative anatomy, psychoanalysis, and other forms of nineteenth-century medical science.[4] As Ato Quayson points out, representations of disability often occasion a type of "discursive nervousness" in which nondisabled persons are faced with their own contingency, an alienation effect in which the autonomous self is revealed as an uncanny fiction. Recognizing such contingency "not only shows us the limit of our autonomy, it perforce enjoins a new mode of language to recognize this limit" (100). I would like to explore this "new mode of language" produced by discursive nervousness in a number of sites—a film about a paraplegic girl in Senegal, a film from Iran about minefield impairments, an AIDS performance from West Africa—to show how the representation of disability, far from serving as a prosthesis for some moral flaw (Oedipus) or character weakness (Richard III), exposes the conditions that create and sustain bodily difference.

A global perspective on disability must begin with some incontrovertible facts. There are more than a half billion disabled people in the world today. One in ten persons lives with a cognitive or physical disability, and according to UN estimates, 80 percent of those persons live in developing countries. More than 50 percent of the people in the world's forty-six poorest countries are without access to modern health care. Approximately three billion people in developing countries lack access to sanitation facilities, and one billion in those countries lack safe drinking water. The developing world carries 90 percent of the disease burden, yet these countries have access to 10 percent of world health resources (Kim et al. 4). As Paul Farmer points out, HIV has become the world's leading infectious cause of adult death, but of the forty-two million people now infected, most live in the developing world and cannot afford the drugs that might extend their lives (xvii). In Africa governments transfer to northern creditors four times more in debt payments than they spend on the health and education of their citizens. In Nicaragua, where three-fourths of the population live below the poverty line, debt repayments exceed the total social-sector budget. In Bolivia, where 80 percent of the highland population lives in poverty, debt repayments for 1997 accounted for three times the spending allocated for rural poverty reduction (Kim et al. 25). Although the United States has pledged two hundred million dollars to the UN Global Aids fund, it receives two hundred million *weekly* from debt repayments (compare this to the $54 billion pledged for homeland security in the wake of the September 11 attacks).[5] There are more than 110 million land mines in sixty-four countries, 1.5 mines per person in Angola, where 120 people per month become amputees. There are 12 million land mines in Afghanistan, one for every two people. It seems hardly necessary to add that land mines are often created not to kill but to disable, thereby maximizing the impact of bodily damage on the extended family and community.[6]

How might the incorporation of such facts into disability studies modify or even challenge some of its primary concerns? What might a critical disability studies perspective bring to the globalization debate? To some extent, the two terms—disability and globalization—are linked in earlier forms of internationalization and consolidation within modernity. U.S. immigration laws in the nineteenth century were often written around bodies deemed "unhealthy" or "diseased" and therefore unfit for national citizenship. New racial panics from without (the Yellow Peril) and within (miscegenation fears during Reconstruction) the United States were often legitimated through narratives of bodily deformity and weakness. Nayan Shah has shown how Chinese migrant laborers in the latter nineteenth century were isolated and segregated, their bodies examined and regulated according to perceived epidemiological hazards that they posed to white America (Shah). The same could be said for international labor history, which is a story of workplace impairments, chronic lung disease, repetitive stress disorders, and psychological damage caused by Fordist modes of production.[7] Taylorized methods of efficiency relied on a hypothetically normal body and set of motor functions upon which production could be rationalized. Such examples suggest that many aspects of what we call modernity are founded upon the unequal valuation of some bodies over others.

At another level, the linking of disability and globalization directs the focus of economic stabilization onto the physical bodies in whose name those strategies are often legitimated. We understand the ways that political violence and civil conflict create disability through warfare, land mines, and displacement, but we need to remember the structural violence that maintains and perpetuates disability through seemingly innocuous economic systems and political consensus.[8] Union Carbide's buoyant motto that I use for my epigraph, "Today, something we do will touch your life," means something very different for the three hundred thousand residents of Bhopal, India "touched" by that company in 1984.[9] The ways that global capital "touches" the body allows us to rethink the separation of bodies and public spaces, of bodies without organs and organizations without bodies. Just as national borders are being redrawn around new corporate trading zones and partnerships, so the borders of the body are being rethought in an age of neonatal screening, genetic engineering, and body modification. Disability studies has monitored such remappings as they affect social attitudes about nontraditional bodies, but it has not paid adequate attention to the political economy of the global body. As a result, disability studies risks remaining a vestige of an earlier identity politics rather than a critical intervention into social justice at large.

A common refrain in disability studies is that disability is the one identity category that, if we live long enough, everyone will inhabit (cf. Berubé, "I Should Live"). White people will not become black, and men will not become women, but most people will become disabled. This has led some disability scholars to posit disability as an ur-identity that, by virtue of its ubiquitousness and fluidity, its crossing of racial, sexual, and gendered categories, challenges the integrity of identity politics. Lennard Davis, for example, believes that disability is a "subset of the instability of identity in a postmodern era," and can serve to extend the class of disabled to the population at large (*Bending* 25). For Davis, disability "dismodernizes" both the humanist belief in a normalized subject as well as the social constructionist belief in identity as performance. What this formulation leaves out—and what the catalog above makes clear—is the overwhelming correlation between disability and poverty.[10] While it is true that many individuals will become disabled, it is just as certain that those who become disabled earlier in life, who have the least access to medical insurance and health care, who suffer longer and die younger, who have the least legal redress, are poor and live in an underdeveloped country. Malnutrition may not be on the minority world agenda of disability issues, but in the majority world defined by the World Health Organization, it is on the front line. Hence the first challenge that globalization poses for disability studies is a consideration of class and the unequal distribution of wealth.

When we consider disability as a global phenomenon, we are forced to reevaluate some of the keywords of disability studies—stigma, normalcy, ableism, bodily difference—from a comparative cultural perspective.[11] We must ask to what extent the discourse of disability is underwritten by a Western, state-centered model that assumes values of individual rights and equality guaranteed by legal contract. The Americans with Disabilities Act (ADA) recognizes both the material and social meanings of disability, but its ability to mitigate issues of access and employment discrimination presumes a level of economic prosperity and political stability that does not easily translate. The independent living concept born out of 1970s civil rights activism may seem a somewhat eccentric value in cultures that rely on community and family support, alternative medicines, and tribal or religious authority. What is considered a disability in the first world may be a physical advantage or blessing in another. As J. Hanks observes, "[The] disfiguring scar in Dallas becomes an honorific mark in Dahomey" (qtd. in Barnes and Mercer 135). Anita Ghai points out that the birth of a disabled child in India is literally a life-and-death situation—a "fate worse than death" (qtd. in Priestley 29)—whereas the same birth in a developed country may be ameliorated by medical intervention. One of the chants of the early disability rights movement was "We're not sick!" but global disability activism often forms around access to medicines to combat infectious diseases such as HIV/AIDS, hepatitis, or malaria. The polio epidemic stemmed in the 1950s in the United States by the Salk vaccine continues to plague many parts of Africa and the Middle East. And when U.S. policymakers attempt to intervene in global health crises in developing countries, they often bring Western assumptions about social normalization that undermine the goodwill gesture. The 1984 Reagan administration's executive order banning government financial support for U.S. and foreign family-planning agencies that provided information about abortion—the so-called Mexico City Policy—is typical of this gesture. Thus the attempt to study disability through the social model as a set of discourses about a hypothetical, normal body must be situated within individual cultural and socioeconomic landscapes.

And it is landscape that motivates the theoretical armature of this chapter. Arjun Appadurai describes the cultural logic of globalization as a series of "imaginary landscapes"—ethnoscapes, mediascapes, technoscapes, financescapes, and ideoscapes—that define "historically situated imaginations of person and groups spread around the globe" (33). He contrasts these overlapping and interdependent categories to earlier global/local, center/periphery models of global relations that rely on dyadic, linear structures of exchange and commerce. Appadurai's theory of scapes is particularly useful for explaining the multiple, interconnected sites in which disability is produced and perpetuated. If we imagine that disability is something that bodies *have* or *display,* then we restrict the meaning of the term to a physiological, medical definition of that impairment. But if we imagine that disability is defined within regimes of pharmaceutical exchange, labor migration, ethnic displacement, epidemiology, genomic research, and trade wars, then the question must be asked differently. Does disability exist in a cell, a body, a building, a race, a DNA molecule, a set of residential schools, a dialysis center, a special education curriculum, a sweatshop, a rural clinic?[12]

The implications of seeing disability spatially forces us to rethink the embodied character of impairment and disease in a number of examples.[13] The increased presence of cognitive disorders among female maquiladora workers along the Mexican-U.S. border or cancers among agricultural workers in the Central Valley of California must be linked to labor and migration in transnational companies, in the weakening of environmental and health standards, in the shift from independent farms to agribusiness.[14] Harlan Lane's description of Deaf persons as constituting a colonial regime invokes the rhetoric of postcoloniality and imperialism to describe a physical condition (deafness) as well as a set of cultural practices relating to the use of manual signing that have little to do with an ability to hear and everything to do with community and culture (31–39). Keith Wailoo's work on sickle-cell anemia in Memphis shows how a disease found predominantly among persons of African descent and characterized by, among other things, acute physical pain became visible as a disease when changes in civil rights laws began to recognize the historic pain of black people. This increased visibility of this genetically transferred disease was enhanced by a regional shift from cotton production in the Delta region to more diversified industries, from arts and entertainment (Beale Street, Graceland) to a boom in hospital construction and health care (Wailoo, *Dying* 10–11). Diabetes, a disease that allows sugar to accumulate in the blood and that leads to kidney failure, strokes, and decaying limbs, has long been known to result from poor eating habits, lack of exercise, and lack of access to medical treatment. The recent upsurge in cases of Type 2 diabetes among children threatens to become a medical epidemic, but it is fueled by an HMO-driven medical establishment that is little interested in prevention and a proactive fast food industry that is not interested in health. Although Type 2 diabetes may be "located" in an individual's pancreas that produces insulin, it is "lived" in poor, working-class neighborhoods in minority communities.[15]

As Stephen Frears's film *Dirty Pretty Things* illustrates, the global market in body parts is inextricable from what Appadurai calls the "ethnoscape"—contexts of labor migration, sexual tourism, and ethnic conflicts through which this market does its business. In such cases, does disability rest with the person with kidney disease or with the so-called donor who sells the kidney, with the wealthy recipient whose life is sustained by an operation or the immigrant whose health is drastically compromised as a result of it? Phrased in this way, disability is as much about national and cultural power differentials as it is a matter of medicine and bodies. As Donald Moore reminds me, when we consider the *place* of disability, we find that the "discursive and material effects of history, culture, and power converge—along with the embodied and experienced sedimentations of physicality and psychic conditionalities imposed in conditions not of subjects' choosing."[16]

Disability Studies in a Global Perspective

The salient feature of U.S., Canadian, and British scholarship in disability studies in the past ten years is a shift from a medical to a social model of impairment. As I have indicated in my introduction, the medical definition of disability locates impairment in the individual as someone who lacks the full complement of physical and cognitive elements of true personhood and who must be cured or rehabilitated. The social model locates disability not in the individual's impairment but in the environment—in social attitudes, institutional structures, and physical or communicational barriers that prevent full participation as citizen subject. Much of this work is reinforced by language in the Americans with Disabilities Act that defines a person with a disability as someone who has a "record of such an impairment" and who is "regarded as having such an impairment." The ADA recognizes that a person in a wheelchair becomes disabled when he or she encounters a building without elevators or when a sight-impaired person tries to use an ATM machine without braille signage. It also recognizes that one may be equally disabled by social stigma.

Phrases like *wheelchair bound, retarded,* or *deaf and dumb* are no less op-
pressive than lack of physical access since they mark how certain bodies
are interpreted and read. The celebrity telethon host who patronizes his
poster child guest disables with one hand while soliciting funds for that
child's rehabilitation with the other.[17]

In the humanities this social model has been accompanied by
significant readings of disabled characters in literature whose nontraditional bodies are sites of moral failing, pity, or sexual panic. David
Mitchell and Sharon Snyder have described this analogical treatment of
disability in cultural texts as a "narrative prosthesis" in which a disabled
character serves as a crutch to shore up normalcy somewhere else. The
disabled character is prosthetic in the sense that he or she provides an illusion of bodily wholeness upon which the novel erects its formal claims
to totality, in which ethical or moral failings in one sphere are signified
through physical limitations in another. In Richard Wright's *Native Son,*
for example, Mrs. Dalton's blindness could be read as a sign of the moral
limits of white liberal attitudes that mask racism. Wright is less interested
in blindness itself than the way that it enables a story about racial violence
and liberal guilt. In *A Christmas Carol* Charles Dickens does not use Tiny
Tim to condemn the treatment of crippled children in Victorian society
but to finesse Scrooge's awakening to charity and human kindness toward
others. By regarding disability as a "narrative prosthesis," Mitchell and
Snyder underscore the ways that the material bodies of blind or crippled
persons are deflected onto an able-bodied normalcy that the story must
reinforce. Indeed, narrative's claim to formal coherence is underwritten
by that which it cannot contain, as evidenced by the carnival grotesques,
madwomen in attics, blind prophets, and mute soothsayers that populate
narrative theory.

Despite Mitchell and Snyder's important warnings about the dangers
of analogical treatments of disability, there are cases in which a prosthesis
is *still* a prosthesis. The first-world texts that have been the site of most
work in disability studies may very well have narrative closure as their telos, but regarded in a more globalized environment, the social meaning of
both disability and narrative may have to be expanded.[18] As I will point
out with reference to Mohsen Makhmalbaf's film *Kandahar,* amputations
due to minefield explosions proliferated in Afghanistan after the Soviet
invasion in 1979. By focusing on the metaphoric use of disability in cul-

tural forms, we may miss lived reality of those metaphors in daily life.

Just as "prosthesis" within a global disability perspective must be looked at historically, so must the term *narrative*. As my final example will show, it is impossible to consider cultural forms in Africa without mentioning the role of AIDS activism and especially the Treatment Action Campaign (TAC) that has legislated for increased access to antiretroviral drugs. Here, representations of disability and social action converge in performances designed to educate, entertain, and create solidarity. Moreover, due to the informational and educational nature of this performance—what some call "edutainment"—issues of reception mean something very different from what they do in traditional narrative theory. Within Theater for Development performances around HIV/AIDS, the stage may be an open clearing or flatbed truck, a movable stage or community center playground where performances occur.[19] Traditional oral and folkloric materials may be fused with references to proper nutrition and safe sex; street protests inspired by U.S. AIDS activism merge with street theater; popular culture (comics, hip-hop) combines with classic theater. The work of art in an age of globalization may be a tape cassette about the need to wear a condom.

If disability studies has been reticent on the subject of globalization, recent literature on globalization has been equally silent about disability. Key critical anthologies such as *The Global Transformations Reader, Dying for Growth, Global/Local, World Bank Literature The Cultures of Globalization,* and Joseph Stiglitz's *Globalization and Its Discontents* mention the ill effects of multinational corporations and structural adjustment policies on health care systems, but they devote no time to disability as a cultural problem. Where disability studies has concentrated much of its attention on the role of stigma and social marginalization, antiglobalist theory tends to treat disabled persons as victims rather than subjects. Often themes of powerlessness and dependency are framed through the rhetoric of disability, as in Gillian Hart's important book on South Africa, *Disabling Globalization,* which, despite its title, never mentions AIDS or the country's active disability rights movement. Richard Wolff's essay "World Bank/Class Blindness" excoriates development theorists who ignore class issues in formulating economic policy, using the word *blindness* throughout the essay to describe ignorance and obtuseness. He uses the word so often that it becomes a verbal tic:

> To ignore the existence of and the changes among and within coex-
> isting kinds of class processes in any society is to blind both analysis
> and policy making. . . . The World Bank cultivates this blindness.
> (176)

I do not mean to dismiss important globalization theory by focusing on
ableist rhetoric but to stress how such usage underscores the ways that a
critique of class blindness may enable obtuseness about blindness. The
danger of these silences around disability is that in arguing against structural violence, globalization theory helps replicate those same institutional features by treating persons with disabilities as "medical problems,"
and "patients"—a form of victimology that all of the texts mentioned
above excoriate.

What would happen if we substituted *disability avoidance* for Wolff's
"class blindness" and looked at the ways that the global capitalist pursuit
of surplus impacts specific bodies in a market system? Two examples
come to mind. In 1983, the Centers for Disease Control (CDC) observed
that pooled blood products (rather than the lifestyles of gay men) were responsible for AIDS among hemophilia patients. In 1984, the Bayer unit of
Cutter Biological sold millions of dollars worth of its blood-clotting factor for hemophiliacs to Asia and Latin America when it discovered that
the company had large stores of product that were now unsalable in the
United States and Europe. Instead of destroying the tainted product and
alerting distributors abroad, Bayer continued to sell factor in Malaysia,
Singapore, Indonesia, Japan, and Argentina, where thousands of hemophiliacs and other patients needing transfusions became infected with
HIV. These events were occurring despite the fact that the company had
developed a safer, heat-treated product that it was selling in the United
States and Europe. In a statement to the *New York Times,* Bayer officials
claimed that they had "behaved responsibly, ethically and humanely" in
continuing to sell the old product in these parts of the world (cf. Bogdanich and Koli). Not only did Bayer continue to sell infected product, it
continued to *make* the old type of factor in order to fill orders from several large fixed-price contracts. The result was a worldwide HIV infection
rate of 90 percent among severe hemophiliacs and a profit for Bayer. Although similar scandals erupted within the United States, Canada, Japan,
and France, the practice of transnational corporations selling unwanted

products to developing countries in order to maintain the bottom line at home is the specter haunting a globalized economy.[20] Supporters of a global marketplace will argue that despite local inequities, a free market will ultimately benefit those most in need, but this assumption obviously depends on what one means by "free." When HIV-infected recipients of blood transfusions become collateral damage in a worldwide trade war, one wonders who is being served by open markets.

My second example concerns the definitions that the World Bank uses for persons with disabilities in order to calculate cost-effective interventions in health policy. In its 1993 World Development Report, "Investing in Health," the World Bank applied the concept of the Disability Adjusted Life Years, or DALY, as an indicator of the "time lived with a disability and the time lost due to premature mortality" (Homedes 3). The language of the report refers to the "global burdens" of disability and the "cost effectiveness of different interventions at reducing the disease burdens due to a particular condition" (Homedes 8). Obviously the World Bank is trying to do the right thing by assessing priorities for intervention in health matters, but by defining individuals by lost productivity instead of medical need, the bank imposes an actuarial value on its largesse. Those deemed least useful in certain cultures—women, children, aged, and disabled persons—will, as Nirmala Erevelles says, "have little or no entitlement to health services at public expense" (5).[21] In both of these examples, the lack of monitoring or quality control on pharmaceutical products, the application of cost-benefit analysis to matters of health and mortality, and the ability of transnational corporations like Bayer to control worldwide distribution and prevent competition are only the most obvious ways that internationalization of health care creates—rather than eliminates—disability and calls into question the degree to which markets can ever achieve the kind of equality that free market economists advocate.

Development, Devaluation, and Disability in the Films of Jibril Mambety ✍

I want now to turn to several cultural examples that read the scapes of globalization through a disability optic. My ocular metaphor calls attention to the importance of performance in all of my examples, but it also reinforces the ways that disability focalizes the inherently unrepresentable quality of global economic processes. The homogenization of commodities, signage, and technology that we associate with globalization creates a placelessness for which mimetic criteria seem inadequate. Lisa Lowe, drawing on Raymond Williams, describes globalization as a "structure of feeling" that cannot be "totalized through a single developmental narrative" (3). We could imagine this structure of feeling around globalization as a kind of phantom limb phenomenon that registers a phantasmatic "whole body" that can no longer be constituted or imagined. When the immigrant workers in *Dirty Pretty Things* describe themselves to the organ broker as being "invisible," they are testifying to the ways that marginal figures in the metropole are ghosts in a global system of exchange. South African Theater for Development projects bring AIDS into public awareness despite administrative refusal to recognize the severity of its presence. In each case, the meaning of the cultural work must be understood not only in terms of formal characteristics or literary history but in terms of how it sees globalization through bodies disabled by it.

The films of Jibril Diop Mambety, one of Senegal's best-known filmmakers, are often based on traditional folktales, yet their retellings of the trickster Yadikoon or the animal fables of rabbit and hyena are placed in contemporary settings. As the title to his incomplete final trilogy indicates, he tells the story of *les petites gens*, the "little people," marginalized by devaluations, both human and economic. In addition to being poor, Mambety's characters are often disabled, played by nonprofessional, disabled actors. In *Hyenes* (1992), a woman with a prosthetic leg and arm returns to her birthplace, the rural town of Colobane, to avenge herself on a former lover who deserted her and their child. *Le franc* (1993) is an allegory about a poor congoma player who wins a lottery ticket from a short person who serves as his guide and goad. In *La petite vendeuse de soleil* (1999) a paraplegic girl displays resilience and pluck by helping her blind grandmother and a mentally disturbed woman. These figures are partly metaphors for an Africa disabled by debt, but their pervasiveness in Mambety's films suggests something more. Disabled characters do not play cameo roles, supporting more able-bodied main characters; they are independent agents who serve as the moral centers for each tale. Their physical impairments do not serve as markers of limit but alternative ways of being in societies handicapped by the residues of colonial authority.

Disability in Mambety's films is used to frame the burdens produced in the social and political infrastructure of Senegal following the 1994 devaluation of the West African franc (CFA) by European and American financial institutions.[22] Almost overnight, the value of domestic products was cut in half, the price of a sack of rice doubled, export prices plummeted. In Mambety's films, the financescape of devaluation is manifested in the various ways that the market is depicted—from the lottery-ticket seller of *Le franc*, who embodies the economic world of poor Africans after devaluation, to the dusty, bustling marketplace of Dakar in *La petite vendeuse*, to the hardscrabble country store that is the centerpiece of *Hyenas*. Framing these local economic sites stand the anonymous corporate buildings of Dakar, looming over the "little" dramas of Mambety's characters. This financescape is combined with both mediascape and ethnoscape through which global information (newspapers, radio) is passed and communal identities (religious institutions, family units) interrupted. In *Le Franc*, the Muslim call to prayer comes via the same public address system that broadcasts the winning lottery numbers. Here, religious and economic rituals vie for a common electronic voice in the marketplace. By situating each of his disabled characters in relation to a massive economic shift in West African finance, Mambety studies the impact of devaluation and development on those most affected.

Mambety's last film, *La petite vendeuse de soleil* (*The Little Girl Who Sold the Sun*), tells of a twelve-year-old paraplegic girl, Sili Laam (Lissa Balera), who begs for money in the crowded market of Dakar with her blind grandmother. Seeing that boys make more money by selling the local paper, *Soleil*, she tries her entrepreneurial hand as a news vendor, arguing, "What boys can do girls can too." Her resilience and toughness carry her through the crowded, competitive world of the market where street vendors vie for the smallest share and where corrupt police lurk at the edges. At one point, after selling her papers, Lily is accosted by a policeman who demands to see her money. She, in turn, demands to be taken to the police station so that she can clear herself. At the station she boldly accuses the chief of police of trying to pilfer her earnings: "What I earn is my own business," she says, displaying her receipt for the newspapers. In the process of clearing herself, she succeeds in intervening on behalf of another woman who had been incarcerated in the police station prison, accused, without proof, of stealing. Lili's forthright demand for justice—her own and that of others—marks her integrity in a world based on competition and corruption.[23]

Sili's paraplegia, possibly a result of polio, suggests the condition of all bodies kept in poverty by structural adjustment, but she is not reduced to being a "cripple." We see her moving forcefully through the crowd, getting a ride to Dakar in a horse cart, dancing in a yellow dress with other girls, defending herself against threatening police and predatory gangs, giving her earnings to various beggars in the market. The theme of structural adjustment is evident through the headlines that Lili shouts and that appear in the papers she sells. In one crucial scene, the paper announces that the CFA has been devalued by half. The economic chaos that this devaluation caused in western Africa is vividly depicted in a shot of imported refrigerators standing unsold alongside the road while Lili lurches past, and in the contrast between an old man breaking rocks with his bare hands while jet planes land behind him. The market in which Lili begs and then sells papers is itself a parodic version of the free market options promised by neoliberalism. Surrounded by tall skyscrapers, Lili's market is dominated by a combination of individual initiative and corruption, not the blessings of free trade. But however flawed, it is also a market in which mixtures of people and products converge—a place where disabled citizens mutually support each other and where exchange of products coincides with sharing of opinions and ideas.[24]

Despite the harsh conditions in which Mambety situates his parable of poverty and globalization, the film presents alternative forms of cooperation and support beyond those of finance. Throughout the film, Lili establishes a friendship with a young boy, Babou Seck (Tayerou M'Baye), who protects her from a gang of threatening news vendors. In the film's last scene, Lili and Babou are selling papers at the port. The headlines read, "Afrique quitte le franc zone" (Africa has left the franc zone), announcing a future, as yet unrealized: francophone Africa, having severed its dependence on the French franc, must adapt to a world economy.[25] Lili is set upon by a gang of boys who knock her down and steal her crutch. Babou tries to retrieve it, but is unsuccessful. "What do we do now?" Babou asks, to which Lili responds, "We continue." He hoists her onto his back and carries her through a crowded arcade of the market. The other vendors fade back into the stalls, leaving only the sound of Babou's footsteps echoing through the hall. The moral of the story—perhaps too baldly stated—is that in a society damaged by fluctuating, international markets and plagued by local corruption (the street boys who harass Lili resemble roving gangs or paramilitary police in any number of African countries), the salvific value is mutual aid and support. But the scene also asks whether former colonies like Senegal can follow an independent economic course without relying on its former colonial infrastructure. Mambety allows us to witness an alternative form of development, one based on self-reliance rather than ruthless competition.

Mambety makes us constantly aware of the relationship between disability and market-driven poverty. The scene just discussed is set at a ferry dock called Goree, a reference to the infamous Goree Island slave port in West Africa from which slaves were sent to the new world. Lili is often observed by a young amputee in a wheelchair who cradles a large boom-box in his arms and who, for a few coins, plays music. He functions as a silent chorus, his music providing entertainment and perhaps a site of resistance (he plays songs by Wasis Diop celebrating African freedom fighters), his disabled perspective providing a vantage from which we too see Lili. And he, like Lily, must negotiate a literally rocky terrain—streets with potholes and puddles of water, garbage strewn about, making the term *access* seem laughable. Clearly, a country that must divert all of its resources to settling its international debts cannot be bothered with providing better infrastructure and curb cuts for any of its population. At the end of the film, Mambety uses his own voice as voice-over moral concerning the role of his film: "This tale is thrown to the sea," suggesting that it is up to the audience to uncork the bottle and read its meanings into the future. But Lili provides the film's last words by saying, "The first to breathe it will go to heaven," providing a redemptive parable of emancipation through mutual (not foreign) aid.[26]

Mambety's parables of development and devaluation situate the disabled body against the backdrop of massive economic inequality. The dusty market of Dakar in which Sili Laam establishes her tenuous authority is flanked by corporate buildings, new refrigerators, and jet planes. Sili sells the government newspaper, *The Sun*, not because she believes its editorial opinions but because, as she says, she hopes to bring the government closer to the people. To this extent, she participates in commodity society without becoming a commodity herself. If the film displays a degree of triumphalism at the end, it nevertheless offers, as Winnie Wood-

hull observes, "provocative images of the bodies of disabled people, allowing them to disturb us, granting them compelling . . . forms of mobility,
and inviting us to imagine Africa profoundly differently" (8). By being
"the little [crippled] girl who sells the sun," Sili's body marks the difficulties of access (to streets, affordable health care, gender equality) in Africa
within the context of currency devaluation. But the word "context" is in-
exact if it simply implies an inert, changeless backdrop. The film illustrates
the degree to which the two markets of Dakar are intertwined. The one Sili
inhabits is fatally connected to the high-rises that surround it.

Living Disability in a War Zone: *Kandahar*

With the attack on the World Trade Center and Pentagon in 2001, the implications of global connectedness gained a new and frightening meaning for U.S. citizens. Global conflict was brought home, inaugurating a
seemingly endless war on terrorism, paranoia around internal security,
and an expanding series of sectarian conflicts throughout the Middle
East. It hardly needs to be said that wars produce disability, and today's
news is filled with images of overcrowded, poorly staffed Iraqi hospitals
and families wailing over loved ones caught in the crossfire. The news is
also replete with stories of American soldiers coming home with missing
limbs and neurological damage. This front-page news is accompanied in
the home and entertainment pages by stories of soldiers amputees learning to walk, ski, play basketball, and return to some semblance of normal
civilian life through the aid of new prosthetic and rehabilitation technologies. David Serlin has pointed out with regard to World War II that
rehabilitation stories are necessary as much for national as for personal
healing. Media accounts of soldiers who triumph over their amputated
limbs imply "a direct relation between physical trauma—and the ability
to survive such trauma—and patriotic duty" (28). Serlin goes on to describe how the U.S. State Department participated in a project to bring a
group of Japanese women who had been disfigured by the A-bomb blasts
in Hiroshima and Nagasaki to the United States for reconstructive
surgery. The "Hiroshima Maidens," as they were called, were enlisted in
U.S. cold war propaganda to soften its involvement in the atomic bomb
blasts and to cement its image as a scientific and humanitarian bulwark

against Soviet totalitarianism. Such examples of rehabilitation and re-constructive surgery are surfacing today as the domestic face of global conflict.

Although the current State Department seems anxious to maintain a distinction between previous conflicts—particularly the cold war—and the war on terror, there are significant parallels in the way that superpower (or G8) interests around oil, port access, drugs, natural resources, and regional security create havoc in the developing world (Korea, Vietnam, Cuba, Iran, Chile) while remaining relatively untouched at home. And although the official rhetoric that joins the two periods is dominated by worries about weapons of mass destruction, the daily accounts of physical suffering concern damage produced by roadside bombs and antiperson-nel mines. If one wanted an image of cold war trauma as it continues to be acted out in the global war on terror, one could point to Bobby Neel Adams's photographs of Cambodian amputees. These images chronicle the massive impact of antipersonnel mines that now litter the Southeast Asian landscape and that have caused, since 1979, the loss of limbs to over forty thousand persons, 1 out of every 234 Cambodians. As David Levi Strauss writes in his catalog introduction to Adams's photographs, the term *minefield* does not adequately describe the situation in Cambodia since there "are minefields *upon* minefields, a patchwork palimpsest of death and destruction" (58). This patchwork includes mines made in the USSR and placed by the North Vietnamese in the early days of the Viet-nam conflict, Chinese-made mines used by the Khmer Rouge in its strug-gles with Lon Nol, and U.S.-manufactured MI6AI mines laid by various resistance groups in more recent opposition to the Phnom Penh govern-ment. Adams's photographs depict the stark daily lives of men, women, and children in a variety of countries—but particularly Cambodia—who have lost limbs while farming, bicycling to work, or playing in fields. Land mines are simple to make and inexpensive to sell, but they inflict massive damage since the person, is more often severely wounded than killed out-right, causing maximum physical and economic hardships on family and community. Moreover, clearing a minefield is extremely expensive, so ex-pensive that some areas of the country remain no-go zones. Finally, there are residual effects of amputation in social costs due to various forms of discrimination, social ostracism, and downright hostility experienced by amputees. As Levi Strauss concludes,

[Land mines] act independently of military tactics and political movements. If a mine victim in Cambodia or Mozambique is asked the question "Who did this to you? Who laid that mine?" they will invariably say they don't know. The original message that the mine was supposed to carry . . . has worn off like a manufacturer's label by the time the mine is activated. The new message is this: you are no longer safe, anywhere, anytime. (64)

The presence of mines is a daily reminder of three decades of warfare in Afghanistan and can be seen in the prevalence of mobility impairments among its citizens. As I pointed out in my introduction, there are more than twelve million unexploded mines in Afghanistan—one for every two people. War injuries from mines account for a large percentage of Afghanistan's seven hundred thousand disabled people, and disabled persons services are dominated by the focus on orthopedic aids and rehabilitation therapy. Due to the constant state of warfare since the Soviet invasion, Afghanistan has been weakened by poverty and war, creating a situation where poor sanitation, malnutrition, malaria, polio, diarrhea are common. The lack of adequate health care, a crumbling or nonexistent infrastructure, the lack of clean, running water and waste removal, the absence of medicine and doctors, and an extremely volatile climate of ethnic and tribal conflict make Afghanistan one of the poorest countries in the world.

The West tends to think of Afghanistan, if at all, in terms of the Taliban's repressive religious regime, but the Iranian film director Mohsen Makhmalbaf has taken a considerably wider view of the country, bringing together the intersecting threads of warfare, minefield disasters, tribal conflict, poverty, and gender difference in his film *Kandahar*. The main character, an Afghani-born female journalist, Nafas (Niloufar Pazira), is traveling from the Iranian border to Kandahar to save her sister from what she fears is an immanent suicide attempt over repressive conditions pertaining to women. Her sister has lost her legs in a mine explosion and has written to Nafas saying that she will end her life at the next eclipse of the sun. The eclipse becomes a powerful metaphor for women's life under the burka, light cloaked in darkness, a world filtered through the veil's meshwork. The film is set during the Taliban regime, and Nafas must wear a burka while traveling, her clothing serving as a metaphor for the limits of female agency but also providing a degree of protection from threatening forces she encounters along the way. Her desert journey is arduous, constantly interrupted by roadblocks, checkpoints, and banditry. She records her thoughts into a tape recorder that she conceals beneath her cloak, yet as the voice-over for the film, her private acts of reflection become the audience's perspective on the film's actions.

The eclipse motif is vividly represented in one scene in which Nafas has gone to a doctor, having become ill from drinking polluted water from a well. In the small village surgery she encounters a black American Muslim who practices medicine in an unofficial capacity (he has no medical degrees) and who has come to Afghanistan as a freedom fighter. Having become disillusioned with armed struggle in service to Islam, he turns to healing and medicine as a way of realizing his spiritual quest. But he encounters severe obstacles, not the least of which are the Taliban's prohibitions against men coming into contact with women. His women patients must be examined behind a sheet of canvas with only a small hole through which he may look at small portions of the woman's face. Furthermore, he may not speak directly to them, requiring an intermediary—often a child—who repeats his questions to the patient and who then relays her answers back. Most of doctor's cases involve illnesses produced by poverty, poor sanitation, and malnutrition. "They don't need a doctor here; they need a baker," he says ruefully, dispensing a sheet of flatbread to one patient. And when Nafas appears through the small hole, she realizes that he speaks English, and so they converse about her plight at trying to get to Kandahar and about his life since leaving the United States. Because their conversation is monitored by the young boy who is enlisted to translate the doctor-patient interview, they must also sustain the fiction—in Arabic—of a professional visit, lest the boy reveal their more intimate conversation to the Taliban authorities. The highly mediated nature of their conversation—in two languages, through a hole in a screen, across global divides, religious affiliations, and genders—is only on the surface a narrative about medicine and illness. Yet that surface narrative—like the burka—hides and protects a woman whose access to language, health care, and agency is eclipsed by historical factors beyond her control.[27]

The doctor agrees to help Nafas reach a Red Cross station where she might find someone to take her the rest of the distance to Kandahar. When she arrives at the station, Nafas witnesses a group of amputated Afghani men on crutches who are waiting for a shipment of prosthetic limbs to arrive. With the help of a Red Cross nurse Nafas meets a man who might take her the rest of the way. He is there to find a pair of prosthetic legs for his wife, but he refuses the heavy, oversized pair that he is given by the Red Cross authorities. Instead, he chooses a smaller pair and tests their adequacy by arranging his wife's burka over them and then putting her shoes on the plastic feet. He then presses his prosthetic wife against himself while looking in a mirror in a gesture that is both tender and tragic. Because the director is working with nonprofessional actors who are improvising their lines based on their actual conditions, this scene is all the more powerful for its invocation of the lived reality of families in which one or more persons are without limbs but whose physical mobility is constrained by rigid prohibitions about social mobility.

The most powerful scene in the movie involves the delivery of prosthetic limbs by parachute from a Red Cross helicopter. Makhmalbaf has already introduced us to several of the men who describe the minefield origins of their amputations to the nurses. As the parachutes begin to open over the desert, the men who have been milling around on their crutches begin to move as quickly as they can, hopping, leaping, and lurching toward the drop site. The image of legs falling gracefully to earth is a powerful, if surreal, image of postcolonial disruptions brought about by the end of the cold war. Makhmalbaf has a keen eye for the mythic implications of crippled men in turbans moving in an erratic wave toward floating prostheses, but for all of its strangeness, the scene is grounded in the realities of Afghanistan's long cycle of occupation and sectarian warfare that continues today. As the men fan out over the desert wasteland, the Red Cross nurses shout, "Where are you going? Where are you going?"—a vain attempt to rein in an unstoppable desire to be made "whole" and perhaps a question about the future of an impoverished nation.

This scene is matched by one at the end of the movie in which a group of women and girls are crossing the desert to attend a wedding in Kandahar. Nafas and her male guide have joined the procession, each wearing a burka to blend in among the other women. Nafas's guide carries a pair of prosthetic legs over his shoulder "as a spare" in case something should happen along the way. Makhmalbaf's camera captures the uncanny beauty of brightly embroidered and colored burkas against a stark desert backdrop. This celebratory procession with children singing bridal songs and the bride in white on horseback is abruptly interrupted by the appearance of Taliban police in dark clothing. They stop the procession and demand that each woman hold up her burka to see if she is carrying any forbidden objects. When the authorities find such objects—a book, a musical instrument—they confiscate them and separate the malefactor from the rest of the group. Nafas's male guide is also discovered and separated from her. Like the previous scene at the Red Cross station, this scene reveals a close connection between prostheses and the burka as agents of gender identity and ambiguity. Both objects make the partial body whole according to normative expectations of gender. Yet while the prosthetic limbs provide only the illusion of phallic potency for the males, the burka provides protection and even a sense of security for the women. The sheer innovativeness of its stitchery and color establishes on its blank surface a creative and differentiating quality that may lie beneath.

Kandahar is a movie made by an Iranian director whose main character is of Afghan birth and Canadian citizenship, conducted in several languages (Farsi, Pashtu, English), and featuring almost exclusively untrained actors. If the acting seems at times stilted, this quality testifies to the collaborative nature of the filmmaking process. Makhmalbaf had to enlist the support of local tribal leaders in order to shoot the film and to engage families who had never seen a film before. Filmmaking was restricted to daylight hours because electricity did not exist in the rural outposts near the Iranian border, and the film had to be shot and relocated several times when Nafas's journey took her to areas notorious for banditry. Land mines were not only a metaphor in the movie, they were a hazard in the making of the movie, necessitating very complicated surveys of the landscape before a shot could be made. These technical aspects of the film are important if we are to understand the degree to which "narrative prosthesis" becomes problematic as a term for the representation of disability. Whatever closure the film's narrative may proffer is discouraged at the end. Nafas never reaches Kandahar, and we last see her looking out at the sunset through the mesh of her veil.[28]

An African Story

At one point in *Dirty Pretty Things,* Senay, the Muslim woman who is the film's lead, asks Okwe why he came to London. He replies, "It's an African story." He is speaking about the diaspora of Africans throughout the Western world, but he could equally be speaking about the spread of HIV/AIDS within Africa. There is a relationship between the two African stories insofar as both are driven by poverty and transnational labor movements. Although HIV/AIDS has expanded throughout the world, the rise of the disease in Africa—especially in sub-Saharan Africa—is spectacular, by any epidemiological standard. It is estimated that of the forty-two million people living with HIV/AIDS, more than twenty-nine million—70 percent—live in sub-Saharan Africa. In 2002 alone, 2.4 million Africans died of AIDS, and 3.5 million new infections appeared in the region. The multiple reasons for the expansion of HIV/AIDS are too large to summarize here, but for our purposes it is worth emphasizing the crucial role that debt repayments have had on the crisis. One-third of all people living with AIDS are in countries heavily indebted to the World Bank.[29] Zambia spends 30 percent more on its annual debt payment than it does on health care. Camaroon spends three and a half times its health budget on debt repayment. Given that one of the first requirements for a fiscal readjustment from the World bank involves a cut in public sector budgets (especially health care and education) it is little wonder that debtor nations find themselves with a pandemic that seems to have no end.

There is cautious optimism among world health authorities that these figures will diminish with renewed emphasis on prevention, the lifting of barriers to generic drugs, and improved communications in rural regions. African governments that ignored or denied the links between HIV infection and AIDS have finally come to acknowledge the connection and, as in South Africa, are mounting an aggressive treatment and prevention campaign. A series of suits against Western pharmaceutical companies have made cheaper generic antiretroviral drugs more available. The formation of the UN Global AIDS fund has committed new resources to treatment. Most important for my concerns of this chapter has been the role of the Treatment Action Campaign (TAC), which has protested aggressively for affordable antiretroviral drugs. Although TAC is largely a political entity, it is supported by a cultural network of education forums, arts advocacy, and performance venues that constitute some of the most significant links between art and politics on a global scale.[30] And TAC joins a number of other political movements in South Africa—including the Landless

People's Movement and the Anti-Privatization Forum—that have utilized public protest and performance around health and welfare issues. What form does this "African story" take? Can Western theories of textuality and aesthetic coherence account for the story of postapartheid Africa, especially when it concerns disability and development? Most importantly, how does the context of AIDS challenge the division between art and politics, cultural forms and social movements? These questions emerge forcefully in Theater for Development projects in which performance has become central to pedagogical efforts to explain government policies or health issues.[31] Although activists are often skeptical about Theater for Development productions as tools of state or NGO interests, there is a growing acceptance of their importance in addressing HIV/AIDS. Theater for Development is reminiscent of other forms of activist theater—Luis Valdez's "actos" or the militant theater of the U.S. black nationalism—that combine pedagogical purpose with audience collaboration. As "edutainment," these new cultural forms challenge formalist aesthetics, their sometimes didactic nature and instrumental character developed through a range of popular genres involving puppetry, dance, hip-hop rhymes, comics, stilt dancing, posters, and mime.[32] Popular television shows like *Soul City* or graphic stories like *Heart to Heart* and *Body and Soul* provide "life skills" education while reinforcing communal formations. As Loren Kruger and Patricia Watson Shariff point out, by "attending to specific local reappropriations of mass-cultural forms," graphic stories "complicate generalized characterizations of 'global culture' and globalization as the standardized dissemination of metropolitan (often American) habits of mass-culture consumption" (480).

In speaking of the film *Kandahar* I referred to Nafas's use of a tape recorder to record her journey among amputees in the desert; I now want to conclude with reference to another tape cassette, forged in Theater for Development arena, whose function, far from representing an outlawed interiority, establishes continuities among travelers. "Yiriba" is a thirty-minute tape cassette developed by several local NGOs and CIDA (the Canadian Agency for International Development) designed to be distributed among long-distance truck drivers who cover routes in West Africa's "AIDS corridor."[33] The tape features the voices of two well-known griots, Djeli Daouda Dembele and his wife, Hawa Dembele, who warn truck drivers of the dangers of sexually transmitted diseases, using traditional oral tales and musical accompaniment. Daouda tells the story of a truck driver, Yiriba, who is approached by a good-looking woman, Korotouma, at a truck stop, who asks for a lift to the next town. They end up at a hotel and begin to engage in sexual activity. When Yiriba produces a condom, Korotouma chastizes him for thinking she might be a prostitute. Yiriba delivers a speech about the need for prudence—"Both of us travel a lot, and we meet many people every day. This condom will protect you and me. I must say we hardly know one another" (Bourgault 134). Korotouma, insulted, leaves Yiriba and takes up with another driver, Seydou. The same scenario occurs, but Seydou does not use a condom and, as a result, becomes infected with HIV. When Yiriba visits his now ailing friend, he learns that Seydou has infected other women as well as his wife, causing her to become infertile. Finally, because of his illness, Seydou has entrusted his truck to his apprentice, who promptly steals it, leaving him without a means of livelihood. Throughout the tale, Hawa Dembele sings a refrain: "I have traveled to the east, to the west, from north to south, and I have never seen a fever like this one, Father of the griots" (Bourgault 135).

There are several stylistic features in the story that link the tape to storytelling traditions and that make this more than a simple cautionary tale. The griot poses as the "great bard of truck drivers," urging solidarity with each other during the long night drives. The Dembeles act both as storytellers and actors who take on various roles. Daouda also praises the AIDS doctors of West Africa and mentions specific truck stops, cities, and health centers that drivers are likely to encounter. He approves of rig owners "who help their drivers when these latter fall ill" (Bourgault 137). According to Louise Bourgault, these epic moments of praise are designed to "affirm the importance of all members of society" (137) and promote communal values. Daouda also describes Korotouma's sexual attractiveness and the flirtation between her and the truck drivers. While this perspective reinforces male stereotypes of the woman as carrier of AIDS, it is countered by the fact that it is the male truck driver, Seydou, who brings the disease to other women, including his own wife. Hawa's musical interludes and refrains give a more global perspective to the cautionary aspects of the tale, showing the effects of the pandemic from a female voice and vantage. Merged into the tale are warnings about the dangers of self-medication or using black market drugs.[34] The tale also explodes myths about sexually transmitted diseases and AIDS, teaching that lack of symptoms does not mean that one is free of infection, that illness has consequences that are both financial and marital.

"Yiriba" raises provocative questions about the work of art in an age of globalization. The cassette exists in a limnal space between several cultural forms, some archaic (the griot tale) and some modern (truck routes, tape recorders). It is, in James Clifford's terms, a form of "traveling culture," crossing national, ethnic, and linguistic boundaries, linking truck drivers from different areas who share the same routes and the same potential for HIV infection. Daouda and Hawa can count on their fame as storytellers among their listeners to validate their message—and along the way, to legitimate the NGOs that sponsor the tape. Thus the cautionary story of "Yiriba," simple though it may seem on the surface, brings the AIDS story and the African story together.

The Work of the ADA in an Age of Globalization ↩

In this chapter I have referred to disability in the singular to emphasize its social and cultural meaning rather than as a synonym for various types of impairments. It is this singular meaning that disability studies studies. Given this distinction, it might have seemed more appropriate for me to speak of the "work of disability *studies*" in an age of globalization, but this usage tends to privilege the work of scholarship over the ideology of ableism it contests. I want to retain the idea that disability—like the aesthetic—challenges ideas of bodily and cognitive normalcy, making both normalcy and disability visible. Tobin Siebers illustrates the distinction by observing that "in a society of wheelchair users stairs would be nonexistent" ("Disability" 740). The fact that stairs are ubiquitous testifies to the success of ableist ideas of architectural design; the fact that stairs, ramps, and communicational technologies are expensive to adapt testifies to the reasons why legal definitions of disability are often about limiting, rather than representing, the class. The claim of expense is often accompanied by the accusation that people with disabilities are selfish and narcissistic— that in seeking greater access they subject small business owners, heritage buildings, and school districts to unnecessary retrofits for their "narrow" bodily concerns.[35] This accusation, often raised by critics of the ADA, becomes one of the more subtle barriers that disability activists have had to negotiate.

In the United States we—at least those of us who are documented citizens—benefit from legal statutes like the ADA as well as section 504 of the 1973 Rehabilitation Act and the 1975 Individuals with Disabilities Education Act that provide a safety net for those who otherwise would fall through the cracks. This safety net is a privilege that a wealthy country can—and should—afford, but as a result, "universal design" remains largely a first-world concept rather than a global reality. And like all legal protections, the ADA is vulnerable to change. In recent years, there have been four major challenges to the ADA, and in the current corporate-friendly administration more are likely to appear. The Rehnquist Court overturned cases on appeal that would expand the class of persons protected, especially plaintiffs with correctable disabilities (high blood pressure, nearsightedness) or cases that would contradict existing state statutes. A more ominous fact is that of the numerous claims made under ADA protection, 95 percent are decided in favor of employers, leading one to conclude that legal arguments for limiting the class and kinds of cases applicable under federal protection are often based on cost-accounting rather than the welfare of the plaintiffs. In an era of increasingly privatized health care, restrictions on Medicare, and the possible evacuation of Social Security, the ADA may become more of a symbolic document than a map for redress.

In my introduction I described disability as a series of sites that include the spaces of the body but that extend into a more public arena of communities and institutions. If we think of disability as located in societal barriers, not in individuals, then disability must be seen as a matter of social justice. The remedy for social justice, as Nancy Fraser points out, involves synthesizing a politics of recognition and the politics of redistribution, a theory of justice based on cultural identities and one based on the reorganization of material resources around those identities (12). Disability would seem to be the test cast for such a synthesis since any recognition of, say, children with developmental disabilities will require, in the words of the Individuals with Disabilities Education Act of 1975, access to "a free and appropriate public education in the least restrictive environment" (Berubé, "Citizenship" 55). Recognition of disability as a civil right entails making sure that a person with a disability has access to the build-

ings, classrooms, and courts where those rights are learned and adjudi-
cated. The demand by activists that disability be included as an identity
category along with ethnic minorities, women, queers, and poor people
has significant implications for a redistribution of property and wealth
that worries employers, legislators, and jurists alike. As Michael Berubé
says, if the ADA "were understood as broad civil rights law . . . [pertain-
ing] to the entire population of the country, then maybe disability law
would be understood not as fringe addition to civil rights law but as its
very fulfillment" (55).

Adapting these remarks to my discussion here, I would suggest that if
disability were considered as a matter of global human rights rather than
as a "health care problem," perhaps the ADA could serve as a road map for
universal design in its best estate. Rather than seeing globalization narrowly as providing greater access to computer chips, phone lines, raw materials, and cheap labor, it could be seen as something relating to all of us
who have bodies, the spirit of inclusion promised by the ADA might extend beyond its current jurisdiction. This would entail a recognition on
the part of wealthier nations that access—to material resources, health
care, social justice—cannot be made contingent on private sector interests
or moral/ideological restrictions. Such recognition is not likely to come
soon, and so we must look to the fruitful alliances among local community organizations, church groups, NGOs, health centers, and political action campaigns that have formed a global disability rights movement. Under the motto "Nothing about us without us," this network of nonaligned
organizations is providing both access and knowledge across—and in
some cases against—the economic landscape that often confuses "development" with "growth."

For the time being, the road map for a global disabilities perspective
may rest with cultural texts such as those that I have discussed in this paper. They would also include Cherrie Moraga's *Heroes and Saints,* a play
set in the California Central Valley during the grape boycott of 1988
protesting pesticide poisoning. It concerns a community of Hispanic
farmworkers whose health has been compromised by toxins sprayed on
the fields and whose human rights are threatened by restrictive immigration practices. Moraga's title character, Cerezita, is a head "positioned on a
rolling, tablelike platform" whose body never developed, due to her
mother's pregnancy while laboring in a pesticide sprayed field. Cerezita is

both a victim of global agribusiness but also a prophet, speaking for those who have no voice. Her gift is her tongue. Speaking to Juan, the priest, Cerezita brags that her tongue has "got the best definition I bet in the world, unless there's some other vegetable heads like me who survived this valley. Think about it, Padre. Imagine if your tongue and teeth and chin had to do the job of your hands" (107–8). She uses her sharp tongue to awaken the members of her community to the plight of migrant workers everywhere. She is the voice of persons disabled by global economics, whose teeth and chin do the work of hands and as such make production difficult to consume. Yet as a character in a play about both disability and global human rights, she imagines her role be both salvific and pedagogical: "put your hand inside my wound. Inside the valley of my wound, there is a people" (148).

Chapter 8
Organs without Bodies
Transplant Narratives in the Global Market

It is impossible to be a person and a thing, the proprietor and
the property. Accordingly, a man is not at his own disposal. He is
not entitled to sell a limb, not even one of his own teeth.
   —KANT, *Lectures on Ethics*

For you can tie me up if you wish,
   but there is nothing more useless than an organ.
   —ANTONIN ARTAUD, *To Be Done with the Judgement of God*

Organs without Bodies:
Transplantation, Disability, Sexuality ⟿

Stephen Frears's movie *Dirty Pretty Things* concerns a black-market organ
trafficking ring that operates out of a London Hotel. In the film, Senor
Juan, the hotel manager who runs the illegal operation, threatens his
Nigerian desk clerk, Okwe (Chiwetel Ejiofor), with deportation unless he
participates in illegal transplant operations. Okwe, who is a doctor in his
native country, balks at becoming involved in this dangerous activity until his friend Seney (Audrey Tautou), a Turkish Muslim woman who
cleans rooms at the hotel, offers to sell her kidney for a passport and
money to escape the immigration police. In order to protect his friend
from unsafe medical procedures, Okwe agrees to perform the operation,
but instead of removing Seney's kidney, he drugs Senor Juan and removes
the hotel manager's kidney instead. With the help of Juliette, a prostitute,
and Seney, Okwe brings the kidney to the organ broker in the basement of
the hotel. When the broker sees Okwe and his subaltern assistants, he says

"I've never seen you before." "Oh yes you have," says Okwe; "we're the ones who drive your cars, clean your rooms and suck your cocks." His linkage of organ sales, prostitution, and menial labor crystallizes a central concern in this film: the "dirty/pretty" relations between global labor migration, new medical technologies, and sexuality. The invisibility of these forces to the consumer of body parts, like Marx's version of the laborer's body in the commodity, maintains the surface glamor of touristic London and finesses the illegal traffic in body parts.

The film's oxymoronic title is based on a remark made by Señor Juan, who explains to Okwe that his wealthy clientele come to the hotel to do "dirty things" in secret, and it is our job to make it "pretty" again the next day. The implications of this insidious remark are evident throughout the movie. The supportive relationship established between Seney, the immigrant cleaning woman, and Juliette, the prostitute, sutures two components of a flexible economy. Both participate in the commodification of the body, whether it is sold for sex, labor, or biomedical ends. Although Seney, as a devout Muslim, is cast as the moral opposite of Juliette, she is subjected to multiple acts of sexual humiliation in her status as an undocumented immigrant. She is raped by Señor Juan prior to the operation, as if to cement her vulnerability within the economic calculus within which she is caught. She is forced to perform sexual acts with the owner of a sweatshop in order to prevent him from turning her in to the immigration police. These links between "dirty" acts and "pretty" surfaces go to the heart, as it were, of organ sales narratives insofar as they merge a dystopic story of global corruption and a redemptive story of biomedical success.

Dirty Pretty Things is one of a number of recent films, plays, and novels that concern the international organ trade. One might say that the organ sale narrative is *the* allegory of globalization in the way that in such works the body itself becomes a commodity, its components—organs, tissue, blood, DNA—exchanged in a worldwide market that mirrors the structural inequality between wealth and poverty. As Nancy Scheper-Hughes says, organ transplantation "now takes place in a trans-national space with both donors and recipients following the paths of capital and technology in the global economy" ("End" 6).[1] Nor is "space" a metaphor. Lawrence Cohen describes the kidney bazaars of India where poor residents undergo kidney operations and where boards post the daily rates for different biological material. At the other end of the spectrum are the specialized private hospitals built throughout the developing world to handle transplant technology and whose luxurious campuses, as we will see with respect to Leslie Marmon Silko's *Almanac of the Dead*, are the subject of dystopic urbanist satire. Cohen discusses the Indraprastha Apollo Hospital in Delhi, a private franchise—one among others in Hyderabad, Chennai, Mumbai, Calcutta and elsewhere in India or Bangladesh—built like a luxury five-star hotel in which wealthy recipients come for transplant operations. "Apollo is not only a hospital that looks like a five-star hotel, it is a five-star hotel that looks like a hospital" ("Other Kidney" 16). When Stephen Frears sets his film about black market organ sales in an upscale London hotel, he marks the thin boundary between sexual and biotourism in the urban metropole at the same time that he links migrant bodies to transient body parts.

Narratives about organ transplants reinforce the links between the body and the global space of capital, between a body regarded as a totality of parts and a communicational and media space in which those parts are sold, packaged in ice chests, and shipped around the world. And organ trafficking is a discursive matter. Rumors of children stolen, soldiers's bodies "looted," hospital patients misdiagnosed for their organs add a gothic element to the organ sale narrative.[2] Urban legends of unscrupulous traders who raid cadavers for usable corneas or livers or tales of tourists who awaken from a drugged sleep with a strange scar revive grave-robbing fears that in poverty-stricken kidney bazaars have provided a literary subgenre that Scheper-Hughes calls "neo-cannibalism" ("Ends" 65). Furthermore, the border between life and death, hospital and mortuary, blurs as pathologists and medical ethicists debate the difference between "brain death" and "cardiac death" to justify harvesting the freshest organs for transplant. With the advancement of immunosuppressive drugs like cyclosporine to facilitate the body's acceptance of the new organ, the concept of "brain death" becomes a necessary category to legitimate the harvesting of organs while the heart still pumps blood. Indeed, as Veena Das observes, the concept of brain death exists for one purpose, "organ retrieval—while it may still be perceived as very much alive for other purposes, such as the maintenance of family ties, affections, religious beliefs, or cultural notions of probity and dignity" (qtd. in Scheper-Hughes, "End" 16). Finally, organs themselves have achieved a certain designer status with cadaveric organs taken from "the state's body"—from anonymous dead donors—disparaged by nephrologists and wealthy recipients alike in favor of organs from living donors and relatives.

We could divide transplantation narratives into two forms. The first, typified by films like *Dirty Pretty Things*, Walter Salles's *Central Station*, Yu Hua's *One Kind of Reality*, and Henning Mankell's *The Man Who Smiled*, and Sanjay Nigam's novel *Transplanted Man*, might be called "organ diaspora stories" that situate body part trafficking within an ethnoscape of transnational labor flows, black market crime, and moral panic. In *Central Station*, a young boy is rescued by a woman who writes letters for poor, illiterate city dwellers in her Rio de Janeiro stall. Her decision to save an orphaned boy is motivated by fears that he will become a victim of unscrupulous body part salesmen in a country where everyone at birth is declared a universal organ donor. In Nigam's novel a wealthy Indian government official is kept alive by multiple organ transplants from poor Indian donors. His transplanted body becomes an elaborate metaphor for the Indian diaspora.[3] In *The Man Who Smiled*, a wealthy global entrepreneur utilizes his pharmaceutical and manufacturing interests in both first- and third-world countries to conduct an illegal traffic in organs—a traffic that, because he controls both supply and demand, escapes detection in his home country of Sweden. In these works—as in *Dirty Pretty Things*— organ sales are a metaphor for unequal class and economic realities that are by-products of globalization.

The second form of transplantation narrative—one that I will discuss in greater detail here—is a more futuristic one that imagines a world in which the ideal of replacing an aging or disabled body with new parts adapts a nineteenth-century eugenics story to a globalized environment. In Manjula Padmanabhan's *Harvest* the play's central character commits his entire body to a giant biotech firm so that his organs may be harvested to pay off debts that have impoverished his family. In Margaret Atwood's *Oryx and Crake*, genetically engineered animals—pigoons—with four or five kidneys are bred for their organs in a society where humans are constructed from spare parts. In Michael Crichton's film *Coma*, patients at a Boston hospital mysteriously become comatose during routine operations. Their bodies are shipped to a high-tech institute where their organs are harvested and auctioned on a worldwide market. Michael Bay's film *The Island* depicts a high-tech science facility occupied by clones whose bodies serve as organ reserves for their human counterparts. In Andrew Niccol's film *Gattaca,* a man with congenital heart disease purchases "pure" DNA stock from an otherwise eugenically perfect male in order to participate in a space program. In Kazuo Ishiguro's *Never Let Me Go,* cloned children are raised in a boarding school so that their organs can be harvested when they are grown. Leslie Marmon Silko's *Almanac of the Dead* describes an elaborate real estate empire constructed around plasma sales, organ transplantation, and southwest real estate. In Karen Tei Yamashita's novel about a dysfunctional Los Angeles, *Tropic of Orange,* a central theme involves the attempt by a Mexican woman to flee with her two-year-old son from an ominous body parts broker. Her northward journey, carrying a cooler with a child's heart stolen from the broker, becomes a magical realist trope for the movement of bodies, labor, and raw materials across the United States–Mexico border.

In these examples, the organ sales narrative plays a partial role in a vision of cultural decay, much as the disabled person—as David Mitchell and Sharon Snyder have pointed out—functions as a prosthetic metaphor for abnormality or deviance in narrative. In their terms, the disabled body carries the symbolic burden of "lack" or "inadequacy" upon which the novel depends in order to return the hero to normalcy, home, and able-bodied wholeness. One might say that the organ sales narrative is to globalization what disability is to narrative. The commodification of body parts defines a form of social panic around surplus bodies that are no longer grounded either by a network of functioning organs nor a unitary Subject. If, for Marx, the prostitute represents the specter of the body as commodity within modernity, the organ donor occupies an analogous position within globalization. In all of the texts that I will discuss, bodily modification, genetic engineering, and cyborg replication threaten "normal" sexual relations and domesticity and posit new queer identities that must be purged from the scene. In *Gattaca,* Jerome (Jude Law), the disabled, queerly marked "donor" of DNA, immolates himself at the end of the film so that the heterosexual recipient, Vincent (Ethan Hawke), can (quite literally) fly off into outer space as an able-bodied astronaut. This is the most overt version of how narratives of body modification often invoke nightmares of sexual violation by "the wrong" sort of body or bodily organ. The science fiction fantasies that I have mentioned here are, of course, present-day potentialities that raise anxieties about the work of embodiment in an era of genetic engineering, physician-assisted suicide, and stem-cell research.

In this chapter I will review three of these texts in order to understand the implications of organ sales on the intersection of disability and globalization.[4] At one important level, these narratives are concerned with the status of embodiment within the economics of global wealth where the third-world body is rendered docile so that the first-world consumer can sustain his futurity. Inverting Deleuze and Guattari's concept of the "body without organs"—the body freed from its productive, organic functions—we might now speak of "organs without bodies," loosed from their role in constituting "Life" and turned into commodities circulated within capital flows.[5] The organ sales narrative often figures genetic research, cloning, and other technologies as a replacement of biological reproduction. Organs are harvested like spare parts and sold through anonymous auction houses and brokers. Sex is no longer tied to reproduction and becomes a free-floating commercial exchange. In the works with which I will deal, sexuality is resited from the body of erotic desire onto the body of capital, subject to its laws of supply and demand, biomedical progress and bioethical consensus.[6]

Of course this phenomenon—the biopolitical colonization of the laboring body—is a hallmark of modernization. As Michel Foucault has pointed out, among the products of industrial capitalism in the nineteenth century are new sexual identities formed through the separation of domestic and industrial production. The family becomes the site of affective, "personal" relations and biological reproduction, whereas the workplace is the site of labor and material production, a division that coincides with the separation of gendered spheres. As John D'Emilio says, when wage labor replaced the household family unit, "it became possible to release sexuality from the 'imperative' to procreate" (470). The creation of new homosocial communities beyond the family unit permitted homosexuality and lesbianism to become visible, not as a set of practices but as identities. Within this modernist paradigm, the privatized, nuclear family unit reinforced capitalist relations of production as well as heteronormal identity categories. With the rise of more flexible forms of accumulation and production and with the globalization of capital, information, and labor, the older market model based on separate gendered and sexual spheres undergoes a transformation. Sexuality is released not only from the imperative to procreate but from the gendered and sexual identities upon which procreation is based. As my discussion of the play *Harvest* indicates, once the third-world organ donor enters the cycle of body part sales, not only is his body modified, his identity as a heterosexual male is destabilized and readjusted to suit the market demands of his buyer.

To what extent are organ sales narratives disability narratives? Looked at from the standpoint of a "medical miracle," transplantation is the epitome of new body and genetic modification occurring in the most developed countries. Looked at from a global perspective, however, organ transplantation always involves an unequal exchange of genetic material, often on a black market and often resulting in the disablement of the organ seller. As Laurence Cohen points out, indebtedness is the primary fact that drives poor organ sellers to sell body parts, even where religious or cultural traditions prohibit such acts. A disability studies perspective thus must expand the social model to include the global politics of structural debt or the legal context of "presumed consent" that exists in a given country.[7] When the donor is a poor resident of an Indian *kidneyvakaam,* or organ bazaar, when the organ is harvested from an organ website or data base, the concept of "gift" loses its redemptive meaning. While we may endorse the liberal ideal by which individuals assert *choice* over their own bodies, we must understand the coercive meaning of that choice in conditions of poverty and structural indebtedness.

Considering organ transfer as a global matter involves the culturally relative meanings of mortality, particularly the impact of "brain death" as a concept determining the end of life. In my introduction, I spoke of the medical-ethical debate around physician-assisted suicide and the fact that, for disability activists, *who* decides when a person is dead accompanies a parallel question of *by what criteria* death is conferred. In a society where the lives of people with severe disabilities are often considered "not worth living," it is a slippery slope to rationalized euthanasia, as the film *Million Dollar Baby* exemplifies. In the case of both physician-assisted suicide and organ transfer, the phrase *brain death* has become a site of contention, especially in those critical care instances following an accident or stroke when split-second decisions must be made on when to cease life supports in order to begin harvesting organs. Prior to the first heart transplant in 1967, cardiac death was considered life's terminal moment, but with the increased use of organ transplantation and the concomitant demand for fresh organs, brain death has assumed greater importance. Brain death and its more controversial synonyms—"vegetative state," "irreversible coma"—occurs when brain stem reflexes and motor responses no longer function, while the heart continues to beat and the lungs, assisted by a ventilator, continue to expand and contract.[8] This "living cadaver" displays many signs of life—as the parents of Terri Schiavo often pointed out—making decisions about when to terminate life supports all the more difficult.

As Margaret Lock points out, attitudes toward brain death in the United States have been dominated by two factors relating less to the cultural meaning of mortality and more to the institutional (and commercial) frame in which death is defined: "the first attempts to assign death to a scientifically deducible and verifiable moment, and thus to make it at once indisputable in medicine and recognizable in law" (7). In Japan, on the other hand, individuals have been more reluctant to accept brain death, not because they repudiate modern science or medicine but because, among other things, "they fear being subjected to abuses of medical power, especially when dying" (6). Moreover, for Japanese persons, death is a process that cannot be isolated in a single moment nor separated from the family and social context in which it occurs (8). And despite the "gift of life" rhetoric that dominates Western rationales for brain death, in Japan gift-giving "is deeply embedded in an economy of reciprocal exchange; thus the idea of giving objects of value to complete strangers with whom one has had no personal contact appears strange to many" (Lock 10). The "rational choice" ideology that often determines the fate of persons living in irreversible comas becomes, in the Japanese context, the substitution of efficiency over long-held cultural values.

In addition to foregrounding the global implications of disability, transplant and organ sale narratives always involve two disabled bodies: the donor/seller and the recipient/purchaser.[9] The recipient body is disabled by any number of physical conditions (renal failure, Parkinson's disease, blindness, lung deterioration, heart failure, leukemia, hemophilia) for which organs and tissue are necessary to sustain life. Once the operation is performed, the recipient body is subject to opportunistic diseases and side effects of immunosuppressive drugs like cyclosporine. The seller body, if not already disabled by malnourishment and disease due to poverty, often becomes vulnerable to any number of infections and chronic diseases—including HIV/AIDS. The fact that poor sellers of a kidney or cornea are also malnourished and lack access to proper, follow-up treatment, and social services means that they often become permanently disabled.[10] Thus the life extended by transplant may, in fact, become doubly impaired. As the transplant surgeon, Thomas Spray has pointed out that patients often trade "one kind of disease for another. Having a transplant is a chronic illness" (qtd. in Wailoo, *Dying* 89).

As I have already suggested with regard to *Dirty Pretty Things*, the illegal sale of body parts is often equated with prostitution and sexual abuse. In this sense, contemporary commodification of the body through biotechnology retrofits a modernist trope of the prostitute as human commodity. In Walter Benjamin's view, modernity, in order to legitimate its exploitation of labor, must cite antiquity. The commodity fetish—sign of a new commercial era—appears in the guise of an archaic religious fetish, imbued with agency and volition. The worker's labor power is effaced in an inert object that, subjected to exchange, becomes a ghostly power that exerts its subtle lure. For Baudelaire the dialectical image of this process is the prostitute, "saleswoman and wares in one," as Benjamin says (157). The globalist version of the dialectical image is visible in Frears's pairing of Seney/Juliette or in Padmanabhan's fantasy of cyborg sex to produce an uncontaminated gene pool.

The sexual politics of organ sales implicates the gendered nature of kidney operations as they relate to questions of agency and nationality. Lawrence Cohen has written extensively about the different ways that poor men and women in India have responded to nephrectomy (the removal of a kidney) in the "performance of agency." For males in rural Tamil Nadu, the operation is experienced as a form of castration, a significant loss of potency linked to conditions of pervasive debt. Women experience the operation as a component of family planning. Poor women in India are often told that in order to sell a kidney they must first undergo tubal ligation or other obstetric operation to prevent future childbirth that would be compromised by the missing organ. Cohen points out that the kidney operation is central to one's relation to the state:

It is not just an example of agency; it is agency's critical ground. In other words, having an operation for these women has become a dominant and pervasive means of attempting to secure a certain kind of future. . . . to be someone with choices is to be operated upon, to be operated upon is to be someone with choices. "Operation" is not just a procedure with certain risks, benefits, and cultural values; it confers the sort of agency I am calling citizenship. ("Where It Hurts" 139–40)

This analysis confirms one of the key issues of the texts I consider here insofar as they negotiate new, as yet unrecognizable subject positions within globalization. The clone children in *Never Let Me Go* attempt to establish some modicum of ordinary life despite the massive biocontrol over their bodies. Jeetu in *Harvest* hopes to grant a future to his family by giving up his body to a transnational biotech firm. Although citizenship is not necessarily the outcome in these works, possibilities for agency and social normalization are.

By reviewing recent organ sale literature from a number of global sites I hope to expand the current discussion of posthuman identities to include disability as a category that, in Lennard Davis's terms, "dismodernizes" the humanist subject.[11] What the organ sale narrative adds to this important critique of identity politics is the role of globalization that under the guise of free market boundary crossing violates the bodily envelope. In their diagnosis of "bodies without organs," liberated from drives and oedipal repressions, Deleuze and Guattari forget those organs that, under the neoliberal banner of borderless trading zones, are removed from bodies and sold on a worldwide market. Antonin Artaud (from whom Deleuze and Guattari derive their concept) makes a plea for man to "remake anatomy" by delivering him from the tyranny of his organs, but he could not have imagined the form that this liberatory impulse would take in the shadow of neoliberal trade and bioengineering.

Harvesting the Body:
Manjula Padmanabhan, *Harvest* ⌐

In 1994, the government of India passed the Transplantation of Human Organs Act, which made the selling of solid organs illegal and authorized the use of organs from patients considered brain dead. The result was a burgeoning trade in illegal body parts and the creation of kidney bazaars where poor Indians, often heavily indebted, could go to offer kidneys for sale to brokers. Donors paid between two and three thousand dollars for a kidney, an amount that constitutes several years' wages and, as Lawrence Cohen reports, is often used to pay for a wedding dowry (reported in Scheper-Hughes, "End" 5). This is the backdrop for Manjula Padmanabhan's 1997 play, *Harvest,* which extends the condition of organ sales to include whole identity purchase and the restructuring of the Indian family.[12] The play situates medical science in a futuristic world where the traffic in organs is handled by transnational conglomerates that take over and maintain the donor body prior to the operation. *Harvest* extends the idea of the body as commodity to absurd lengths where transplant surgery, genetic engineering, prosthetics, in vitro fertilization, virtual reality, and commodity culture have created the possibility for *whole body* replacement. As a postcolonial allegory, the play seizes upon the mediascapes and technoscapes by which poor countries become the outsourcing centers for body parts and labor in the first world.[13] At one point, Virgil, the wealthy organ recipient says, "[We] support poorer sections of the world, while gaining fresh bodies for ourselves" (246). Virgil's reference links contemporary organ trafficking to the earlier transatlantic slave trade, but it also annexes, as well, the current expansion of high-tech corridors and microchip processing that is the hallmark of multinational development in India.

Padmanabhan divides her cast into two groups: Donors and Receivers, a poor Indian family and a rich North American couple. The former live in a single room of a crowded Bombay apartment building; the latter only appear as images on a video screen. There are also anonymous "guards" and "agents" who facilitate the transplant operation and deliver high-tech goods. The division of roles in the play mirrors the relation between debtor (donor) and G8 (receiver) countries, with a class of managers and support staff in the middle to perform the technical work. The Donors consist of the family of Om Prakesh, a lower-level clerk who has just lost his job as the play begins. He is accompanied by his wife, Jaya, his mother, Ma, and his brother, Jeetu, the latter of whom earns money as a male prostitute. Facing unemployment and sudden poverty, Om enters into a Faustian contract with InterPlanta, a giant biotech conglomerate that agrees to support his family in exchange for the option of harvesting his organs for transplant purposes. According to the contract, Om must not be married, so he lies, calling his wife Jaya his sister and "marrying her" in his contract to his brother, Jeetu. In order to monitor the family's activities, InterPlanta installs a "Contact Module" in the apartment that beams the image of the Receiver, "Gini," into the apartment. Gini is a Stepford Wife parody of the rich American with time on her hands and money to spend on health and fitness.[14]

The play's three acts develop Virgil's remark about "gaining fresh bodies" through an exfoliating series of fantasies that explore the ways that developed countries procure raw materials, bodies, and wealth from donor countries. At each level, the donor body is a phantasmatic space for colonization. The first frame—the organ transplant stage—involves the fiction that Om will save his family from starvation by donating his superfluous organs to a first-world patient who is dying of some unspecified disease. Here, Padmanabhan explores the disruption of the nuclear family through poverty-induced destruction of the physical body. In order to sell his organs to InterPlanta, Om undermines the traditional patriarchal family structure, turning his wife into his sister, his brother into her husband and lover, his mother into a television-addicted harridan. The renovated home, according to this new biologic, is an elaborate metaphor for the colonial transformation of domestic space into sites of production and outsourced capital.

The second frame—the whole body transplant fantasy—involves the substitution of Om's single organs for Jeetu's entire body. When the InterPlanta guards come to take Om's body for organ harvesting, they mistake him for his brother Jeetu, and take the latter instead, returning him without his eyes but with electrodes implanted so that he may receive images beamed directly into his brain. Gini projects sexually alluring images of herself so that Jeetu will give himself over to her image and donate his entire body to her. The irony here is that Gini, instead of receiving pure, carefully protected organs, will inherit those that have been compromised by Jeetu's promiscuous life on the street—the very opposite of what Inter-Planta promises to guard against.

The final frame—what we might call the gender transplant fantasy—involves the substitution of the Receiver's first-world body for the Donor's subaltern female body. It turns out that the bouncy, trophy wife Gini, is actually an electronically modified voice of Virgil, a North American male who, as he says, has already gone through three bodies in fifty years and who now needs a fresh, young body to go on living. In a Burroughsian fantasy of cyborg sex, Virgil appears to Jaya through the Contact Module in the form of her former lover and brother-in-law, Jeetu. Virgil explains that he has transplanted Jeetu's body into his own in order to propagate children, but because he lives in a world where reproduction is no longer possible ("We secured Paradise—at the cost of birds and flowers, bees and snakes!"), he needs Jaya's reproductive system to extend the gene pool (246). Having discovered that Jaya actually loves Jeetu, Virgil believes he may achieve his biological goal by producing desire in Jaya for the now vacated body of her former love. But in a final, humanist protest, Jaya resists the lure of biological propagation with Virgil unless he comes to her in his embodied form. For Virgil, such physical contact is impossible. "The environment you live in is too polluted for me," Virgil says and sends his sperm by courier to Bombay for in vitro fertilization (247). Jaya holds firm, saying that she will commit suicide and ruin the entire project unless he accepts the risk of proximity: "There is no closeness without risk," she says (247).

This allegorical scenario at times becomes bogged down in its own artifice. Although Padmanabhan has a good eye for the surreal possibilities of a totally biomanaged life, she becomes enamored with the very gadgetry she satirizes. To take one example: at one point, VideoCouch Enterprises enters the apartment to install a virtual reality unit for Om's mother. This elaborate device is a self-contained habitat, complete with breathing tubes, virtual reality zones, and food dispensers in which Ma seals herself, presumably, for the rest of her life. It is a clever inversion of the organ sale scenario where, instead of divesting oneself of organs, one is simply attached to a commodity body that satisfies all sensory and biological needs—an elaborate variation on Deleuze and Guattari's de-oedipalized body. The nurturing mother becomes the nurtured child, attached by tubes to a technological mediator between herself and reality. Such elaborate biotech scenarios offer a degree of humor, but they exist solely to exploit a local bit of pop culture and not to complicate the darker allegory of power and control.

Harvest's satire depicts a world sustained by images, produced in the developed West and beamed into the homes and minds of the developing world. Much of the play concerns the mediascapes through which ideas of health and disease are disseminated, a technology of bio-power that merges subject production with surveillance. What the Contact Module manufactures as the allure of new products, sex, technology, it also witnesses, by eavesdropping on the Prakesh family. Here, Foucault's panopticon is retrofitted to include electronic media as a technology of surveillance at the same time that it encourages docility among its viewers. Padmanabhan links the technological to the sexual and racial to suggest that the sale of bodies across class lines must be legitimated by images. Om's slavish dedication to Gini's health (his willingness to undergo privation for his "receiver's" well-being) is not far from the Uncle Tom stereotype who accepts the plantation logic of benign owners and loyal slaves. It is through the first-world buyer's ability to create desire in the subaltern body, realized here by Virgil's reproduction of himself as Jeetu, that the commodification of the body can be completed. And it is through the fantasy of eternal youth—of a medical and technological prosthesis—that disability can be perpetuated in others. In the play, the possibility of bodily "improvement" in the developed world is purchased through the poor, third-world body, a scenario that updates and extends a logic first seen in the eugenics movement of the nineteenth century and realized in the Nazi Final Solution.

Told and Not Told: Kazuo Ishiguro, *Never Let Me Go* ✍

Padmanabhan creates her biodystopia out of a futuristic Bombay. In Kazuo Ishiguro's *Never Let Me Go*, the setting is a relatively familiar contemporary Britain. Like Ishiguro's previous novels, *Never Let Me Go* is about the not said, the unlived life, now given new meaning in a world where "life" is mediated by bioengineering. Set in the 1990s but looking back to the 1970s and early 1980s, the novel is told from the standpoint of Kathy H., a thirty-one-year-old "carer" for patients undergoing organ donation operations. As she drives from one clinic to another, she reflects nostalgically on her upbringing at a boarding school called Hailsham located in some unnamed rural setting outside of London. Kathy remembers with fondness the small details of school life,

our guardians, about how we each had our own collection chests under our beds, the football, the rounders, the little path that took you
all round the outside of the main house ... the duck pond, the food,
the view from the Art Room over the fields on a foggy morning. (5)

In particular, she describes the close childhood relationship with her will-
ful, often deceitful friend, Ruth, and her devoted, more passive friend,
Tommy. They form a band of outsiders within the school, and before they
graduate, they also form a sexual ménage à trois, first between Tommy and
Ruth and then between Tommy and Kathy.

Hailsham, as its name implies, is more than it appears. Despite its Victorian residential school trappings, it is actually a home for bodies cloned
so that their organs may be harvested once they reach adulthood. Although the children gradually come to realize their difference from "normals," they are given meager information about the outside world and
their ultimate fate within it. In Ishiguro's dystopic Britain, cloning is a
thriving industry whose morality has already been rationalized. Indeed,
Hailsham itself is an important dimension of this rationalization as an experiment to give the clone children a semblance of normal life and, more
insidiously, to provide a patina of humanism around its Frankenstein-like
rationale. By providing the clone children with education, arts and crafts,
and a nurturing environment, Hailsham creates the comforting illusion of
civilized scientific progress. Artworks produced by the children are saved
and displayed by the guardians to skeptical normals who need reassurance
of the civilizing function of the school. By posing as a proper British
boarding school, Hailsham is a simulacrum of the smug, class-conscious
environment of bourgeois society with its own versions of clones and
replicants in business and social service.

At one point, Miss Lucy, one of the teachers (who are called
"guardians") at the school, becomes impatient when some of the students
fantasize about becoming actors when they grow up. Although guardians
are not supposed to discuss the reality of their students' destinies, Miss
Lucy disabuses them of their dreams:

The problem, as I see it, is that you've been told and not told. You've
been told, but none of you really understand, and I dare say, some

people are quite happy to leave it that way. But I'm not. If you're going to have decent lives, then you've got to know and know properly.
. . . Your lives are set out for you. You'll become adults, then before
you're old, before you're even middle-aged, you'll start to donate
your vital organs. That's what each of you was created to do. (81)

For her presumption in telling such truths, Miss Lucy is dismissed from
the school, but the students remember her words as they try to make sense
of the absolute barrier that separates them—as products—from biologically reproductive humans. The idea that they will donate their organs is,
of course, a kinder, gentler term for the industrial exploitation of their
bodies that the novel depicts. In this respect, they represent more domes-
ticated versions of the androids or replicants in Ridley Scott's futuristic
Blade Runner. They are "told and not told" about their future, but because
as readers we occupy Kathy's naive point of view, we share her questions.
How are the "guardians" different from their students? What does it mean
to be a "carer"? Why are the children's art projects taken away from them?
Can one defer donation? By adopting Kathy's perspective, Ishiguro combines a coming-of-age story about a female adolescent with a coming-
into-consciousness allegory of bioengineering. In this sense the micro-rit-
uals in which the children stave off consciousness are similar to Stevens,
the butler in *Remains of the Day,* whose endless polishing of silver and setting of tables occludes the fact of his complicity in working for a Fascist
employer.

Most critics have read *Never Let Me Go* as a dark fable about the
specter of cloning. Ishiguro has warned against such programmatic interpretations, hoping that readers see it as vaunting resilience and decency in
the face of mortality ("Interview"). Both of these responses—the humanist warning about scientific excess and the triumphalist belief in human
resilience—avoid a more menacing story about disability in a society that
reinforces compulsory able-bodiedness and one in which a proscribed
model of normalcy produces narratives to reinforce it. In this sense, *Never
Let Me Go* is true to its boarding-school novel predecessors—from
Nicholas Nickleby and *Jane Eyre* to *Harry Potter*—in focusing extensively
on the emerging sexuality of adolescent children. The clone children are
subjected to extensive monitoring of their bodily health and are warned

against excesses that might compromise their internal organs. Although they are, to all outward appearances, normal and are able—even encouraged—to have sex, the children are instructed in what forms sexuality can take. They learn that they are different from normals—who can have babies—and that they must "respect the rules [pertaining to normals] and treat sex as something pretty special" (84).

Sex among the students at Hailsham becomes confused with organ donation. Miss Emily, one of the guardians, gives the students a clear-eyed lecture on sexuality but then suddenly warns them to be careful about whom they have sex with:

> Not just because of the diseases, but because, she said, "sex affects emotions in ways you'd never expect." We had to be extremely careful about having sex in the outside world, especially with people who weren't students, because out there sex meant all sorts of things. Out there people are even fighting and killing each other over who had sex with whom. And the reason it meant so much—so much more than, say, dancing or table-tennis—was because the people out there were different from us students: they could have babies from sex. (84)

As Kathy muses on this scene, she remembers that they would "be focusing on sex, and then the other stuff would creep in. I suppose that was all part of how we came to be 'told and not told'" (84). This scene of instruction is not only about sexual difference but about the difference between disability and normalcy, between a body that, in order to be productive, must not be *reproductive*. Imitating an earlier racial logic, the story implies that sex must not occur across eugenically monitored lines. For the clones, sex must be seen as equivalent to "dancing or table-tennis"; once it is connected to reproduction, people begin to "fight and kill each other" over it. Kathy's insouciant voice belies her growing awareness of the links between children with "special needs" and the normals whose status quo must be supported.

Many of the narratives that dominate the bioethics of organ sales come together in one scene that provides the novel's title. Kathy H. remembers a moment when she was eight or nine years old when she was dancing by herself in her dorm room while listening to a popular song

"Never Let Me Go." She imagines that the title refers to a woman who has been told she cannot have babies, but by a miracle she has one anyway, and in Kathy's fantasy the woman holds her baby to her breast while she sings, "Never let me go. Oh baby, baby, baby. Never let me go." Kathy holds a pillow to herself in imitation of the mother, while she dances by herself, but she is overseen by one of the matrons, known only as "Madame." When Kathy realizes that her solitary dance is being watched, she discovers that Madame is weeping. Much later, when Kathy is grown, she tracks Madame to her home and confronts her with this scene, wondering why she had wept at the sight. Kathy of course thinks it is because Madame understands the plight of the clone child denied the possibility of reproduction, but Madame has another explanation for her sadness:

> I was weeping for an altogether different reason. When I watched you dancing that day, I saw something else. I saw a new world coming rapidly. More scientific, efficient, yes. More cures for the old sicknesses. Very good. But a harsh, cruel world. And I saw a little girl, her eyes tightly closed, holding to her breast the old kind world, one that she knew in her heart could not remain, and she was holding it and pleading, never to let her go. That is what I saw. It wasn't really you, what you were doing, I know that. But I saw you and it broke my heart. And I've never forgotten. (272)

The disparity between the lyrics of the song, which are about erotic desire, and Kathy's interpretation (they they are about mothering) and Madame's interpretation (that they are about the pain of new biotechnologies) explores meanings of sexuality in an age of genetic engineering. As bodies become dispensable spare parts to keep normals alive, the "old kind world" becomes, like the song itself, a nostalgic remnant. Ishiguro's quiet, often deadpan narrative mediates between nostalgia and futurity. Sexuality has become disabled, unmoored from the body and from the humanism that supports it, and superimposed onto a narrative of scientific advancement. Madame's tears are those of progressive humanists who understand the costs of science but do nothing to qualify its ascendency. The children will produce progeny—their organs—and the novel charts how this "gift of life" story must be cited by donors and receivers alike.

Bio-Materials, Inc.: *Almanac of the Dead* ↩

In countries that permit the harvesting of cadaveric organs through "presumed consent" laws, the body becomes a property of the state. In the neoliberal world order, the market subsumes ethical issues in an ideal of rational choice. Within this logic, as summarized by Nancy Scheper-Hughes, "Paying for a kidney 'donation' is viewed as a potential 'win-win' situation that can benefit both parties. Individual decision making has become the final arbiter of medical bioethical values. Social justice hardly figures into these discussions" ("Ends" 61). The politicization of the body occurs, according to Michel Foucault, when power is detached from juridical and state institutions and imposed onto the body itself: "For millennia, man remained what he was for Aristotle: a living animal with the additional capacity for political existence; modern man is an animal whose politics calls his existence as a living being into question" (143). The origins of this tendency can be found in the emergence of hospitals and asylums and, as Giorgio Agamben points out, culminate at Auschwitz. The operatic version of biopolitics for a global era is developed in Leslie Marmon Silko's 1991 novel, *Almanac of the Dead*.

In *Almanac of the Dead* Silko understands biopolitics as a late vestige of new world colonialism where the bodies of indigenous and mestizo people have become, for five hundred years, collateral damage of expansion and colonization. Written at a moment when Fordist modes of production are giving way to forms of flexible production and distribution, *Almanac* imagines a new social imaginary produced by the rise of biotech industries and privatized health care, a world that relies on the labor of migratory, border-crossing populations. Instead of indicting specific institutions—like the clinic and the asylum—where bodies become docile, Silko diagnoses the transnational movement of labor, drugs, and capital as fluid sites for a body not only without organs but without borders. Critics have called attention to the novel's weblike narrative technique in which different voices in distant locations are brought together, paths crossing in ways that mimic new cosmopolitan movements in the global market.[15] Indigenous peoples' struggles in southern Mexico merge with recruitment of a homeless army in the Southwest; stories of real estate development in Arizona merge with mercenary armies in South America; legacies of the

Vietnam War intersect with the current war in Iraq; Native American religious traditions merge with New Age healing. Like *Dirty Pretty Things,*
global instabilities in one part of the world are acted out in first-world
tourism and commodity society.

It would be difficult to summarize the many intersecting strands that
constitute this vast, sprawling novel, but one important theme that per-
tains to our topic is the collusion of real estate and medicine in colonizing
the global body. This theme is intricately worked out in the "Africa" section of the novel, which concerns the development and sale of biomaterials. One of the novel's sleaziest characters, Trigg, "the realtor in a wheelchair," owns a series of plasma centers and biotech corporations with
names like Alpha-Bio Products, Alpha-Hemo-Science Limited, and Bio
Mart. He not only supplies his buyers with blood products but provides
tissue and human organs to the local research hospital. As a person disabled by a spinal cord injury, he dreams of developing new technologies
that will help him walk again. For the time being, he uses the profits from
his successful plasma centers to finance a vast "health and beauty capital"
in Tucson that will service a new biotourist industry in the Southwest
(663). In Trigg's fantasy there would be a research center for nerve-tissue
transplants, cosmetic surgery clinic, a giant hospital, detox centers for various addictions, and not insignificantly, collection center for body parts.
The wealthy transplant surgeons and patients who live in this medical
utopia will need a place to live, and here Trigg enlists the aid of his mistress, Leah, who is a successful real estate developer and wife of a gangster
hit man. She has a utopian dream of planning a giant water-themed housing development, Venice, Arizona, that will bring water from deep wells to
the desert in a network of canals and waterways that will transform the
desert landscape. Silko's projection of a new exurban space based on the
modification of the body is not too distant from the model health villages,
retirement communities, and spas that already exist throughout the
Southwest.

In order to fulfill his corporate dreams, Trigg must deal with the laws
of supply and demand:

> The secret was how to obtain the enormous supply of biomaterials
> and organs which was necessary, and the civil war in Mexico was al-
> ready solving that. Even if there were no war, still Trigg had come up

with a brilliant solution. Trigg had a gold mine. Hoboes or wetbacks could be "harvested" at the plasma centers where a doctor had already examined the "candidate" to be sure he was healthy. (663)

Here is the imperialist scenario revised for a global era. The wealthy real estate impresario can benefit from civil unrest elsewhere by—quite literally—obtaining cheap bodies to service his organ-harvesting factory while, at home, he may fill his plasma centers with the blood of the "human refuse . . . cast-off white men, former wage earners from mills and factories" that are the result of downsizing and free-trade agreements (461). Such cultural ethnic cleansing provides, as Ann Stanford says, "a menacing pragmatism—getting rid of certain (radically unstable) categories of people" (32).

Trigg employs a Vietnam vet, Rambo Roy to seek out possible donors. Because many of the transients that Rambo recruits are veterans like him, he uses his green beret and combat fatigues to rekindle a vestigial military desire to "sacrifice their blood for their country." Roy becomes fixated on organizing a guerrilla army of the dispossessed to overthrow the government and wealthy entrepreneurs like his employer.[16] Roy's partner in this operation is a black vet named Clinton who has lost a foot during the war. Like Roy, Clinton also seeks to use the homeless army to revolutionary ends, only he wants to use black soldiers to oppose racism, drawing on religious traditions from Africa. Clinton's revolutionary spirit, based on the "great serpent spirit" of Damballah, is linked to that of other native people in southern Mexico elsewhere in the novel who similarly hope to drive out European capitalism and restore the rights of indigenous people.

Trigg's enterprise is fueled by a functionalist view of sex that becomes a component of the industrial-grade medical industry he controls. His plasma centers help finance his commerce in biomaterials—"fetal-brain material, human kidneys, hearts and lungs, corneas for eye transplants, and human skin for burn victims" (398). Trigg's demonic method of transforming plasma donor into organ donor is by "bleeding his patients dry," often by performing fellatio on them until they are too relaxed to realize that they are being drained of all their blood. This Dracula-like parallel between organ procurement and sexual servicing is a heavy-handed version of that link between disability and sexuality that I've already mentioned in *Dirty Pretty Things*. Although Silko realizes that the transplantation narratives often have a sexual subtext, she indulges in all-too-familiar stereotypes of disabled persons as "defective" and "dependent." Trigg is in a wheelchair, and although paralyzed, he is still able to maintain an erection that he uses to satisfy his insatiable mistress. In Silko's allegory, Trigg's disability permits him to divert his sexual potency from an erotic body he has lost onto real estate he hopes to procure. His feelings of masculine inferiority are compensated by his ability to sustain an erection without orgasm, thus securing the erotic and financial help of his mistress and the political support of her husband's political contacts and wealthy friends. Following their first night together, Trigg and Leah discuss his plans for a new health-care theme park. Leah admires Trigg's conflation of sex and real estate: "She had not felt so good in months. Trigg had fucked her one way, and in typical Tucson fashion he was ready to try to fuck her with a slick real estate deal too" (382).

If real estate demands sex, urban development requires culture. The building of Rockefeller Center, as Rem Koolhaus has pointed out, relied on the glamor of Radio City Music Hall and the Rockettes with their "plotless theatrical energy" (216). As a contemporary version of this scenario Trigg wants to convert a defunct Tucson shopping mall into a "Pleasure Mall," adjacent to his hospitals, clinics, and plasma centers:

> The Pleasure Mall would feature a gallery of erotic art. Sex toy stores would offer live demonstrations to promote safe sex. If all that wasn't educational enough, Trigg had been negotiating with a promoter in London to lease a rare collection of specimens in jars and under glass consisting of the scrotums and penises of all species, including a number of human specimens. (664)

Trigg's idea of a sex and pleasure mall is not that different from his body parts industry. In the Sex Mall, body parts are on display, eroticizing for specular pleasure the medical transplantation operations going on in the nearby hospital. In the context of the novel as a whole, Trigg's fantasy parallels those of other characters who indulge in forms of perverse voyeurism and sexual deviance: a character who enjoys watching films of abortions and sex change operations; a gay man who takes photographs of his lover's bloody body after he has committed suicide; a local judge who has sex with his loyal basset hounds. Sex has becomes real estate speculation, the body a property to be developed. Unfortunately, in Silko's elaborate allegory of global corruption and greed, disabled characters carry the heavy metaphoric burdens of deviance and repressed sexuality that have been their roles in much previous literature.

For all of its fragmented narrative, *Almanac* features a rather traditional conclusion in which all of the major characters converge at an International Holistic Healers Convention in Tucson and await a spiritual and political revolution that is on the horizon:

> The people came from all directions, and many claimed they had been summoned in dreams. . . . People from tribes farther south, peasants without land, *mestizos,* the homeless from the cities and even a busload of Europeans, had come to hear the spirit macaws speak through Wacah. (710)

German root doctors, Celtic leech handlers, ecoterrorists, landless peasant movement leaders, latter-day ghost dancers. and Yupik Eskimo medicine women are on hand to remember ancestors killed in the name of civilization and to agitate for an ecological reclaiming of land lost to pollution and development. This apocalyptic conclusion marks the end of the "Reign of Death-Eye Dog" and the worship of the "Destroyer" who, like Trigg and his Bio-Materials, Inc., drains the blood of its victims. Anticipating the WTO protests in Seattle, the Healers Conference brings together constituencies from around the world with different political agendas. Marx is a kind of titulary spirit, a European who reported on "the suffering of English factory workers the way a tribal shaman might have, feverishly working to bring together a powerful, even magical, assembly of stories" (520). Somehow all of this syncretism and cultural synthesis goes against the novel's discontinuous narrative and dislocated geography. But in its dark comedy of transnational bio-power, *Almanac* provides a capacious, Boschian canvas for seeing the specters of globalization as they inhabit the most vulnerable bodies.

Imagining the Present

In *Oryx and Crake,* Margaret Atwood's two main characters, Snowman and Glenn (Crake), surf the Net, enjoying scenes of torture, sexual humiliation, and violence—as though violation of the body has become a new form of entertainment. Beaufrey in *Almanac* enjoys watching "surgical fantasy movies" of sex change operations and abortions (103). Atwood's and Silko's linkage of sexual fetishism and body part sales speaks to the ways that the posthuman body has become an object of specular as well as commercial fascination. Judith Halberstam and Ira Livingstone note that "posthuman bodies are the causes and effects of postmodern relations of power and pleasure, virtuality and reality, sex and its consequences" (3). They might add to their list the consequences of globalization, insofar as bodies sold as spare parts are organizing the futuristic fantasies of neoliberal embodiment.

It is worth remembering that Foucault developed his theory of bio-power—the writing of power on the body—in his research on sexuality. The regularization of body and species, through taxonomy, comparative anatomy, and eugenics, that he associates with the modern era coincides with the invention of sex as a political fact. In the nineteenth century "sexuality was sought out in the smallest details of individual existences; it was tracked down in behavior, pursued in dreams; it was suspected of underlying the least follies, it was traced back to the earliest years of childhood; it became the stamp of individuality" (146). These "technologies of sex" discipline the body and regulate populations, yet they are not imposed by juridical means but by consent. This ratio of bio-power to sexuality is most obviously manifested in the attempt to render bodies docile within nationalist movements like Naziism or scientific regimes like eugenics, but we could see something of the same connection within globalization as bodies become subjected to vicissitudes of labor migration, medical intervention, and global warfare conducted within and across national borders.

With the expansion of transplant technologies, in vitro fertilization, genetic engineering, and cloning since the 1970s, sexuality seems increasingly removed from the body and embedded in institutions and technologies (the lovers in *Coma* have clandestine assignations on the eighth floor of the transplant hospital; Virgil prefers virtual sex over the Internet to physical contact; Trigg enjoys fantasizing about real estate while having sex). The proliferation of organ procurement / theft narratives expresses how that sexuality is transferred onto exchange that organizes a new set of bioethical questions: What is death? *When* is death? Who owns the body?

Whose life is "worth living"? The texts considered here imagine such questions in an allegorical or fabulous manner through a body that no longer coincides with the humanist subject.[17] Like the comatose patients suspended in air in Michael Crichton's *Coma* or the clone students of *Never Let Me Go*, bodies resemble meat hung in the abattoir, manikins behind plate glass. Their inert bodies and blank stares are the biotech versions of George Romero's zombies.

To some extent these works are contemporary variants of cold war science fiction like *Invasion of the Body Snatchers* or *The Thing* in which aliens from outer space serve as thinly disguised fantasies of Communist subversion. As Michael Rogin observes of such films, "Biology is out of control" (264). Fears of bodily contamination by fluoridation or the Salk polio vaccine that fueled many a John Birch Society pamphlet have not entirely disappeared, but in the absence of a Communist menace, globalization itself seems to have provided a new doomsday scenario for an age of AIDS and genomics. The current administration is defining that scenario around the threat of worldwide terrorism and is orchestrating its own biotech nightmare scenario around stem-cell research and abortion. In this script the twin threats of stateless terrorism and secular humanist bioengineering are the enemies of democratic, Christian society. Given this conflation of geopolitical and biopolitical discourses, it is little wonder that disability advocates, who have forcefully argued against physician-assisted suicide and genetic engineering, have found themselves in an unholy alliance with the religious Right. The dystopic worlds that organ sales narratives envision complicate the easy segue from global terror to bioterror and warn of a world in which biotechnology becomes an end in itself, and bioethics a satellite of cost accounting. Like cold war works that tried to imagine a world outside of superpower dominance and conflict, these tales of biological violation negotiate the increasingly thin border between the capitalized body and the state.

Afterword

Disability and the Defamiliar Body

The poem must resist the intelligence
Almost successfully.
—WALLACE STEVENS, "Man Carrying Thing"

Thus far in *Concerto for the Left Hand* I have resisted mentioning my sub-title almost successfully. "Disability and the *Defamiliar* Body" is my clumsy attempt to characterize the uncanny nature of disability, as a both personal and social form of estrangement. I come to the defamiliar body late in the book because I had to write the book in order to understand the concept. The uncanny, as we know from Freud, is the return of something so familiar that it is rendered strange—a sudden encounter with oneself in a mirror in a dark hallway. The uncanny comes in two forms, repressed childhood castration anxieties that the ego keeps at bay and atavistic, primitive cultural forms upon which civilization erects its edifice. This doublet could also define the two forms in which disability appears: as a confrontation with one's own body experienced as other and as an embodied relationship to an alien society. For the person who becomes disabled later in life, impairment is a sudden reminder of mortality, an awakening to what Ato Quayson calls "the tyranny of contingency" (100). For the person who is born deaf or with a congenital disease, disability is a constant reminder of the intractability of the social, legal, and built environment and its reliance on a one-size-fits-all model of embodiment. That model was forged in nineteenth-century medical science and reinforced by industrial design, comparative anatomy, ugly laws, freak shows, and immigration health policies, but its uncanny doppelgänger is reappearing in current debates over applications of the Human Genome Project and the wonders of genetic engineering.

In this book I have also resisted mentioning my own stake in the defamiliar body almost successfully. As I have already mentioned, Georgina Kleege, in her introduction to *Sight Unseen*, remarks, "In writing this book I became blind," and adapting her formulation, I might say that in writing this book I became disabled. Kleege points out that it was not the exertion of writing that made her blind but that the research involved in writing *Sight Unseen* permitted her to understand what seeing means in a sighted world. In my own case, I became aware of cultural meanings associated with hemophilia and deafness, conditions with which I have lived my entire life but seldom acknowledged. When I was growing up, chronic bleeds and the deterioration of joints and cartilage curtailed the "exercise" of young manhood that dominated postwar gender codes. It was only when hemophilia became joined to HIV/AIDS through a threatened blood supply that I began to regard what had been a lifelong medical nuisance as a set of imbricated social and cultural attitudes of which genetic mutation is only a part. My opening chapter began as an attempt to discover the cultural history of the bleeder, but it turned into a larger encounter with American attitudes toward race and sexuality as they have been deployed in sedimenting nationhood. Similarly, when I began to lose my hearing, due to bilateral tumors growing on each of my auditory nerves, I had to rethink every aspect of my personal and professional life—from my love of music and conversation to my teaching and scholarly work on poetry. Discovering the rich heritage of Deaf poets and performers completely altered my view of the text and sound basis of poetics and forced me to think about the visual, spatial, and communal nature of poetic production. I could not have come to this awareness had I not become estranged from what is most familiar.

Of course the problem with my subtitle is that it reinforces the idea that there is something familiar of which disability is a variant, a conundrum implicit in the term *dis-ability* itself with its negative prefix casting ability into the default position. Disabled people do not think of themselves as "variants" from some norm, yet they live surrounded by triumphalist narratives of athletes or public figures who have conquered their "handicaps" to live "normal" lives. These narratives do an injustice to those who, because of chronic pain, autoimmune deficiencies, cognitive disorders, or paralysis cannot so easily participate in these activities—and by extension the humanity such acts legitimate. To many disabled people, the triumphalist version of disability is an insidious rebuke—as though to say, "Buck up! if you'd stop whining and get on with your therapy (and stop asking for expensive accommodation) you could be one of us." This is the rebuke of narcissism with which disabled people must struggle on a daily basis. Claiming disability, as Simi Linton says, involves reassigning meaning, turning "wheel-chair bound" into "wheel-chair user," and, more recently, into "crip"; it means transforming "AIDS victim" into someone "living with AIDS," it implies challenging the stereotype of disabled people as lonely and depressed and showing their active participation in a richly diversified public sphere; it means rethinking the idea that people with disabilities can't (or shouldn't) have sex or children; it means repudiating the celebrity telethon image of pathetic childhood and testifying to disability as a collective movement. As Linton says,

> We are everywhere these days, wheeling and loping down the street, tapping our canes, sucking on our breathing tubes, following our guide dogs, puffing and sipping on the mouth sticks that propel our motorized chairs. We may drool, hear voices, speak in staccato syllables, wear catheters to collect our urine, or live with a compromised immune system. We are all bound together, not by this list of our collective symptoms but by the social and political circumstances that have forged us as a group. (*Claiming Disability* 4)

And increasingly, claiming disability means claiming intersectional alliances with communities formed around queer, raced, gendered, classed, and—as I've tried to indicate in my last chapters—subaltern identities.

Perhaps the most intractable term in need of reassignment is "dependency." In a society that values autonomy and independence, the idea that we depend on others is anathema. Those of us with aging parents (or who *are* aging parents) will know how complicated it is, as the body becomes more fragile, to become reliant on caregivers, drivers, lawyers, doctors, hospice providers, text enlargers, and our own children for basic human needs. Eva Kittay speaks of these as "inevitable dependencies" that everyone, sooner or later, experiences, yet we live as though dependent relations are the severest burden, a sign of one's uselessness and nonproductivity. At my father's retirement community, the greatest existential trauma of old age is not retirement or even the loss of a spouse but the nonrenewal of one's driver's license. In a culture that defines self-reliance as mobility, relying on a taxi or shuttle driver is a bitter pill to swallow. Because such relations of dependency are felt to be a diminution of agency, the labor that attends it—"dependency work"—is the most disparaged, least remunerative work of all. Kittay points out that dependency work is invariably gendered as "women's work," the onus thus extended to the one being cared for as well.

The stigma of dependency is one of the greatest barriers to achieving disability rights. If rights are defined as the province of independent rational agents, do they apply to those who, in varying degrees, require the care of others? What about the rights of attendants and family members of persons with severe dementia or Down syndrome or cancer, caregivers who become so closely bound to the disabled individual that they become, in effect, disabled themselves? Not all disabled persons require such aid, but to deny dependency as a component of embodied life is to privilege a narrowly prescriptive view of independent living. Martha Nussbaum regards the erasure of dependent relations as a severe obstacle to liberal theories of social justice and urges a reversal of the contractarian norm that presumes that all individuals have equal access to rights. If the social contract means anything, it means acknowledging reciprocal dependencies and validating the role of caregiving—from parenting to teaching to paid professional help.

If disability demands reassigning meaning, it also means challenging the metaphors that have been developed to control and stigmatize human variation. Throughout this book I have used the trope of aesthetic defamiliarization as it was applied to the modernist avant-garde to speak of the ways that disability lays bare the body as an unstable, uncontainable site. There are historical reasons within modernity for joining these two forms of materialization. The threat of an emergent mass public, with its immigrants, new women, and racial others that threatened national integrity in the late nineteenth century, also helped create that great divide between high art and mass culture that is a defining feature of modernism.[1]

The crisis of language diagnosed by Mallarmé is also a crisis about the stability of categories and genres for which an aesthetics of the pure word, disconnected from all forms of contingency and instrumental reason, was a remedy. The threat of the social body to art—the destruction of originality by mass reproduction—also threatened national projects formed around bodily and racial standardization. Eugenics, by marking different types of bodies according to a hierarchy of bodily features, cognitive abilities, and facial types, supported processes of acculturation and national solidity. The Progressive Era is filled with well-intentioned social reformers like Margaret Sanger, Charlotte Perkins Gilman, and Victoria Woodhull who, like their modernist artist counterparts, Gertrude Stein, D. H. Lawrence, and W. E. B. DuBois, endorsed the findings of Francis Galton, Otto Weininger, and other racialists of the day.

The uncanny nature of disability produces what Ato Quayon calls "discursive nervousness" among able-bodied persons, but the concept attends the unruly work of art as well. Aesthetic perfection is supported by an ideal of physical proportion, and when such perfection cannot be achieved, its inadequacy is often figured as physical disfigurement. In 1678 Anne Bradstreet described the publication of her book—the first literary work published by an American author—as a disabled child:

I wash'd thy face, but more defects I saw,
An rubbing off a spot, still made a flaw,
I stretcht thy joints to make thee even feet,
Yet still thou run'st more hobbling than is meet.

And as Tobin Siebers observes, a recent review of Elizabeth Bishop's uncollected poems and fragments, *Edgar Allan Poe and the Juke-Box*, laments, "[The] real poems will outlast these, their maimed and stunted siblings" ("Disability Theory" 279). The idea that "real poems" transcend their textually disabled variants testifies to the ways that aesthetics depends on a certain kind of body in order to transcend it. But as much as the aesthetic is underwritten by an able body, so it is revised when the photographer is blind, the poet is deaf, the pianist has one arm. The defamiliarization of the normate body is also the generative force in new cultural production.

"Limits /are what any of us / are inside of," Charles Olson recognized, and while the social model of disability disparages such limits, a cultural model—in terms developed by David Mitchell and Sharon Snyder—offers a way of considering the meanings produced by the defamiliar body cultural locations (17). A cultural model builds on disabled persons' experiences of disability, "a site of phenomenological value that is not purely synonymous with the processes of social disablement" (6). As such, a cultural model negotiates between the two poles of impairment and disability to stress "the ways disabled people experience their environments and bodies" in specific cultural locations: residential schools or oral education programs or hospitals as well as social movements such as the independent living movement or Deaf President Now (6). I would add that the cultural model includes the performances, dance, poetry, music, and art produced out of those experiences. As I point out with regard to the poet Larry Eigner in chapter 5, this cultural work need not address disability directly but may register the effects of (in Eigner's case) cerebral palsy through the imposition of new formal limits on the poem, alternative ways of responding to an inaccessible world. The problem for the cultural critic is how to honor the poet's reticence about a physical condition that severely restricted his movements while reading that reticence as itself a function of disability.

Considering the cultural locations of disability becomes particularly important when studying disability in a global context. As I have noted in my final two chapters, to study the condition of AIDS in Africa or transplant surgery in India or cognitive disorders in the maquiladora border zones requires consideration of institutional sites and public documents in which disabled persons are interpellated, incarcerated, quarantined, and made citizens. In such locations disability is defined as much by conditions of unequal distribution, structural indebtedness, and trade as by physical incapacity or cognitive impairment. In the case of global organ sales the question becomes "What is the body?" and what does it mean when its organs become commodities in a worldwide global trade? Can disability be dissevered from issues of poverty and malnutrition, and equally, can disability studies, in its repudiation of the medical model, dismiss the role of healthcare or NGOs or transnational aid groups like Médecins Sans Frontières?

Globalization, as Robert McRuer observes, is haunting disability studies, but the specter of disability haunts global discourse as well (*Crip Theory* 199). Take for example Alejandro González Iñárritu's recent movie *Babel,* in which disability—in this case deafness—becomes an integral

part of an attempt to imagine a new world order of global interconnect-
edness. The ghostly aspect of the film involves its attempt to suture discontinuous events occurring in various parts of the world without posit-
ing a totalizing narrative ("we are the world") or telos of development.
Iñárritu expands the biblical metaphor of the Tower of Babel to describe
the allure—and failure—of global communications. What neoliberal
boosterism offers as a narrative of global interchange and mutual understanding becomes, in *Babel*, a series of mis- and cross-communications
with fatal consequences. A Winchester rifle given as a gift by a Japanese
businessmen to a Moroccan goatherd ends up in the hands of the latter's
sons, whose target practice accidentally wounds an American tourist, Susan (Cate Blanchett). In a panic, Susan's husband, Richard (Brad Pitt)
phones their Mexican nanny, Amelia (Adriana Barraza), in San Diego and
urgently asks her to stay with the children until Susan's wound can be
cared for. Amelia ends up taking the children across the border with her
nephew Santiago (Gael Barcia Bernal) to attend her son's wedding in Tijuana. On her return following the wedding, she and Santiago are de-
tained by border guards. Unable to explain why they have two American
children asleep in the back seat and scrutinized for his inebriated condition, Santiago guns the car across the border and leaves Amelia with her
charges alone in the desert. Meanwhile, the goatherd's sons, because the
victim of their target practice is an American, are presumed to be terror-
ists and are hunted down in the desert by Moroccan police, who kill one
of them. The film's simultaneous deployment of three interconnected stories, set in different parts of the world (Japan, the southwest border region, Morocco) and seven languages provides a discontinuous look at
temporalities being created by global conditions, at the same time that the
film maps the unequal relations among individuals who are otherwise
widely separated. The gun that links the various characters in the film is a
kind of global pharmakon, a gift that is also a poison. A child is caught in
the crossfire.

What concerns us most in the context of disability issues concerns the
Japanese businessman's daughter, Chieko (Rinko Kikuchi), who is deaf
and whose relationship to her father is estranged, partly as a result of her
mother's suicide. She lives in a subculture of other deaf teenagers who
roam the urban technoscape of Tokyo, dropping into bars and clubs or
hanging out on the neon-drenched streets. The film's sound track alter-

nately cuts in and out to contrast the loud, electronic soundscape of a global city to Chieko's experience. Although her deaf friends maintain a degree of community, Chieko actively and perilously seeks out male sexual companionship. Frustrated by the dismissive looks of boys who, when they discover she is deaf, reject her ("They think we are monsters," she says to one of her friends), she proceeds to remove her underpants and expose herself to them in a restaurant. In a dentist's office she grabs the dentist's hand and places it between her legs. When a detective comes to her apartment to investigate the gun that wounded Susan in Morocco, Chieko suddenly appears before him naked. This overt display of her body could be read as a compensatory response to deafness, performing one kind of abject communication in place of the "inadequacy" of the other. It could also be seen as a rather transparent attempt to gain attention from men as a surrogate for Chieko's distant father.[2] As the source of the phallus—the rifle that causes chaos on another part of the globe—he is positioned as the *nom du père* that organizes all signification. But he is less the *source* of the gun's violence than a participant in its global circulation. The Winchester rifle as a famously American weapon, essential to the winning of the West, participates in a circuit of violence of which the current war on terror is the latest example. At the end of the film, he and his daughter stand on a balcony looking out over the city, suggesting a tentative rapprochement between them, but the mood is still haunted by her previous scene of sexual abasement.

Their silence speaks to the crisis of communication between parents and children that runs throughout the film—from the goatherder and his children, to Susan and Richard, whose global tourism leaves them far from their children in San Diego, or Amelia, whose undocumented labor in the United States leaves her distant from her son in Tijuana. But the failure of communication cannot be ascribed to the usual generational divide of an earlier domestic model; rather, it is a direct result of turbocharged technological and capital expansion that promises connectedness but instead reinforces social inequalities and divisions. The air conditioned tour bus that brings affluent Western tourists to Morocco may, in touristic parlance, "shrink the globe," but when two of its passengers need immediate medical help in a remote, impoverished village, it affords little protection from the realities of ongoing, structural inequality. Susan's nearly fatal wound makes her a figure of tragic motherhood among nameless poor Moroccans, while her Mexican nanny—also a mother—is deported for being an illegal alien after attending her son's wedding. Two mothers in crisis, yet two different trajectories for their fate.[3]

 Babel is one among many recent works attempting to confront the as yet unreadable text of globalization. Critics of the film felt that its discontinuous stories lack narrative cohesion and rely, instead, on what David Denby in the *New Yorker* called "trivial contingency." In short, what critics wanted, apparently, is a film that provides a telos for contingency, a satisfying narrative for the discontinuities wrought by globalization. But this seems a misreading of its most salient contribution to the debate—that there are no such convenient stories to tell. The film refuses the familiar bromides of globalization and raises, instead, the specter of those caught in its perilous logic. Iñárritu dedicates the film to his children, and given the film's focus on the fraught relationship between parents and children, he seems to be offering a grim parable about the future. That future, unfortunately, seems increasingly written through the long shadow cast by 9/11, and although the perpetual war on terror is not overtly mentioned in *Babel*, it is the beast in the jungle, always ready to leap. The daily media display of soldiers returning from the Middle East missing limbs or suffering neurological damage suggests that disability *is* the news, whether the news recognizes it as such. Whether we have the will and intelligence to connect the lives of those caught in the crossfire with the lives we hope our children will lead remains an open question.

Notes

1. By focusing her attention on severely cognitively and physically disabled persons, Nussbaum addresses only one component of the Whitmanian pool and not the large population of persons variously positioned in relation to disability. Obviously someone who is hard of hearing or who has progressive macular degeneration occupies a very different level of participation with a social contract from the person with Down syndrome or cerebral palsy. In these cases, the issue of dependency—the disabled person's reliance on caregivers, family members, and social services—creates another kind of barrier to independent living and to the ideal of social equality advanced by Rawls. Nussbaum's emphasis on dependency, however, risks reinstating a more paternalistic view of disability that has been the subject of criticism by disability activists. Thinking of disability through the optic of dependency challenges American ideals of self-reliance and individualism and may explain why claims for civil rights have been so fraught. In a society based on autonomy and self-reliance, anyone perceived to be dependent—unemployed single mothers, elderly persons on pensions, persons with disabilities—will be regarded as a drain on resources, a burden to society. Because of this stigma, disability activists have argued that Nussbaum's definition of dependence reinforces this paternalistic view and does not account, adequately, for the independence or interdependencies within the disability community. Furthermore, critics have observed that her conversation is too much with Rawls and not enough with the work of disability scholars who have raised many of these issues in specific instances for the past twenty years.

Introduction

1. This metaphoric transfer has been described by David Mitchell and Sharon Snyder as "discursive dependency" (*Narrative Prosthesis* 5).
2. A good introduction to the relationship between aesthetics and the body can be found in Tobin Siebers's introduction to his anthology *The Body Aesthetic*.
3. On the one-handed piano repertoire, see Edel.
4. At this level, one-armed pianist Paul Wittgenstein joins his two-armed

brother, the philosopher, for whom language was always a system of physical acts in highly situated contexts. On the body in the aesthetic, see Eagleton 5–8.

5. On the relationship between Winckelmann and National Socialism see Siebers, "Hitler."

6. Colin Barnes and Geoff Mercer describe the emergence of a social model of disability with the manifesto of the Union of the Physically Impaired Against Segregation, whose manifesto of 1976, *Fundamental Principles of Disability*, asserts, "It is society which disables physically impaired people. Disability is something imposed on top of our impairments by the way we are unnecessarily isolated and excluded from full participation in society" (14).

7. The most infamous example occurs in Louis Simpson's review of Brooks's *Selected Poems* in the *New York Herald Tribune Book Week*. Simpson remarked, "I am not sure it is possible for a Negro to write well without making us aware he is a Negro; on the other hand, if being a Negro is the only subject, the writing is not important" (27).

8. Tobin Siebers has observed that debates over the National Endowment of the Arts funding of "objectionable art" have been motivated largely by fears of nontraditional bodies violating the pristine enclaves of art museums. Chris Ofili's *The Holy Virgin Mary*, with its depiction of the Virgin Mother decorated in elephant dung, or Karen Finley's performance as Aggie, a woman in a wheelchair who needs her diaper changed, or Andres Serrano's *Piss Christ*—targets of conservative critics of the NEA—all involve bodies that have "gone awry" and that challenge the passive gaze of the museum viewer ("What Can Disability Studies Learn" 184).

9. For a critique of Davis's position, see Sandahl, "Black Man" 580–82.

10. For a thorough treatment of "quality of life" issues as they pertain to genetic testing, see Wasserman, Bickenbach, and Wachbroit.

11. For the disability rights perspective, see Hershey; Hentoff.

12. Robert McRuer points out that this restrictive view of euthanasia as the only alternative offered to Maggie in the film is part of a more general neoliberal tendency to finesse medical ethical questions by reference to the bottom line. He points out that in a world where the market dominates everything, Maggie's condition (and Frankie's complicity in her death) is circumscribed the following ethos: "You get your shot: you take a risk, you put yourself out there, and if it pays off, it pays off, but regardless, you get your shot. The second lesson is that you best get that shot in a deregulated environment" ("Neoliberal Risks" 12). McRuer observes that the film validates free choice for the disabled Maggie while permitting no alternative models for her future as a quadriplegic.

13. A number of medical professionals have pointed out that Maggie's high-priced hospital care is far from adequate, given the various ailments she incurs there, not to mention the isolation from hospital staff that allows Frankie to administer his lethal injection. See Weiss.

14. Indeed, the film features at least five forms of disability: Maggie's paralysis, Eddie's missing eye, Maggie's mother's obesity, and the mental illness of a member of the gym, Danger, who is the butt of jokes by the gym's patrons but who is befriended by Eddie. The fifth example would include disabilities of gender, race, and class that mark the lives of the hardscrabble characters, and while

these may not be classified as disabilities, in the film they serve as limits to what the ADA calls "major life activities."

15. Eastwood's problematic conclusion may reflect his own negative attitudes about disability, inspired by a 1990 case in which he was sued under the ADA by a patron of his Mission Ranch Inn in Carmel for inadequate facilities. Eastwood was cited for violations of the ADA, but the major claims were ultimately dismissed. In a subsequent attempt to lobby Congress to modify the ADA, Eastwood called the 1990 law "a form of extortion" (Davis, "Why 'Million Dollar Baby' Infuriates" 6).

16. Susan Schweik develops the implications of Davis's remark by looking at the work of poet Josephine Miles, who lived with severe rheumatoid arthritis throughout her life. Schweik notes that in Miles's poetry, the bringing into vision of the author's visible disability is "also a spoken moment, one made in discourse" (486).

17. Foucault begins *The Birth of Clinic* by saying, "This book is about space, about language, and about death; it is about the act of seeing, the gaze" (ix). On the visibility of mental illness through IQ testing, see Carlson.

18. On the theatricalization of disability, see Sandahl, "From the Streets."

19. In *Precarious Life* Judith Butler extends Emmanuel Levinas's theory of "the face" from a realm in which the other makes ethical claims on us to one in which the other's face reveals the precariousness of life within a precarious history. For Butler, this situation is dramatically evident in the post-9/11 era, in which the faces of Middle Eastern figures circulate through the media, marshaled "in the service of war, as if bin Laden's face were the face of terror itself, as if Arafat were the face of deception, as if Hussein's face were the face of contemporary tyranny" (141).

20. Martin Jay, on the other hand, sees Levinas's idea of "face" as profoundly anti-ocularcentric, deriving from Talmudic prohibitions against images and the kinds of formal reciprocity associated with Buber's I-Thou principle. "Rather than the shame induced by a Sartrean reifying look, real ethical responsibility [for Levinas] came from an eminently non-visual source" (557).

21. In a personal communication, Grigely has said that Calle responded positively to his postcards and has seen them as very much the kind of dialogue she had hoped to establish around issues of photography, museums, and looking.

22. This is the claim of Moynihan and Cassels's *Selling Sickness.*

23. On the social production of disease see Rosenberg and Golden.

24. On Roberts and the independent living movement, see Shapiro, 41–73.

25. On the limits of implant technology, see Lane 216–30.

26. On the other hand, as A. Philip Aiello and Myrna Aiello have written, cochlear implants needn't be described in black-and-white terms as either genocidal or liberatory but can be seen as permitting a useful biculturality or bilingualism that will expand, rather than limit, deaf experience.

27. This encounter occurred at a lecture-demonstration by the artist at the University of California, San Diego, March 3, 2000.

28. A variant of this idea has been the subject of Wendy Brown's *States of Injury.* She argues that rights claims among minorities often rely on a middle-class ideal that remains untheorized: The middle class is "not a reactionary identity in

the sense of reacting to an insurgent politicized identity from below. Rather, it precisely embodies the ideal to which nonclass identities refer for proof of their exclusion or injury." She goes on to name homosexuals, women, and racial minorities, all of whom lack the protections that are taken for granted by straight, white, middle-class families (61). Lennard Davis develops Brown's ideas extensively in *Bending Over Backwards*.

CHAPTER 1

1. Factors are proteins manufactured in the body that are necessary for blood clotting. There are twelve factors of which two—Factors VIII and IX—are among those most commonly absent in hemophiliacs. The quantity of factor in the blood determines the severity of a bleeding disorder.

2. As in any area involving disabilities the question of nomenclature is a vexing question. In this essay I will refer alternatively to *hemophiliacs* and *persons with hemophilia*, recognizing that within the community so defined, the latter term is preferred.

3. Cryoprecipitate was discovered in 1965 by Judith Graham Pool, working as a researcher at Stanford University. She noticed that in the process of thawing frozen plasma to obtain Factor VIII—a process known as "fractionating"—there was a thick residue left that was rich in factor. This factor-rich residue became cryoprecipitate, and its discovery led to the development of freeze-dried concentrates. On the history of cryoprecipitate see Resnik 37–55.

4. For a severe Factor VIII hemophiliac who weighs 150 pounds, a normal dosage would cost $3,500. For a Factor IX hemophiliac at the same weight, the cost would be $7,000.

5. Richard Titmuss's study *The Gift Relationship* is an important pre-AIDS look at the blood-distribution industry. Titmuss asks why people donate their blood to strangers. He concludes that blood donation involves a "gift relationship" that, unlike so many other transactions in capitalist societies, transcends market considerations. When blood donation becomes a matter of economic policy— when donors give only for profit—then social policy is divorced from moral considerations and leads "to an ideology to end all ideologies" (12).

6. The term *severe* refers to individuals who have less than 1 percent of the normal range of clotting factor. Persons with hemophilia are designated as severe, moderate, and mild.

7. The most thorough study of this narrative is provided by Susan Resnik, whose *Blood Saga* is the only full-scale institutional history of hemophilia.

8. Cindy Patton has provided the most thorough study of the effects of such pronominalization as it affected research. She notes that the New Right and Moral Majority opposed funds for AIDS research since in their minds it was an "elective disease created by homosexuals who might just as well die off" (*Sex and Germs* 69).

9. All three levels of this shift had profound implications for AIDS research. If the disease could be restricted to constituencies regarded as socially deviant— homosexuals, IV drug users, prostitutes—it could be ignored or, more insidiously,

used as a moral lesson and even a genocidal corrective. Once AIDS touched the blood supply—and hemophiliacs in particular—the epidemic became general. Despite the fact that heterosexuals around the world had been dying of AIDS since the late 1970s, it was represented in the popular media as a gay-marked syndrome for which funding, health care, and education need not be not a priority.

10. The Hemophilia Foundation was formed in 1948, but was renamed the National Hemophilia Foundation in 1959.

11. Hemophilia is X-linked, which means that the gene for the disease is passed on through the X chromosome. Since a male has both an X and a Y chromosome, there is a fifty-fifty chance that he will receive the hemophilia gene from a carrier mother. In women, the presence of a second X chromosome masks the effects of hemophilia on the other chromosome, and although they carry the defective gene, they do not become hemophilic. Although cases of female hemophilia have been recorded (in which the second X chromosome failed to mask the effects of the disease), examples are rare. Hence, for all intents and purposes, hemophilia is a male disease.

12. A former executive director of the National Hemophilia Foundation interviewed by Susan Resnik describes the way these "hemo-homo wars" were conducted:

They (the media) tried to pit hemophiliacs against homosexuals. We were then approached by . . . right-wing groups to engage The National Hemophilia Foundation in this war against "sin." . . . I'm really proud of the role of the hemophilia community in resisting these demagogues in trying to exploit this horrible situation. (128)

13. Cindy Patton quotes a hemophiliac who describes "the growing fear that hemophiliacs are dangerous to employ or to have in schools as 'hemophobia,' and speaks wryly of coming out of the 'clot closet'" (*Sex and Germs* 23). In Andrew Puckett's mystery novel *Bloodstains* the main character, Tom, is asked to investigate the theft of blood from a transfusion center. Tom's task is made the more difficult due to his "haemophobia" or fear of blood. Whether referring to a phobia of blood or a fear of bleeders, the term is metonymically linked to homophobia by a series of displacements involving anxiety over penetration. In popular media representations of AIDS such as those on television shows of the 1980s like *Hill Street Blues* or *St. Elsewhere,* a standard AIDS scenario involved the threat of needle sticks from potentially infected blood. The drama that ensues involves the innocent nurse or policeman negotiating conflicting attitudes not only about infection but about gays.

14. On hemophilia in the Talmud see Rosner; on hemophilia in early North America see A. McKusick; on hemophilia in eugenics see Kevles; on germ theory see Kraut; Burbick. Robert Gluck has reminded me that kosher dietary laws prohibit the eating of certain "bloody" parts of cows or chickens that have not been cleaned of blood.

15. In the *Ithaca Journal,* May 1, 1986, White was photographed at a benefit for AIDS research, the accompanying caption of which reads: "Ryan . . . is a homophiliac [*sic*] who contracted AIDS through a blood transfusion" (qtd. in Gilman 105).

16. Massie was moved to write his book by his own son's hemophilia. Curiosity about his son's disease led him, as he says in his introduction, "to curiosity about the response of the parents of the boy who was the most famous hemophiliac of all" (vii).

17. On hemophilia camps, see Resnik. See also "Hemophiliacs Lead Fairly 'Normal' Lives."

18. The dialogue excerpted here is from *The Donahue Show,* October 1, 1993.

19. On new coalitional alliances see Cohen. On AIDS activism in general see Epstein.

20. This optimistic mood is best represented by the 1996 International AIDS Conference in Vancouver, BC. Articles in the *New York Times* (July 7, 1996) and *Los Angeles Times* (July 4, 1996) describe advances made in combination therapies as they were outlined by researchers at the conference. But both articles go on to point out that while AIDS may be contained in the United States, it is expanding in staggering rates in Africa, Southeast Asia, and the Middle East. Ninety percent of HIV infections are in the third world, and the high cost of new drugs will place them out of the reach of most affected individuals.

Chapter 2

1. The music that sets Buzz off is referred to as "jungle music," clearly a reference to jazz and black music in general. The movie implies that Buzz's music trauma is due not only to his combat experiences but to his having served in an integrated army, of which black music is a troublesome reminder.

2. In addition to the films that I discuss in this chapter, a brief survey of disabled figures in films noirs would include the following: in *Ministry of Fear* (1944), the spy who pursues Stephen Neale (Ray Milland) is blind; in *Gilda* (1946) the title character (Rita Hayworth) marries a crippled casino owner, Ballin Mundson (George Macready), who dispenses rough justice to his enemies by means of a spring-loaded knife in his cane; in *Somewhere in the Night* (1946) an ex-marine, George Tayler (John Hodiak), suffers from amnesia; in *The Spiral Staircase* (1946), a mute servant, Helen Capel (Dorothy McGuire), lives in a small town where a number of disabled people are murdered; in *The Big Sleep* (1946), Raymond Chandler's detective, Philip Marlowe (Humphrey Bogart), works for General Sternwood (Charles Waldron), who is confined to a wheelchair; Sternwood's daughter Carmen (Martha Vickers) suffers from some undiagnosed mental condition and drug addiction; *The Brasher Doubloon* (1947) features Marlowe in a blackmail scheme involving a secretary who is mentally disturbed; in *Kiss of Death* (1947) a deranged man, Tommy Udo (Richard Widmark), pushes a woman in a wheelchair down a flight of stairs; in *Ride the Pink Horse* (1947), a deaf mob figure, Frank Hugo (Fred Clark), uses a primitive hearing aid attached to his ear; in *Sorry Wrong Number* (1948), a bedridden woman, Leona Stevenson (Barbara Stanwyck), overhears a telephone conversation that concerns a plot to kill her; in *They Live By Night* (1949) features Chicamaw Mobley (Howard Da Silva), a demented robber and sadist with one eye; in *Thieves Highway* (1949) Nick Garcos (Richard Conte) returns from the war to find his father crippled from a truck accident; in

The Big Heat (1953), Detective Sergeant Dave Bannion (Glenn Ford) obtains crucial information on a crime from a crippled secretary, and Vince Stone (Lee Mar-
vin) scalds his girlfriend, Debby Marsh (Gloria Graham) with coffee, thus "ruin-
ing her looks"; in *Rear Window* (1954) Jeff Jeffries (Jimmy Stewart), in a cast after
an accident, observes a plot to conceal a murder of a bedridden woman in a neigh-
boring building; in *The Big Combo* (1955), Joe McClure (Brian Donlevy), a crime
boss's enforcer who is deaf, tortures his victims by forcing them to listen to loud
music through his hearing aid; in *The Manchurian Candidate* (1962), Raymond
Shaw (Laurence Harvey) is a brainwashed Korean War vet programmed to be an
assassin. In these films, disability, invariably a sign of weakness or evil, often serves
as a metonymic reflection of the noir hero's own flaws. Although cognitive disorders and mental illness exist in a separate category of disability, they form the
backbone of many noir films, including Alfred Hitchcock's *Spellbound* (1945),
Strangers on a Train (1951), *Vertigo* (1958), and *Psycho* (1960).

3. On the making of *The Blue Dahlia* see Naremore 107–14.

4. Although some films of this period—*Sorry Wrong Number*, *The Spiral
Staircase*, or *Rear Window*—feature a main character who is disabled, it is usually
the bit character whose deafness or limp marks the hero's psychic wounds.

5. The first description of the phantom limb phenomenon was provided in
the mid–sixteenth century by the French surgeon Ambroise Paré, whose patients
"imagine they have their members yet entire, and yet due complaine thereof"
(Gorman 30). The fullest early discussion of the phenomenon was provided in the
late nineteenth century by the American physician S. Weir Mitchell, who noted
that almost all of his patients who lost organs or limbs experienced the phenomenon. Although the phrase itself refers to arms and legs, Mitchell's patients experienced comparable sensation with the loss of eyes, internal organs, rectum, and
uterus following hysterectomy. It was reported also in cases of missing penises. On
phantom limb and body image see Gorman. See also Grosz 70–79.

6. The Motion Picture Production Code was implemented in 1930 by the
Motion Picture Producers and Distributors of America under the administration
of Will Hays. As Vito Russo says, the "Code survived under different names until
the late Sixties, often taking the name of its current administrator. Thus, at various times it was called the Johnston Office, the Hays Office and the Breen Office"
(31).

7. I adapt Corber's terms about homosexuality here to speak of the ways
that the disabled body in film noir turns performance into spectacle, supplanting
a gaze between viewer and unruly body with one between viewer and queer bodies elsewhere in the film.

8. I discuss this phenomenon in relation to cold war literary communities
in *Guys Like Us*, chapter 1.

9. I am grateful to Liberty Smith for her own work on the intersection of
queer and disabilities issues in *Gattaca*.

10. An excellent disabilities reading of the film is provided by Mark Jeffreys.

11. *Richard III*, 1.1.16.

12. As a sign that later films in the noir cycle developed their own self-conscious critique of the genre's masculinist character, Robert Aldrich's *Kiss Me
Deadly* (1955) features the character of Christina (Cloris Leachman) who skewers

macho Mike Hammer (Ralph Meeker). Fleeing from unknown pursuers, she is picked up on the road by a sneering, self-indulgent Hammer in his sports car. Noting his dismissive tone and male accouterments, she ventriloquizes his misogyny, "Woman, the incomplete sex. What does he need to complete her? A man of course—wonderful man."

13. A variation on this use of flashback and voice-over occurs in *Mildred Pierce* (1945), whose title character, played by Joan Crawford, narrates a story of domestic trials while raising an ungrateful daughter and running a restaurant. But since her voice-over narration is told to a police inspector who suspects her of killing her husband, it is still contained within the figure of the masculine Law, although it offers, as Pam Cook observes, a corrective version of the noir crime frame. On *Mildred Pierce* and voice-over see Cook.

14. That Lisa herself decides to assume a more active role in Jeff's fantasy is merely a consequence of the way that the male gaze structures the terms of agency.

15. On the epistemological implications of feminist film criticism see White.

16. As Jennifer Nelson, Timothy Melley, Robert Corber, and others have pointed out, acts of looking during the cold war were often underwritten by a surveillance ideology that placed communists and queers as the inevitable objects of a national gaze.

17. As Paul Starr notes, the defeat of a national health insurance plan during the 1930s (and opposed by the AMA) led to the expansion of private health insurance companies during the postwar years. Defined as "socialized medicine," the idea of a national plan could now be perpetually demonized during the anti-Communist decades (280–89). It is worth pointing out that Wilder returned to the image of the vast, impersonal insurance company in his 1960 film, *The Apartment*, in which Fred MacMurray appears again, this time as the head of the office.

18. Claire Johnston reinforces the idea that the relationship between Neff and Keyes is to some extent determined by the compulsorily homosocial nature of the insurance company for which they work, a business in which women are distrusted: "Women represent the possibility of social excess which the insurance business seeks to contain" (91).

19. On polio in general see Gould.

20. On the Oedipal triangle between Michael and the Bannisters see West.

21. Grisby's telescope is a self-conscious commentary on Welles's filmic technique and perhaps on the surveillance of the film by Columbia Pictures and Harry Cohn, who demanded editing and cuts that Welles was loathe to make. Furthermore, Cohn insisted on adding a musical score that "interpreted" every action. As a result, the film is oddly disjunctive, studio sets juxtaposed to on-site shots, static portraits of Hayworth juxtaposed to fluid camera movement. On the making of *The Lady from Shanghai* see Naremore 125–76.

22. Bannister is also ethnically typecast as a "clever Jewish lawyer" in distinct contrast to O'Hara's honest Irishness (complete with brogue). Although this fact is never explicitly stated, it can be supported by the fact that the actor who plays Bannister, Everett Sloane, portrayed Bernstein, the lawyer in *Citizen Kane*, whose Jewishness is central to his characterization.

23. Lennard Davis speaks about the way that volatile bodies arrest the gaze in

an essay that links the Venus de Milo, epitome of classical beauty, and disabled body, site of fragmentation. Davis notes that art historical accounts of the Venus de Milo such as those of Kenneth Clark, attempt to replace the missing limbs of the classical sculpture with the ideal "normal" body it displaces, "an act of re-formation of the visual field, a sanitizing of the disruption in perception." Davis concludes that the "mutilated Venus and the disabled person in general . . . will become in fantasy a visual echo of the primal fragmented body—a signifier of castration and lack of wholeness" ("Nude Venuses" 57). Although I am unsatisfied with the castration definition, I recognize that Davis is trying to link the disabled body with a pervasive condition of fragmentation that all humans experience prior to the stage of self-objectification that Lacan figures as the mirror stage. For Davis, the disabled body, "far from being the body of some small group of victims, is an entity from the earliest of childhood instincts" (61). In this sense, disability is a social and cultural construction the encounter with which provides an uncanny memory of preoedipal condition.

24. On Kennan's own health, see Stephanson 44–45.

CHAPTER 3

1. On the DPN protests see Brueggemann 151–200; Christiansen and Barnartt; Lane. In the period since the writing of this chapter, student protests have once again brought international attention to Gallaudet University, and once again the issue is the appointment of a new president. The appointment of Jane K. Fernandes to replace outgoing president E. King Jordan offended many students and, ultimately, a majority of the faculty. Although Fernandes is deaf and does use ASL, students who blockaded the school and boycotted classes complained that she was not a fluent signer, having learned ASL late in life, and that she maintained a rather distant, cold administrative style. The result of these protests is that the Gallaudet board of governors rescinded their offer to Fernandes and appointed interim president Robert R. Davila. For an overview of the recent protests, see Davis, "Deafness."

2. For this reason I will capitalize the word *Deaf* when referring to deaf persons as a distinct culture and use a small *d* when speaking of the physiological condition of deafness.

3. On the issue of voice and sign language see Ree. On the NAD films see Burch 57–61.

4. A good introduction to the situation of children of deaf parents can be found in Lennard Davis's memoir, *My Sense of Silence.*

5. *I Am Ordered Now to Talk* can be seen on the DVD included in *Signing the Body Poetic,* edited by Dirksen Bauman.

6. Brenda Brueggemann has provided an excellent reading of this performance, as she has of many other ASL poets. I am indebted to her readings of both performances as I am to videotapes loaned me by her and by Kenny Lerner. In the absence of commercially available tapes by deaf performers, the student of sign-literature must rely on a limited set of videos, circulated in an ad hoc manner

among friends and colleagues. While this limits the number of performances available for commentary, it points to the limits of video documentation and to the site-specific nature of such performances. The important interactive character of Deaf performance can hardly be rendered in a video.

7. According to Brenda Brueggemann, the use of two signers signing is a standard "deaf ventriloquist" act used in many forms of Deaf storytelling, and the Flying Words Project uses it in a number of their performances (207). "Poetry around the World" can be seen on the Flying Words collection, *The Can't Touch Tours*, where it is listed as "4 Arms."

8. In several of his performances, Williamson utilizes musicians and dancers. In a recent collaboration, Williamson worked with a drummer, Craig Astill, which produced "a kind of Beckettian reduction of my capacity to hear or sense music. Craig played a frame drum directly into the floor (we insisted on hollow wooden stages only) and I picked up a barefoot vibrational signal from varying distances from the drum, thus stimulating degrees of animation in the improvised performance" (private correspondence, January 18, 2000).

9. "Wave" can be seen on the DVD included in *Signing the Body Poetic*.

10. A portion of *Hearing Things* can be seen on the DVD included in *Signing the Body Poetic*.

11. Although Derrida does not refer to deaf persons in his various critiques of phonocentrism, he might well consider a population that relies on nonphonetic means to signify and that bases its meaning-production on visual rather than audible information. Derrida's "phonocentrism" is usually equated with speech, but Williamson foregrounds "voice" as a multifaceted producer of meaning, not limited to linguistic signs. For further discussion of deafness and Derrida, see Bauman.

12. Grigely's book *Textualterity: Art, Theory, and Textual Criticism* discusses the transformations of cultural texts through various processes of writing, editing, and publishing. Although deafness is not his subject, Grigely does provide a theoretical justification for his creation of installations based on conversation slips and ephemeral notes exchanged between himself and interlocutors. The premise of the book is that the uniqueness of the unique art object or literary text is constantly undergoing transience as it ages, is altered by editors and conservators, and is resituated or reterritorialized in different publications and exhibition spaces (1). Translated into Grigely's art installations, such "reterritorialization" would involve the transformation of public spaces where his "conversations with the hearing" take place (bars, cafés, parks) into the art gallery. It would equally involve the ways his art destroys the aura of the unique artwork by its deployment of actual conversations and communications between the deaf and the hearing.

13. A good survey of Grigely's work can be seen in the catalog for his 1998 Whitney Museum Exhibition, *Conversation Pieces*.

14. This is very much the theme of Grigely's installation *Barbicon Conversations* (1998), in which his conversation slips appear in various public spaces of London's vast Barbicon Centre. Examples can be found on advertising kiosks, information pamphlets, and docent sheets as well as in the restrooms, bars, and lobbies of the building. Thus Grigely is able to refer to the conversational focus of his work in those spaces where such conversations actually occur.

CHAPTER 4

1. On modernist ocularcentrism see Levin; Jacobs; and Jay.

2. Jay's *Downcast Eyes* is a cultural history of an anti-ocularcentric tendency within modernism, specifically among French intellectuals from Bergson to Bataille and Levinas and based, to some extent, on unseating the privileging of Cartesian perspectivalism within which much late-nineteenth-century French intellectual life was formed. Duchamp's "antiretinal" art is the epitome of this antiocular tendency. My emphasis is much more on Anglo-American poets and their deployment of ocular metaphors as a hedge against particular rhetorical forms.

3. On the meeting of Ginsberg and Panara, see Cohn's *Sign Mind* 28–29.

4. This series can be seen on the Flying Words Project's collected videos, *The Can't Touch Tours: Current Works (1990–2003)*. Lacking a printed version of the poem and relying on Lerner's spoken version of it, I have created my own lineation based, admittedly, on English syntactic patterns. This raises the interesting question of what constitutes the "line" in ASL poetry and whether it can be mapped onto print. Clayton Valli, in "The Nature of the Line in ASL Poetry," has attempted to relate signed poetry to traditional English versification, finding in the repeated patterns of handshapes an equivalent to traditional English lines. However important Valli's thesis, it is based on a rather traditional, blank verse model (indebted, no doubt, to his own affection for Robert Frost) and does not deal with the manifold differences between pattern in manual signing and in English prosody.

5. Jennifer L. Nelson remarks that Derrida's theory of meaning as *différance* can be applied to social identities as well. "We 'see' black as a color because we have red to compare with, for example, and we can classify people as deaf because we have hearing as a counterpoint or frame of reference. . . . 'Deaf' thus necessarily carries 'hearing' with it as something from which it draws meaning, and the same with 'hearing' as well, although in the latter, this process is unconscious" (123).

6. After writing this chapter, I discovered Jim Cohn's excellent study of disability, *The Golden Body: Meditations on the Essence of Disability*, which features a chapter titled "Sun Tangled in Sun: Disability Freedom in the ASL Poetry of Peter Cook and Kenny Lerner."

7. On the connection of orality and ASL poetry see Krentz.

8. "Snowflake" can be seen on Valli's videotape *Poetry in Motion: Clayton Valli*. I have been aided in my reading of this poem by David Perlmutter, to whom I extend my thanks.

CHAPTER 5

1. Manuel Gamiz, Jr., "Torch Relay for Disabled Arrives by Land and Sea." *Los Angeles Times*, June 20, 2000, B7.

2. Eigner was a reluctant participant in the independent living movement in Berkeley. His first communal living situation with other disabled persons was not

successful, and he left to form a household with poets Robert Grenier and Kathleen Frumkin. Nevertheless, he continued to visit local community centers, working with disabled senior citizens at the Berkeley Outreach Recreation program in Live Oak Park (*areas* 140–41).

3. The best overall survey of the disability rights movement is Fleischer and Zames. Other sources include Longmore and Umansky; Campbell and Oliver; Charlton, *Nothing about Us;* Davis, *Enforcing Normalcy;* Linton *Claiming,* Shapiro.

4. This condition is the subject of Duncan's poem "Crosses of Harmony and Disharmony" in *The Opening of the Field:*

> so that the lines of the verse do not meet,
> imitating that void between
>   two images of a single rose near at hand, the one
> slightly above and to the right . . .
>
> "The double vision
> due to maladjustment of the eyes" like
> "Visual delusions arising from some delirium
> illustrates surrounding spatial regions"
>
>   (45)

5. These line are from Allen Ginsberg's "Howl" 126.

6. The poetry movements mentioned here received their inaugural appearance in Donald Allen's 1960 anthology, *The New American Poetry,* which first divided poets into groups (Beat, Black Mountain, New York school, San Francisco Renaissance) and provided an appendix of poetics statements at the end. Although each of these groups claimed different literary antecedents, they were all influenced, in one way or another, by modernist free verse poets such as Ezra Pound, William Carlos Williams, Marianne Moore, H.D., and Gertrude Stein, within the American tradition, and surrealism and Dadaism within the European avant-garde tradition. They strongly dissented from the then-reigning New Critical position that stressed formal cohesion, structural complexity, and impersonality in favor of a free verse line, cadential rhythm, and expressive—even vatic—use of language.

7. George Hart has written an excellent article on Eigner as a nature poet, "Reading under the Sign of Nature," and Benjamin Friedlander has written a useful encyclopedia entry on him in the Gale Dictionary of Literary Biography series. The latter is the best introduction to Eigner's life and work.

8. This critical disregard may change soon when Stanford University brings out Eigner's *Collected Poems,* edited by Robert Grenier and Curtis Faville.

9. Kenny Fries, *Staring Back: The Disability Experience from the Inside Out,* features four poems by Eigner.

10. Eigner's reticence in foregrounding his cerebral palsy aligns him with another Berkeley poet, Josephine Miles, who lived with rheumatoid arthritis from an early age but who did not identify as disabled or with the disability rights movement. Susan Schweik has made the case that despite her reticence, Miles's early work often anticipates "conditions for the emergence of a new contemporary social group—but only if that group is understood in both broad and complex

terms" (489). If we understand "disability rights" in the contemporary, post–civil rights sense, then Miles does not accept the label "disabled." Schweik locates Miles's acknowledgment of disability in a discursive resistence to the language of reason and rationality. "In [Miles's poem] 'Reason' and other colloquial poems, Miles devises a vigorous alterative to this particular tradition, one in which colloquy replaces soliloquy. The poem deflects identification, or at any rate renders it elastic and provisional. In 'Reason' . . . Miles develops a (counter)narcissistic poetic that challenges a dominant equation of disability with aggrieved self-absorption, not by evacuating narcissism, but by revealing and reveling in it—as the basis of *all* (un)reasonable spoken interaction, and as a force that both generates and is tempered by conversation" (500).

11. Benjamin Friedlander notes that in 1962 Eigner underwent cryosurgery to freeze part of his brain in order to control his spastic movements (121). The successful operation is described in a letter to Douglas Blazek:

> Sept. 62 cryosurgery, frostbite in the thalamus (awakened to see if i was numbed, test whether they had right spot, felt much like killing of a tooth nerve!), tamed (and numbed some) my wild left side, since when I can sit still without effort, and have more capacity for anger etc. Before, I had to be extrovert, or anyway hold the self off on a side, in this very concrete, perpetual sense. A puzzlement of the will. (Qtd. in Friedlander, 121)

Friedlander notes that prior to the surgery, "Typing, of all activities, provided relief from the wildness, from the distraction of the flailing, and from the effort of holding the body still, or trying to" (121).

12. According to Bob Grenier, who is editing the forthcoming collected edition of Eigner's poems, Stanford University will honor his page size by printing all three volumes in an 8ž by 11 format and in a font that approximates his typewriter font (personal communication, January 7, 2006).

13. In his letters, some of which have been published, Eigner tends to fill the page, writing even in the margins and blank spaces of the page:

> Well letters get crowded just from attempt to save time, i.e., cover less space, avoid putting another sheet in the typewriter for a few more words as I at least hope there will only be. There've always been so many things to do. For instance with only my right index finger to type with I never could write very fast—to say what I want to when I think of it, before I forget it or how to say it; I sometimes say 2 things at about the same time, in two columns. It'll be from not deciding or being unable to decide quickly anyway what to say first, or next. Or an after thought might as well be an insert, and thus go in the margin, especially when otherwise you'd need one or more extra words to refer to a topic again. (*areas* 149)

Here is a good instance of how a textual parataxis that one associates with the Pound/Olson tradition can be read differently by a poet for whom the act of changing a sheet of paper or typing a few more words is a considerably more difficult task. The desire to render the phenomenological moment remains the same for Eigner and Olson, and certainly the look of the page is similar, but the physical circumstance of writing must be factored in as well.

14. Ezra Pound quotes Chaucer's lines in his imagist manifesto "A Retrospect," 10.

15. Ben Friedlander was the instigator of this second round of the "Plan for the Curriculum of the Soul," which was to feature, among other topics, Andrew Schelling on "Walking," Gail Sher on "cf. Weyl" and Friedlander on "The Dogmatic Order of Experience." In the original series the subject of "Dance" was chosen by Lewis MacAdams. Other pairings included Robert Duncan on "Dante" and Olson on "Pleistocene Man."

16. This is not to say that there weren't isolated examples of disability activism before the 1950s. See, for example, Longmore and Goldberger. See also Longmore and Umansky's *The New Disability History: American Perspectives,* which offers a number of essays on pre–cold war disability activism. My point in speaking of the silence of poets like Larry Eigner or Josephine Miles around disability is to contextualize the absence of a fully developed social movement around disability rights until the early 1970s.

CHAPTER 6

Parts of this chapter were presented at the "Blind at the Museum" Conference, March 11 and 12, 2005, at the Berkeley Art Museum. The conference was organized by Georgina Kleege, Cathy Kudlick, Susan Schweik, and Katherine Sherwood. I am grateful to them for organizing this event.

1. Included in this category would be "Shooting Blind: Photographs by the Visually Impaired" at the New York Museum of Natural History (2000); "Seeing without Eyes" at the Palo Alto Cultural Center (May 5–June 6, 1991); "Blind at the Museum" at the Berkeley Art Museum (March 11–June 24, 2005); "Art beyond Sight: Multi-modal Approaches to Learning" at the Metropolitan Museum in New York (October 14–15, 2005).

2. Carrie Sandahl has analyzed the implications of race, disability and visibility as they challenge post-identity politics in "Black Man, Blind Man: Disability Identity Politics and Performance."

3. This representation was circulated by members of the Moral Majority, who used such images to read AIDS as God's anathema against gay lifestyles. But the image of wasting men with AIDS appeared, as well, in a Benetton ad as well as in the photographs of Nicholas Nixon. For a critical account of such representations, see Crimp.

4. The Zone Zero website, from which this quotation and others are taken, is an excellent introduction to Bavcar's work and contains a wide range of photographic examples. Most of the images I discuss in this chapter can be seen in the exhibit. Benjamin Mayer-Foulkes has curated the website and provides an excellent introduction to Bavcar.

5. These swallow photographs can be seen in Bavcar's memoir, *Le voyeur absolu.*

6. This series of Parisian photographs was made while Bavcar was the official photographer of the City of Light's Photography Month in 1988.

7. This detail is recounted in Benjamin Mayer-Foulkes's essay that is part of the "Mirror of Dreams" website.

8. Another artist whose blindness was caused by CMV is John Dugdale, whose photographs have been exhibited extensively and who has written several books along with being active in the Archive Project, which collects the work of artists with HIV/AIDS.

9. On *Blue*'s relationship to representations of AIDS see Lawrence.

10. The text of *Blue* is contained, in its entirety, in the chapter, "Of Being Blue," of Jarman's 1994 book, *Chroma*. Thus we could regard the film as an extension of the director's color theory or as an application of color theory directly to social protest.

11. In writing this chapter, I have benefited from the help of Georgina Kleege, Signe Mayfield, Ryan Knighton, Simi Linton, Susan Schweik. A special note of thanks is extended to Norma Cole who first introduced me to the work of Evgen Bavcar.

CHAPTER 7

1. A word about nomenclature. The term *globalization* has both a limited and more general meaning. The limited and more recent usage refers to neoliberal economic policies of the World Bank and the International Monetary Fund in confronting debt relief and creating new trade relations. In this usage, globalization refers to forms of spatial interconnection made possible through networks of capitalist accumulation, post-Fordist production, and economic restructuring. What we might call "cultural globalization" refers to more general social and cultural amalgamations linked to changes in media, commodities, and national borders. This latter definition includes the integration of information, the global traffic in ideas and products. The two definitions are obviously related, but I will be focusing largely on the first, more narrow definition.

2. Anita Ghai notes that "globalisation has constructed a world that offers open-ended possibilities and new life patterns, like access to information and technology. However the paradox is that its emphasis on power and profit has systematically dislodged vulnerable groups from access to even basic resources such as food and livelihood" (26).

3. On recolonization through economics, see Khor.

4. Lisa Lowe notes that failure to achieve modernization often marked the "backwardness" of a culture or civilization and could be found in anthropological ideas of "the primitive" and the "native" as the result of a 'lack' in the given culture" (10). The same anthropological language was used to justify the genocide of persons who were mentally or physically impaired during the Nazi genocide.

5. Cf. Bourgault 261.

6. Cf. Charlton 5. See also Levi Strauss.

7. On silicosis and the Great Depression see Markowitz and Rosner.

8. Johan Galtung distinguishes between "personal or direct" violence and "structural or indirect" violence. In the latter case, "[There] may not be any person who directly harms another person in the structure. The violence is built into the structure and shows up as unequal power and consequently as unequal life chances" (171). See also Kim et al. 102–4; and Farmer 29–50.

9. This ad appeared in *Scientific American*, July 1974, 9. I am grateful to Peter Middleton for alerting me to its appearance. This is not the first time Union Carbide caused a massive environmental disaster. In the 1930s, while building a hydroelectric dam near Gauley Junction, West Virginia, miners were exposed to large amounts of silica through unsafe mining practices (the tunnel was not ventilated, and miners were not required to wear masks). Many miners contracted silicosis and died. The miners sued Union Carbide, but the small settlement they received was absorbed by court and lawyer's fees. The event resulted in a congressional subcommittee hearing on the case. Muriel Rukeyser makes the Gauley Junction disaster the subject of her 1938 poem, "Book of the Dead."

10. Davis discusses the importance of class in disability elsewhere in his essay "Nation, Class, and Physical Minorities" (28–29) and more extensively in *Enforcing Normalcy* (85–89).

11. For discussions of global disability from a social science perspective see Holzer, Vreede, and Weight; Ingstad and Whyte; Priestley.

12. Considerations of genetics in chronic illness make locating a disease in an individual difficult. Keith Wailoo points out that sickle-cell disease, prevalent in persons of African heritage, may have evolved by "its value in fighting malaria on the African continent" and that it may have begun "as a beneficial evolutionary protection against malaria" (*Dying* 6). People with the trait who showed no symptoms ("heterozygotes" or "carriers") seemed immune to malaria, yet when this trait was passed on to their children from two carriers, the sickle-cell anemia appeared. On the "space" of disease, see Wailoo, "Inventing the Heterozygote." See also essays in Rosenberg and Golden.

13. In *The Cultural Locations of Disability*, Sharon Snyder and David Mitchell provide an in-depth study of charity systems, eugenics-era institutions for the feebleminded, documentary films about disability, and other spaces. They point out that despite the avowed aims of such institutions to rehabilitate and educate, "these locations exist largely at odds with the collective and individual well-being of disabled people" (4).

14. A 1995 case study on maquiladoras and health reveals that the labor-intensive nature of assembly processes has created a number of physical hazards, including repetitive motion problems, exposure to solvents, acids, metals. Increases in neurotoxicity, musculoskeletal disorders, dermatides, cancer, and renal and hepatic toxicity have also been noticed, especially among workers who have moved from rural areas where workers lack both education and proper technical training. See Frumkin, Hernandez-Avila, and Torres. See also Brenner et al.

15. On the rise in type 2 diabetes in New York City, see Kleinfield.

16. Donald Moore, email correspondence, December 12, 2003.

17. While the attack on the medicalized version of disability in favor of a social constructionist stance is an important development in disability studies, it tends to dismiss the significance of medical science and health for individuals who

lack access to it. We may decry the reliance in psychiatry on antidepressant drugs, but these medicines allow many individuals previously institutionalized for bipolar disorder to function. We worry, rightly enough, at the ethical implications of the Human Genome Project on a new eugenics movement, but for persons with genetically transmitted diseases such as hemophilia and sickle-cell anemia, the possibility of genetic intervention may be lifesaving. In a global context, the social constructionist view of disability needs to be tested against the realities of inadequate sanitation, health care, and social infrastructure. Joseph Priestly points out that while activists in the United Kingdom are criticizing the principle of charitable support from the National Lottery, "disabled people in Thailand are protesting to maintain employment of disabled lottery sellers" (4). I am not arguing for a return to a medical or rehabilitation definition of disability but for a more nuanced approach that considers the disabling process in terms of individual impairments and medical regimes.

18. Narrative prosthesis would seem to be a key trope for many postcolonial texts where a disabled figure provides an analogy for divisions and ruptures within new national formations. A short list of texts would include the following: John Coetze's *Waiting for the Barbarians* features a woman who has been blinded and crippled through political torture within a colonial setting; Jose Saramago's *Blindness* is set in a city in which everyone suddenly becomes blind; in Bapsi Sidhwa's *Cracking India*'s the girl narrator's crippled condition seems to stand for partitioned India; Edwidge Danticat's "Carolyn's Wedding" is a tale about Haitian immigrants in New York whose divided condition is represented through the eponymous heroine's missing left forearm; the Egyptian novelist Naguib Mahfouz's *Midaq Alley* features a character who "creates" cripples who then make their living by begging; the main character of Cherrie Moraga's play *Heroes and Saints*, Cerezita, is a young woman whose body has been destroyed in utero by her mother's exposure to pesticides while working in California agribusiness fields.

19. In Fernando Meirelles's film *The Constant Gardener* (2005), one can see such a play being performed in the background of a health clinic where medicines are being dispensed. The film's heroine, Tessa Quayle (Rachel Weisz), has come to the open-air clinic to see if doctors are forcing villagers to take a dangerous tuberculosis drug, Dypraxa, as a condition for their receiving antiretroviral drugs. As Tessa wanders though the chaotic scene, an AIDS education play is being performed in one corner of the marketplace.

20. In contrast, Cuba initiated an HIV screening program early, once it was suspected that HIV was blood borne. According to Paul Farmer (70), in 1983 Cuba "banned the importation of factor VIII and other hemo-derivatives, and the Ministry of Public Health ordered the destruction of twenty thousand units of blood product." These actions have resulted in Cuba's having one of the lowest incidence of HIV infection in the Western Hemisphere.

21. For useful surveys of DALY's see Groce, Chamie, and Me; and Wasserman, Bickenbach, and Wachbroit.

22. Mantha Diawara calls the 1994 devaluation "the most serious economic and cultural crisis in Franco-African relations since the 1960s when most African countries assumed their independence from France" (65).

23. This is the most uncanny scene in the film since it flies in the face of al-

most every expectation of what Sili's fate would ordinarily be when confronted by repressive police authority. I see this scene as directly commenting on those expectations by providing a conclusion so improbable that it forces the viewer to imagine a different form of power and a different resolution. At the same time, the police arrest and incarceration of the "crazy woman" is observed by everyone in the marketplace, all of whom laugh and point without showing the least concern for her fate. This would appear to be Mambety's critique of a certain complicity between the community and the police that contrasts with Sili's acts of solidarity and resistance.

24. On the cultural function of West African markets, see Diawara 73–80.

25. Manthia Diawara explains that following devaluation, France's prime minister, Edouard Balladur, reassured Francophone countries that "devaluation was not a bad thing; its aim was to bring Africa back into the world economy, and it had done that. Francophone Africa was now exporting more goods to Europe, America, and Asia; the lowered cost of the currency had the potential to attract investors and to create jobs in Africa" (69). Such Afro-boosterism is satirized by Mambety in *Le franc* when the short-statured lottery seller and congolum player who has just won the lottery get together and make a point of "eating African."

26. Mambety figures social death in terms of a parable of hyenas and elephants. "You know the Hyena is a terrible animal. He is able to follow a lion, a sick lion during all seasons. And during the lion's last days it comes down and jumps on him and eats him, eats the lion peacefully. That is the World Bank. They know we are sick and poor and we have some dignity. But they can wait" ("Interview"). In *La petite vendeuse*, Sili Laam is like the lion, fierce in her determination, and although weakened by polio, refuses to lie down. Rather, she asserts herself and, most important, forms alliances. The marauding gangs of news vendors who menace her—the hyenas in Mambety's parable—are not the World Bank, but they represent what happens to a collective enterprise in such a world (Mambety, "Interview").

27. The doctor himself wears a kind of burka himself in the form of an artificial beard that he must, according to Islamic law, wear, despite the fact that he is unable to grow facial hair.

28. For an excellent survey of development and disability in Afghanistan in the recent period, see Coleridge.

29. See, for example, Irwin, Millen, and Fallows 5.

30. Significantly, TAC has shifted the focus from prevention to treatment, a shift that has implications for disability studies insofar as the politics of AIDS can now directed *both* at those who already test positive for HIV as well as at those are who vulnerable to infection.

31. On Theater for Development, see Banham, Gibbs, and Osofisan; Gunner; and Bourgault.

32. Perhaps the most famous crossover between popular entertainment and AIDS awareness can be found in the fame of Congolese singer Franco's (L'Okanga Landju Pene Luambo Makiadi) last song, "Attention Na Sida" ("Beware of AIDS"), which reached a worldwide audience when it was released in 1987. It is available on a Rough Guide anthology of Franco's music.

33. "Yiriba" is discussed in Bourgault 132–38. A CD-ROM accompanies the book that includes clips of plays, dances, songs, and "edutainment" performances.

34. Louise Bourgault explains that "Foot," or "Anything Goes," pharmacy refers to drugs, often expired, "that are readily available in the markets, taxi stands, and long distance trucks and bus stations in many parts of Africa." These drugs are often called "Foot Pharmacy" because they are carried on the head of the vendor "who ambles about the stations" (135).

35. On the accusation of narcissism against persons with disabilities, see Siebers, "Tender Organs."

CHAPTER 8

1. In this essay I refer to two versions of Schepher-Hughes's work on organ sales; they have similar titles ("End of the Body: The Global Traffic in Organs for Transplant Surgery" and "Ends of the Body: Commodity Fetishism and the Global Traffic in Organs") but include different areas of research.

2. On rumor and organ trafficking see Scheper-Hughes, "Theft of Life" 3–11; and Castaneda.

3. Not only does his longevity enhance his power as an Indian politician; he becomes famous for having multiple foreign body parts. In contrast to Western leaders who would be regarded as "weakened" by so many operations, the transplanted man makes capital out of his uniqueness as a kind of political cyborg.

4. I have discussed some of these issues in chapter 7.

5. Slavoj Žižek has already inverted Deleuze and Guattari's phrase to different ends in his book *Organs without Bodies*. He is not thinking organ trafficking in the global sphere but, rather, of pornography, in which "the entire human body, inclusive of the head, is nothing but a combination of such partial organs—the head itself is reduced to just another partial organ of *jouissance*" (172). The combination of pornography and organ trafficking comes together in Silko's *Almanac of the Dead*.

6. In the short space of time since transplant surgery has been practiced, demand for organs has increased. According to a *New York Times* article, "In 2005 more than 16,000 kidney transplants were performed in the United States, an increase of 45 percent over 10 years. But during that time, the number of people on a kidney waiting list rose by 119 percent. More than 3,500 people now die each year waiting for a kidney transplant" (Dubner 20). Nancy Scheper-Hughes points out that the rising demand for organs and the threat of "organ scarcity" are artificially constructed, "invented by transplant technicians and dangled before the eyes of an ever expanding sick, aging, and dying population" ("End" 4).

7. "Presumed consent" is the policy in a number of countries (Spain, Austria, Germany, Brazil, among others) by which the state is given authority to dispense with bodies, organs, and tissues in the case of death. In Brazil, according to Scheper-Hughes, one hears disparaging references to "the state's body" as that which comes from an anonymous dead body rather than from a living relative or friend ("End" 15).

8. On varying definitions of brain death, see Sharp 59.

9. Most texts on organ transplantation refer to the one whose kidney is removed as the *donor*, but this only applies to those cases where there is no financial transaction. I have chosen to refer to *seller* when speaking of strictly commercial contexts of organ transplantation and *donor* when referring to nonremunerated organ transfer.

10. Lawrence Cohen discusses the "impoverishment" of the flesh when sellers have no access to postoperation hospital care and who rely on strenuous physical labor for their livelihoods ("Other Kidney" 6).

11. Davis develops this idea in *Bending Over Backwards*.

12. *Harvest* won the prestigious Onassis Prize for Theatre in 1997. The play had its U.S. premier at La MaMa E.T.C. in New York in February 2006.

13. On "mediascapes" and "technoscapes" see Appadurai 33.

14. The schematic, sci-fi nature of Padmanabhan's characters may derive from her earlier career as a cartoonist with a daily comic strip in a Delhi newspaper.

15. Silko discusses the web as a model for Pueblo storytelling in "Notes on *Almanac of the Dead*," which appears in *Yellow Woman and a Beauty of the Spirit*.

16. Roy's partner, Clinton, is also a Vietnam vet who has lost one foot during the war. He mounts a severe critique of Deep Ecology and its attacks on overpopulation, which, to Clinton, seems like another form of genocide in the name of health: "Human beings had been exterminated strictly for 'health' purposes by Europeans too often" (415). As a black, disabled person himself, he remembers the linkage of race and disability in various forms of cultural genocide throughout history.

17. One of the most brilliant realizations of this disjunction occurs in Ridley Scott's *Blade Runner* in a scene in which the replicant Pris meets the genetic engineer, Sebastian, who has designed her. Sebastian asks her to "do something" to show her genetic superiority, and she proceeds to quote Descartes: "I think therefore I am." If, as Descartes thought, thinking constitutes being, the replicant may, by her ability to quote from the very heart of Enlightenment rationality, indeed be superior to the human.

AFTERWORD

1. On the "great divide," see Huyssen 3–15.

2. Chieko's nakedness is a kind of silent speech act demanding a response that cannot be reciprocated, either from the electronic phantasmagoria of Tokyo or from her alienated father. Her signing adds one more language to the globalized Babel of tongues in the film, and although the film makes deafness a sign of miscommunication, Iñárritu does show sign language's importance to a community that can cut across the literally "deafening" soundscape. Moreover she and her deaf girlfriends maintain active contact through the digital technology of videophones that permit them to stay in touch in ways that have been heretofore impossible.

3. I am grateful to Lisa Lowe for sharing her thoughts on *Babel* with me.

Works Cited

Agamben, Giorgio. *Homer Sacer: Sovereign Power and Bare Life.* Trans. Daniel Heller-Roazan. Stanford: Stanford University Press, 1998.

"AIDS Suit Accuses Companies of Selling Bad Blood Products." *New York Times,* October 4, 1993, A18.

Aiello, A. Philip, and Myrna Aiello. "Cochlear Implants and Deaf Identity." *Deaf World: A Historical Reader and Primary Sourcebook.* Ed. Lois Bragg. New York: New York University Press, 2001. 406–12.

Antin, David. "whos listening out there." *Tuning.* New York: New Directions, 1984. 269–96.

Appadurai, Arjun. *Modernity at Large: Cultural Dimensions of Globalization.* Minneapolis: University of Minnesota Press, 1996.

Atwood, Margaret. *Oryx and Crake.* New York: Doubleday, 2003.

Banham, Martin, James Gibbs, and Femi Osofisan, eds. *African Theatre in Development.* Bloomington: Indiana University Press, 1999.

Barnes, Colin, and Geoff Mercer. *Disability.* Cambridge: Polity, 2003.

Bauman, H. Dirksen. "Toward a Poetics of Vision, Space, and the Body: Sign Language and Literary Theory." *The Disability Studies Reader.* Ed. Lennard J. Davis. New York: Routledge, 1997. 315–31.

Bauman, H. Dirksen, Jennifer L. Nelson, and Heidi Rose, eds. *Signing the Body Poetic: Essays on American Sign Language Literature.* Berkeley and Los Angeles: University of California Press, 2006.

Bavcar, Evgen. "Images of Elsewhere." Introduction to *Enlightened Visions* Exhibition Catalogue. TCDD Sanat Galerisi, Gar, Ankara, September–October, 1992.

Bavcar, Evgen. "Mirror of Dreams." http://www.zonezero.com/exposiciones/fotografos/bavcar/bavcar36.html, consulted August 1, 2007.

Bavcar, Evgen. *Le voyeur absolu.* Paris: Seuil, 1992.

Baynton, Douglas C. *Forbidden Signs: American Culture and the Campaign against Sign Language.* Chicago: University of Chicago Press, 1996.

Beckett, Samuel. *Happy Days.* New York: Grove Press, 1961.

Belgrad, Daniel. *The Culture of Spontaneity: Improvisation and the Arts in Postwar America.* Chicago: University of Chicago Press, 1998.

Benjamin, Walter. "Paris, Capital of the Nineteenth Century." *Reflections: Essays,*

Aphorisms, Autobiographical Writings. Trans. Edmund Jephcott. New York: Schocken, 1978.

Berger, Jan. "Uncommon Schools." *Foucault and the Government of Disability*. Ed. Shelley Tremain. Ann Arbor: University of Michigan Press, 2005. 153–71.

Berlant, Lauren. *The Anatomy of National Fantasy: Hawthorne, Utopia, and Everyday Life*. Chicago: University of Chicago Press, 1991.

Berlant, Lauren, and Elizabeth Freeman. "Queer Nationality." *Fear of a Queer Planet: Queer Politics and Social Theory*. Ed. Michael Warner. Minneapolis: University of Minnesota Press, 1993. 193–229.

Berubé, Michael. "Citizenship and Disability." *Dissent* 50.2 (2003): 52–57.

Berubé, Michael. "I Should Live So Long." *Disability Studies: Enabling the Humanities*. Ed. Sharon L. Snyder, Brenda Jo Brueggemann, and Rosemarie Garland-Thomson. New York: Modern Language Association, 2002. 337–43.

Berubé, Michael. *Life as We Know It: A Father, a Family, and an Exceptional Child*. New York: Random House, 1996.

Bogdanich, Walt, and Eric Koli. "2 Paths of Bayer Drug in 80's: Riskier Type Went Overseas." *New York Times*, May 22, 2003, C5.

Bourgault, Louise. *Playing for Life: Performance in Africa in the Age of AIDS*. Durham: Carolina Academic Press, 2003.

Bradstreet, Anne. "The Author to Her Book." *The Norton Anthology of Poetry*. 5th ed. Ed. Margaret Ferguson et al. New York: Norton, 2005. 465.

Bragg, Lois. *Deaf World: A Historical Reader and Primary Sourcebook*. New York: New York University Press, 2001.

Brenner, Joel, Jennifer Ross, Janie Simmons, and Sarah Zaidi. "Neoliberal Trade and Investment and the Health of *Maquiladora* Workers on the U.S.-Mexico Border." *Dying for Growth: Global Inequality and the Health of the Poor*. Ed. Jim Young Kim et al. Monroe, Maine: Common Courage Press, 2000. 261–90.

Breslauer, Jan. "Your World, His View." *Los Angeles Times*, May 27, 2001, Calendar 1.

Brown, Wendy. *States of Injury: Power and Freedom in Late Modernity*. Princeton: Princeton University Press, 1995.

Brueggemann, Brenda Jo. *Lend Me Your Ear: Rhetorical Constructions of Deafness*. Washington, DC: Gallaudet University Press, 1999.

Burbick, Joan. *Healing the Republic: The Language of Health and the Culture of Nationalism in Nineteenth-Century America*. Cambridge: Cambridge University Press, 1994.

Burch, Susan. *Signs of Resistance: American Deaf Cultural History, 1900 to World War II*. New York: New York University Press, 2002.

Butler, Judith. *Bodies That Matter: On the Discursive Limits of "Sex."* New York: Routledge, 1993.

Butler, Judith. *Precarious Life: The Powers of Mourning and Violence*. London: Verso, 2004.

Campbell, Jane, and Mike Oliver. *Disability Politics: Understanding Our Past, Changing Our Future*. London: Routledge, 1996.

Carlson, Licia. "Docile Bodies, Docile Minds: Foucauldian Reflections on Mental Retardation." *Foucault and the Government of Disability*. Ed. Shelley Tremain. Ann Arbor: University of Michigan Press, 2005. 133–52.

Castaneda, Claudia. *Figurations: Child, Bodies, Worlds.* Durham, NC: Duke University Press, 2002.

Castronovo, Russ. *Fathering the Nation: American Genealogies of Slavery and Freedom.* Berkeley and Los Angeles: University of California Press, 1995.

Central Station (Central do Brasil). Dir. Walter Salles. France and Brazil: Sony Pictures, 1998.

Charlton, James I. "The Disability Rights Movement as a Counter-hegemonic Popular Social Movement." Unpublished manuscript.

Charlton, James I. *Nothing about Us without Us: Disability, Oppression, and Empowerment.* Berkeley and Los Angeles: University of California Press, 1998.

Children of a Lesser God. Dir. Randa Haines. Los Angeles: Paramount Pictures, 1986.

Christiansen, John B., and Sharon N. Barnartt. *Deaf President Now! The 1988 Revolution at Gallaudet University.* Washington, DC: Gallaudet University Press, 1995.

Clifford, James. *Routes: Travel and Translation in the Late Twentieth Century.* Cambridge: Harvard University Press, 1997.

Cohen, Cathy J. "Punks, Bulldaggers, and Welfare Queens: The Radical Potential of Queer Politics?" *GLQ* 3 (1997): 437–65.

Cohen, Lawrence. "The Other Kidney: Biopolitics beyond Recognition." *Commodifying Bodies.* Ed. Nancy Scheper-Hughes and Loïc Wacquant. London: Sage, 2004. 9–29.

Cohen, Lawrence. "Where It Hurts: Indian Material for an Ethics of Organ Transplantation." *Daedalus* 128.4 (1999): 135–65.

Cohn, Jim. *The Golden Body: Meditations on the Essence of Disability.* Boulder, CO: Museum of American Poetics Publications, 2003.

Cohn, Jim. *Sign Mind: Studies in American Sign Language Poetics.* Boulder, CO: Museum of American Poetics Publications, 1999.

Coma. Dir. Michael Crichton. Los Angeles: Metro-Goldwyn-Meyer, 1978.

Coleridge, Peter. "Development, Cultural Values and Disability: The Example of Afghanistan." http://www.eenet.org.uk/key_issues/cultural/coleridge1.shtml, consulted 3/23/2004.

Cook, Pam. "Duplicity in *Mildred Pierce.*" *Women in Film Noir.* 2nd ed. Ed. E. Ann Kaplan. London: British Film Institute, 1999. 69–80.

Corber, Robert J. *Homosexuality in Cold War America: Resistance and the Crisis of Masculinity* Durham, NC: Duke University Press, 1997.

Crane, Hart. *The Bridge. The Complete Poems and Selected Letters and Prose.* Ed. Brom Weber. New York: Liveright, 1966.

Creeley, Robert. *The Collected Poems of Robert Creeley, 1945–1975.* Berkeley and Los Angeles: University of California Press, 1982.

Crimp, Douglas. *AIDS: Cultural Analysis, Cultural Activism.* Cambridge: MIT Press, 1991.

Crimp, Douglas. "Portraits of People with AIDS." *Cultural Studies.* Ed. Lawrence Grossberg, Cary Nelson, and Paula Treichler. New York: Routledge, 1992. 117–33.

Davidson, Michael. *Guys Like Us: Citing Masculinity in Cold War Poetics.* Chicago: University of Chicago Press, 2004.

Davidson, Michael. "Hearing Things: The Scandal of Speech in Deaf Performance." *Disability Studies: Enabling the Humanities.* Ed. Sharon Snyder, Brenda Jo Brueggemann, and Rosemarie Garland-Thomson. New York: Modern Language Association, 2002. 76–87.

Davidson, Michael. "Universal Design: The Work of Disability in an Age of Globalization." *The Disability Studies Reader.* 2nd ed. Ed. Lennard J. Davis. New York: Routledge, 2006.

Davis, Lennard. *Bending Over Backwards: Disability, Dismodernism, and Other Difficult Positions.* New York: New York University Press, 2002.

Davis, Lennard. "Deafness and Identity in the Postmodern World." *Chronicle of Higher Education,* January 12, 2007, B6–B8.

Davis, Lennard. *Enforcing Normalcy: Disability, Deafness, and the Body.* New York: Verso, 1995.

Davis, Lennard. *My Sense of Silence: Memoirs of a Childhood with Deafness.* Urbana: University of Illinois Press, 2000.

Davis, Lennard. "Nation, Class, and Physical Minorities." *Beyond the Binary: Reconstructing Cultural Identity in a Multicultural Context.* Ed. Timothy B. Powell. New Brunswick, NJ: Rutgers University Press, 1999. 17–38.

Davis, Lennard. "Nude Venuses, Medusa's Body, and Phantom Limbs: Disability and Visuality." *The Body and Physical Difference: Discourses of Disability.* Ed. David T. Mitchell and Sharon L. Snyder. Ann Arbor: University of Michigan Press, 1997. 51–70.

Davis, Lennard. "Why Disability Studies Matters." *Inside Higher Education,* February 21, 2005. http://www.insidehighered.com/views/why_disability_studies_matters, consulted August 1, 2007.

Davis, Lennard. "Why *Million Dollar Baby* Infuriates the Disabled." *Chicago Tribune,* February 2, 2005. http://www.chicagotribune.com/services/site/premium/access_registered.intercept.

de Lauretis, Teresa. *Alice Doesn't: Feminism, Semiotics, Cinema.* Bloomington: Indiana University Press, 1984.

DeLay, Tom. "It Is More Than Just Terri Schiavo." *Time,* March 23, 2005. Http://www.time.com/time/nation/article/0,8599,1040968,00.html.

Deleuze, Gilles, and Felix Guattari. *A Thousand Plateaus: Capitalism and Schizophrenia.* Trans. Brian Massumi. Minneapolis: University of Minnesota Press, 1987.

Denby, David. "Battle Fatigue: 'Flags of Our Fathers' and 'Babel.'" *New Yorker: Printables.* http://www.newyorker.com/printables/critics/061030crci_cinema, consulted August 1, 2007.

D'Emilio, John. "Capitalism and Gay Identity." *The Lesbian and Gay Studies Reader.* Ed. Henry Abelove et al. New York: Routledge, 1993. 467–76.

Derrida, Jacques. "Différance." *Margins of Philosophy.* Trans. Alan Bass. Chicago: University of Chicago Press, 1982.

Derrida, Jacques. *Memoirs of the Blind: The Self-Portrait and Other Ruins.* Trans. Pascale-Anne Brault and Michael Naas. Chicago: University of Chicago Press, 1993.

Derrida, Jacques. *Of Grammatology.* Trans. Gayatri Chakravorty Spivak. Baltimore: Johns Hopkins University Press, 1976.

Diawara, Manthia. "Toward a Regional Imaginary in Africa." *World Bank Literature.* Ed. Amitava Kumar. Minneapolis: University of Minnesota Press, 2003. 64–81.

Didion, Joan. "The Case of Theresa Schiavo." *New York Review of Books,* June 9, 2005, 60–69.

Dirty Pretty Things. Dir. Stephen Frears. London: Miramax and BBC Films, 2003.

Dmytryk, Edward. *It's a Hell of a Life but Not a Bad Living.* New York: Times Books, 1978.

The Donahue Show. October 1, 1993. Multimedia Entertainment.

Double Indemnity. Dir. Billy Wilder. Los Angeles: Paramount Pictures, 1944.

Dubner, Stephen J. "Flesh Trade: Why Not Let People Sell Their Organs?" *New York Times Magazine,* July 9, 2006, 20–21.

Duncan, Robert. *The Opening of the Field.* New York: New Directions, 1960.

Dunning, Jennifer. "Bodies, Imperfect but Still Moving." *New York Times,* March 10, 2002, Arts, 8.

Dyer, Richard. "Homosexuality and Film Noir." *The Matter of Images: Essays on Representations.* New York: Routledge, 1993.

Eagleton, Terry. *The Ideology of the Aesthetic.* London: Blackwell, 1990.

Eigner, Larry. *air the trees.* Los Angeles: Black Sparrow Press, 1968.

Eigner, Larry. *areas lights heights.* New York: Roof, 1989.

Eigner, Larry. *readiness enough depends on.* Ed. Robert Grenier. Copenhagen: Green Integer, 2000.

Eigner, Larry. "Dance." Unpublished MS.

Eigner, Larry. *Selected Poems.* Ed. Samuel Charters and Andrea Wyatt. Berkeley: Oyez, 1972.

Eigner, Larry. *Things Stirring Together or Far Away.* Los Angeles: Black Sparrow Press, 1974.

Edel, Theodore. *Piano Music for One Hand.* Bloomington: Indiana University Press, 1994.

Epstein, Steven. *Impure Science: AIDS, Activism, and the Politics of Knowledge.* Berkeley and Los Angeles: University of California Press, 1996.

Erevelles, Nirmala. "Disability in the New World Order: The Political Economy of World Bank Intervention in (Post/Neo)colonial Context." Unpublished manuscript.

Farmer, Paul. *Pathologies of Power: Health, Human Rights, and the New War on the Poor.* Berkeley and Los Angeles: University of California Press, 2003.

Franco. *The Rough Guide to Franco.* London: World Music Network, 2001.

Fraser, Nancy Fraser. *Justice Interruptus: Critical Reflections on the "Postsocialist" Condition* New York: Routledge, 1997.

Faulkner, William. *Absalom, Absalom!* New York: Vintage, 1986.

Feldman, Douglas A. *Culture and AIDS.* New York: Praeger, 1990.

Fenollosa, Ernest. *The Chinese Written Character as a Medium for Poetry.* Ed. Ezra Pound. San Francisco: City Lights Books, 1936.

Fleischer, Doris Zames, and Frieda Zames. *The Disability Rights Movement: From Charity to Confrontation.* Philadelphia: Temple University Press, 2001.

Flying Words Project. *The Can't Touch Tours: Current Works (1990–2003).* N.p., n.d.

Foucault, Michel. *The Birth of the Clinic: An Archaeology of Medical Perception.* Trans. A. M. Sheridan Smith. New York: Random House, 1973.

Foucault, Michel. *The History of Sexuality.* Vol. 1, *An Introduction.* Trans. Robert Hurley. New York: Vintage, 1980.

Foucault, Michel. *Technologies of the Self: A Seminar with Michel Foucault.* Ed. Luther H. Martin, Huck Gutman, and Patrick H. Hutton. Amherst: University of Massachusetts Press, 1988.

Frank, Joseph. *The Widening Gyre: Crisis and Mastery in Modern Literature.* Bloomington: Indiana University Press, 1963.

Friedlander, Benjamin. "Larry Eigner, 1926–1996." *Dictionary of Literary Biography.* Vol. 193, *American Poets since World War II.* Ed. Joseph Conte. Detroit: Gale Research, 1998. 114–27.

Fries, Kenny, ed. *Staring Back: The Disability Experience from the Inside Out.* New York: Penguin, 1997.

Frumkin, Howard, Mauricio Hernandez-Avila, and Felipe Espinsoa Torres. "Maquiladoras: A Case Study of Free Trade Zones." *Occupational and Environmental Health* 1.2 (1995): 96–109.

Galloway, Terry. *Annie Dearest.* Tallahassee: Faust Films / Diane Wilkins Productions, n.d.

Galloway, Terry. "Making a Claim on the Empty Space: An Interview with Terry Galloway." *Theatre InSight* 18 (Fall 1997–Spring 1998): 50–54.

Galloway, Terry. "Tough." Lecture delivered at the Gay Shame Conference, University of Michigan, 2003.

Galtung, Johan. "Violence, Peace and Peace Research." *Journal of Peace Research* 3 (1969): 167–91.

Gates, Henry Louis Jr. *The Signifying Monkey: A Theory of African-American Literary Criticism.* New York: Oxford University Press, 1988.

Ghai, Anita. "Marginalisation and Disability: Experiences from the Third World. *Disability and the Life Course: Global Perspectives.* Ed. Mark Priestly. Cambridge: Cambridge University Press, 2001. 26–37.

Gilman, Sander L. "AIDS and Syphilis: The Iconography of Disease." *AIDS: Cultural Analysis, Cultural Activism.* Ed. Douglas Crimp. Cambridge: MIT Press, 1991. 87–107.

Ginsberg, Allen. *Collected Poems, 1947–1980.* New York: Harper and Row, 1984.

Goffman, Erving. *Stigma: Notes on the Management of Spoiled Identity.* Englewood Cliffs, NJ: Prentice-Hall, 1963.

Gorman, Warren. *Body Image and the Image of the Brain.* St. Louis: Warren H. Green, 1969.

Gould, Tony. *A Summer Plague: Polio and Its Survivors.* New Haven: Yale University Press, 1995.

Graybill, Patrick. "Paradox." *Poetry in Motion: Patrick Graybill.* Sign Media, 1989.

Grenier, Robert. "Afterword." *readiness enough depends on,* by Larry Eigner. Los Angeles: Green Integer, 2000.

Grigely, Joseph. *Conversation Pieces.* Tokyo: Center for Contemporary Art, 1998.

Grigely, Joseph. *Deaf & Dumb: A Tale.* New York: White Columns, 1994.

Grigely, Joseph. "Postcards to Sophie Calle." *Points of Contact: Disability, Art, and*

Culture. Ed. Susan Crutchfield and Marcy Epstein. Ann Arbor: University of Michigan Press, 2000. 31–58.

Grigely, Joseph. *Textualterity: Art, Theory, and Textual Criticism.* Ann Arbor: University of Michigan Press, 1995.

Groce, Nora Ellen, Mary Chamie, and Angela Me. "Measuring the Quality of Life: Rethinking the World Bank's Disability Adjusted Life Years." *Disability World* 3 (June–July 2000). http://www.disabilityworld.org.

Grosz, Elizabeth. *Volatile Bodies: Toward a Corporeal Feminism.* Bloomington: Indiana University Press, 1994.

Gunner, Liz. *Politics and Performance: Theatre, Poetry, and Song in Southern Africa.* Johannesburg: Witwatersrand University Press, 2001.

Hacking, Ian. *The Social Construction of What?* Cambridge: Harvard University Press, 1999.

Halberstam, Judith. *Skin Shows: Gothic Horror and the Technology of Monsters.* Durham, NC: Duke University Press, 1995.

Halberstam, Judith, and Ira Livingston, eds. *Posthuman Bodies.* Bloomington: Indiana University Press, 1995.

Harraway, Donna J. *Simians, Cyborgs, and Women: The Reinvention of Nature.* New York: Routledge, 1991.

Hart, Gillian. *Disabling Globalization: Places of Power in Post-Apartheid South Africa.* Berkeley and Los Angeles: University of California Press, 2002.

Heidegger, Martin. *The Question concerning Technology and Other Essays.* Trans. William Lovitt. New York: Harper, 1977.

"Hemophiliacs Lead Fairly 'Normal' Lives." *Antioch, Ill. News Tribune,* July 1, 1993.

Hall, Stuart. "Cultural Studies and Its Theoretical Legacies." *The Cultural Studies Reader.* Ed. Simon During. London: Routledge, 1993. 97–109.

Hart, George. "Postmodern Nature / Poetry: The Example of Larry Eigner." *Reading under the Sign of Nature: New Essays in Ecocriticism.* Ed. John Tallmadge and Henry Harrington. Salt Lake City: University of Utah Press, 2000. 315–32.

Held, David, and Anthony McGrew, eds. *The Global Transformations Reader: An Introduction to the Globalization Debate.* Cambridge: Polity, 2000.

Hentoff, Nat. "Terri Schiavo: Judicial Murder." *Village Voice,* March 29, 2005. Http://villagevoice.com/generic/show_print?id=62489&page=hentoff&issue=05, consulted 8/17/2005.

Hershey, Laura. "Killed by Prejudice." *The Nation,* April 14, 2005. Http://www.thenation.com/docprint.mhtml?i=20050502&5=hershey1, consulted 8/18/2005.

Hockenberry, John. "And the Loser Is . . ." http://www.milliondollarbigot.org/loser.html, consulted 2/17/2005.

Hollinger, Karen. "The Look, Narrativity, and the Female Spectator in *Vertigo.*" *Journal of Film and Video* 39.4 (1987): 18–27.

Holzer, Brigitte, Arthur Vreede, and Gabriele Weight, eds. *Disability in Different Cultures: Reflections on Local Concepts.* New Brunswick, NJ: Transaction, 1999.

Homedes, Nuria. "The Disability-Adjusted Life Year (DALY) Definition, Measurement and Potential Use." Human Capital Development and Operations Pol-

icy Working Papers. www.worldbank.org/html/ extdr/hnp/hddflash/workp/
wp_00068.html, consulted 4/26/04.

Huyssen, Andreas. *After the Great Divide: Modernism, Mass Culture, Postmodernism*. Bloomington: Indiana University Press, 1986.

Ingstad, Benedicte, and Susan Reynolds Whyte, eds. *Disability and Culture*. Berkeley and Los Angeles: University of California Press, 1995.

Irwin, Alexander, Joyce Millen, and Dorothy Fallows, eds. *Global Aids: Myths and
Facts*. Cambridge, MA: South End Press, 2003.

The Island. Dir. Michael Bay. Los Angeles: Dreamworks, 2005.

Ishiguro, Kazuo. Interview with Karen Grigsby Bates, NPR, "Day to Day," May 4,
2005.

Ishiguro, Kazuo. *Never Let Me Go*. New York: Vintage, 2005.

Jacobs, Karen. *The Eye's Mind: Literary Modernism and Visual Culture*. Ithaca, NY:
Cornell University Press, 2001.

Jameson, Fredric, and Masao Miyoshi, eds. *The Cultures of Globalization*.
Durham, NC: Duke University Press, 1998.

Jarman, Derek. *Blue*. Woodstock, NY: Overlook Press, 1994.

Jarman, Derek. *Chroma: A Book of Color*. Woodstock, NY: Overlook Press, 1995.

Jay, Martin. *Downcast Eyes: The Denigration of Vision in Twentieth-Century French
Thought*. Berkeley and Los Angeles: University of California Press, 1993.

Jeffreys, Mark. "Dr. Daedalus and His Minotaur: Mythic Warnings about Genetic
Engineering from J.B.S. Haldane, Francois Jacob, and Andrew Niccol's *Gattaca*." *Journal of Medical Humanities* 22.2 (2001): 137–52.

Johnston, Claire. *"Double Indemnity." Women in Film Noir*. Ed. E. Ann Kaplan.
2nd ed. London: British Film Institute, 1999. 89–98.

Joyce, James. *Ulysses*. New York: Random House, 1986.

Kandahar. Dir. Mohsen Makhmalbaf. Iran and France: Makhmalbaf Film House
(Ira Films), 2001.

Kant, Immanuel. Extracts from "Analytic of Aesthetic Judgment" and "Dialectic of
Aesthetic Judgment." *The Contental Aesthetics Reader*. Ed. Clive Cazeaux.
London: Routledge, 2006. 16–34.

Kennan, George. "Moscow Embassy Telegram #511, Feb. 22, 1946." *Containment:
Documents on American Policy and Strategy, 1945–1950*. Ed. Thomas H. Etzold
and John Lewis Gaddis. New York: Columbia University Press, 1978. 50–63.

Kevles, Daniel J. *In the Name of Eugenics: Genetics and the Uses of Human Heredity*. New York: Alfred A. Knopf, 1985.

Khor, Martin. "Colonialism Redux: Reconquering the Third World with Protocols
Instead of Gunboats." *The Nation*, July 15–22, 1966, 18–20.

Kim, Jim Yong, Joyce Millen, John Gershman, and Alec Irwin, eds. *Dying for
Growth: Global Inequality and the Health of the Poor*. Monroe, Maine: Common Courage Press, 2000.

Kirp, David. "Look Back in Anger: Hemophilia, Rights, and AIDS." *Dissent* 44.3
(1997). 65–70.

Kiss Me Deadly. Dir. Robert Aldrich. Los Angeles: United Artists Corporation,
1955.

Kittay, Eva Feder. *Love's Labor: Essays on Women, Equality, and Dependency*. New
York: Routledge, 1999.

Kleege, Georgina. *Sight Unseen*. New Haven: Yale University Press, 1999.

Kleege, Georgina. "What We Talk about When We Talk about Art: Blind Access to the Visual Arts." Keynote address, "Blind at the Museum" conference, Berkeley Art Museum, March 11, 2005.

Klein, Yves. *Yves Klein: Long Live the Immaterial.* Ed. Gilbert Perlein and Bruno Cora. New York: Delano Greenidge Editions, n.d.

Kleinfield, N. R. "Diabetes and Its Awful Toll Quietly Emerge as a Crisis." *New York Times,* January 9, 2006, A1, A18–A19.

Koolhaus, Rem. *Delirious New York.* New York: Monacelli, 1994.

Kraut, Alan M. *Silent Travellers: Germs, Genes, and the "Immigrant Menace."* New York: Basic Books, 1994.

Krentz, Christopher. "The Camera as Printing Press: How Film Has Impacted ASL Literature." *Signing the Body Poetic: Essays on American Sign Language Literature.* Ed. Dirksen Bauman, Jennifer Nelson, and Heidi Rose. Berkeley and Los Angeles: University of California Press, 2006. 51–70.

Kruger, Loren, and Patrica Watson Shariff. " 'Shoo—This Book Makes Me to Think!': Education, Entertainment, and 'Life-Skills' Comics in South Africa." *Poetics Today* 22.2 (2001): 475–509.

Kumar, Amitava, ed. *World Bank Literature.* Minneapolis: University of Minnesota Press, 2003.

Ladd, Barbara. " 'The Direction of the Howling': Nationalism and the Color Line in *Absalom, Absalom!" Subjects and Citizens: Nation, Race and Gender from "Oroonoko" to Anita Hill.* Ed. Michael Moon and Cathy N. Davidson. Durham, NC: Duke University Press, 1995. 345–71.

The Lady from Shanghai. Dir. Orson Welles. Los Angeles: Columbia Pictures, 1947.

Lane, Harlan. *The Mask of Benevolence: Disabling the Deaf Community.* New York: Random House, 1992.

Lanzmann, Claude. *Shoah: An Oral History of the Holocaust.* New York: Pantheon, 1985.

Lawrence, Tim. "AIDS, the Problem of Representation, and Plurality in Derek Jarman's *Blue." Social Text* 52–53 (1997): 241–64.

Levin, David Michael, ed. *Modernity and the Hegemony of Vision.* Berkeley and Los Angeles: University of California Press, 1993.

Levi Strauss, David. "Broken Wings." *Between the Eyes: Essays on Photography and Politics* New York: Aperture, 2003.

Linton, Simi. *Claiming Disability: Knowledge and Identity.* New York: New York University Press, 1998.

Linton, Simi. "What Is Disability Studies?" *PMLA* 120 (March 2005): 518–22.

Lock, Margaret. *Twice Dead: Organ Transplants and the Reinvention of Death.* Berkeley: University of California Press, 2002.

Lott, Eric. "The Whiteness of Film Noir." *Whiteness: A Critical Reader.* Ed. Michael Hill. New York: New York University Press, 1997. 81–101.

Longmore, Paul K. *Why I Burned My Book and Other Essays on Disability.* Philadelphia: Temple University Press, 2003. 53–101.

Longmore, Paul K., and Paul Goldberger. "The League of the Physically Handicapped and the Great Depression: A Case Study in the New Disability His-

tory." *Journal of American History* 87.3 (2001). Http://www.historycoopera
tive.org/journals/jah/87.3/longmore.html.

Longmore, Paul K., and Lauri Umansky. *The New Disability History: American Perspectives*. New York: New York University Press, 2001.

Lorde, Audre. *The Cancer Journals*. San Francisco: Aunt Lute, 1980.

Lott, Eric. *Love and Theft: Blackface Minstrelsy and the American Working Class*. New York: Oxford University Press, 1998.

Lowe, Lisa. "The Metaphoricity of Globalization." Unpublished manuscript.

MacIntyre, Alasdair. *Dependent Rational Animals: Why Human Beings Need the Virtues*. Chicago: Open Court, 1999.

MacKinnon, Kenneth. *The Politics of Popular Representation: Reagan, Thatcher, AIDS, and the Movies*. Rutherford, N.J.: Farleigh Dickinson University Press, 1992.

McKusick, Victor A. "Hemophilia in Early New England: A Follow-up of Four Kindreds in Which Hemophilia Occurred in the Pre-Revolutionary Period." *Journal of the History of Medicine* 17 (1962): 342–65.

McRuer, Robert. "Compulsory Able-Bodiedness and Queer/Disabled Existence." *Disability Studies: Enabling the Humanities*. Ed. Sharon Snyder, Brenda Jo Brueggemann, and Rosemarie Garland-Thomson. New York: Modern Language Association, 2002. 88–99.

McRuer, Robert. *Crip Theory: Cultural Signs of Queerness and Disability*. New York: New York University Press, 2006.

McRuer, Robert. "Neoliberal Risks: *Million Dollar Baby, Murderball*, and Anti-national Sexual Positions." Unpublished manuscript.

Mairs, Nancy. *Plain Text: Essays by Nancy Mairs*. Tucson: University of Arizona Press, 1986.

Mambety, Djibril Diop. "Interview with Djibril Diop Mambety." *Remembrances Filmography*. http:/www.itutu.com/djibril/Interview.html, consulted August 1, 2007.

Mambety, Djibril Diop, with June Givanni, "African Conversations." *Sight and Sound* 5.9 (1995): 30–31.

Markowitz, Gerald, and David Rosner. "The Illusion of Medical Certainty: Silicosis and the Politics of Industrial Disability, 1930–60." *Framing Disease: Studies in Cultural History*. Ed. Charles E. Rosenberg and Janet Golden. New Brunswick, NJ: Rutgers University Press, 1992. 185–205.

Massie, Robert K. *Nicholas and Alexandra*. New York: Atheneum, 1967.

Medoff, Mark. *Children of a Lesser God*. Clifton, NJ: James T. White, 1980.

"The 'Miracle' of Ryan White." *Time*, April 23, 1990, 39.

Million Dollar Baby. Dir. Clint Eastwood. Los Angeles: Warner Brothers, 2005.

Melley, Timothy. *Empire of Conspiracy: The Culture of Paranoia in Postwar America*. Ithaca, NY: Cornell University Press, 2000.

Mitchell, David, and Sharon Snyder. *Narrative Prosthesis: Disability and the Dependencies of Discourse*. Ann Arbor: University of Michigan Press, 2000.

Modelski, Tania. *The Women Who Knew Too Much: Hitchcock and Feminist Theory*. New York: Methuen, 1988.

Moraga, Cherríe. *Heroes and Saints*. *Heroes and Saints and Other Plays*. Albuquerque: West End Press, 1994.

Moynihan, Ray, and Alan Cassels. *Selling Sickness: How the World's Biggest Pharmaceutical Companies Are Turning Us All into Patients.* New York: Nation Books, 2005.

Mulvey, Laura. "Visual Pleasure and Narrative Cinema." *Film Theory and Criticism: Introductory Readings,* 4th ed. Ed. Gerald Mast, Marshall Cohen, Leo Braudy. New York: Oxford University Press, 1992. 746–57.

Narmemore, James. *The Magic World of Orson Welles.* Dallas: Southern Methodist University Press, 1978.

Naremore, James. *More Than Night: Film Noir in Its Contexts.* Berkeley and Los Angeles: University of California Press, 1998.

Nelson, Jennifer. *Pursuing Privacy in Cold War America.* New York: Columbia University Press, 2002.

Nelson, Jennifer L. "Textual Bodies, Bodily Texts." *Signing the Body Poetic: Essays on American Sign Language Literature.* Ed. Dirksen Bauman, Jennifer Nelson, and Heidi Rose. Berkeley and Los Angeles: University of California Press, 2006. 118–29.

Nigam, Sanjay. *Transplanted Man.* New York: Morrow, 2002.

Nussbaum, Martha C. *Frontiers of Justice: Disability, Nationality, Species Membership.* Cambridge: Harvard University Press, 2006.

Olson, Charles. *The Maximus Poems.* Berkeley and Los Angeles: University of California Press, 1983.

Omi, Michael, and Harold Winant. *Racial Formation in the United States: From the 1960s to the 1990s.* New York: Routledge, 1994.

Ott, Katherine, David Serlin, and Stephen Mihm. *Artificial Parts, Practical Lives: Modern Histories of Prosthetics.* New York: New York University Press, 2002.

Padden, Carol, and Tom Humphreys. *Deaf in America: Voices from a Culture.* Cambridge: Harvard University Press, 1988.

Padden, Carol, and Tom Humphreys. *Inside Deaf Culture.* Cambridge: Harvard University Press, 2005.

Padden, Carol, and Tom Humphreys. *Learning American Sign Language.* Englewood Cliffs, NJ: Prentice-Hall, 1992.

Padmanabhan, Manjula. *Harvest. Postcolonial Plays: An Anthology.* Ed. Helen Gilbert. London: Routledge, 2001. 214–48.

Patton, Cindy. *Inventing AIDS.* New York: Routledge, 1990.

Patton, Cindy. *Last Served? Gendering the HIV Pandemic.* London: Taylor and Francis, 1994.

Patton, Cindy. *Sex and Germs: The Politics of AIDS.* Montreal: Black Rose Books, 1986.

Pencak, William. *The Films of Derek Jarman.* Jefferson, NC: McFarland, 2002.

Pernick, Martin. *The Black Stork: Eugenics and the Death of "Defective" Babies in American Medicine and Motion Pictures since 1915.* New York: Oxford University Press, 1996.

La Petite vendeuse de Soleil [*The Little Girl Who Sold the Sun*]. Dir. Djibril Diop Mambety. Senegal: California News Reel, 1999.

Pollitt, Katha. "Backward Christian Soldiers." *The Nation,* April 18, 2005. Http://www.thenation.com/docprint.mhtm/?i=20050418&5=pollitt, consulted 8/18/2005.

Pound, Ezra. "A Retrospect." *Literary Essays of Ezra Pound.* New Directions, 1968.
Priestley, Mark, ed. *Disability and the Life Course: Global Perspectives.* Cambridge: Cambridge University Press, 2001.
Proof. Dir. Jocelyn Moorhouse. Victoria: Australian Film Commission, 1992.
Puckett, Andrew. *Bloodstains.* New York: Doubleday, 1987.
Quayson, Ato. *Calibrations.* Minneapolis: University of Minnesota Press, 2003.
Ree, Jonathan. *I See a Voice: Deafness, Language, and the Senses—a Philosophical History.* New York: Henry Holt, 1999.
Resnik, Susan. *Blood Saga: Hemophilia, AIDS, and the Survival of a Community.* Berkeley and Los Angeles: University of California Press, 1999.
Rogin, Michael. *Blackface, White Noise: Jewish Immigrants in the Hollywood Melting Pot.* Berkeley: University of California Press, 1998.
Rogin, Michael. *Ronald Reagan, the Movie: And Other Episodes in Political Demonology.* Berkeley and Los Angeles: University of California Press, 1987.
Rosenberg, Charles E., and Janet Golden, eds. *Framing Disease: Studies in Cultural History.* New Brunswick, NJ: Rutgers University Press, 1992.
Rosner, Fred. "Hemophilia in the Talmud and Rabbinic Writings." *Annals of Internal Medicine* 70 (April 1969): 833–37.
Rubinstein, Raphael. "Visual Voices." *Art in America,* April 1996, 95–100, 133.
"Ruling Bars HIV-Infected Hemophiliacs from Suit." *New York Times.* Sunday, March 19, 1995, A16.
Russo, Vito. *The Celluloid Closet: Homosexuality in the Movies.* New York: Harper and Row, 1981.
Sandhal, Carrie. "Ahhhh Freak Out! Metaphors of Disability and Femaleness in Performance." *Theatre Topics* 9.1 (1999): 11–30.
Sandhal, Carrie. "Black Man, Blind Man: Disability Identity Politics and Performance." *Theatre Journal* 56.4 (2004): 579–602.
Sandhal, Carrie. "From the Streets to the Stage: Disability and the Performing Arts." *PMLA* 120.2 (2005): 620–24.
Saramago, José. *Blindness.* Trans. Giovanni Pontiero. New York: Harcourt, 1997.
Saussure, Ferdinand de. *Course in General Linguistics.* Ed. Charles Bally and Albert Sechehaye. Trans. Wade Baskin. New York: McGraw-Hill, 1966.
Saxton, Alexander. *The Rise and Fall of the White Republic: Class, Politics, and Mass Culture in Nineteenth-Century America.* London: Verso, 1990.
Scheper-Hughes, Nancy. "The End of the Body: The Global Traffic in Organs for Transplant Surgery." http://sunsite.berkeley.edu/biotech/organsswatch/pages/cadraft.html, consulted 6/25/2003.
Scheper-Hughes, Nancy. "The Ends of the Body: Commodity Fetishism and the Global Traffic in Organs." *SAIS Review* 22.1 (2002): 61–80.
Scheper-Hughes, Nancy. "Theft of Life: The Globalization of Organ Stealing Rumours." *Anthropology Today* 12.3 (1996): 3–11.
Sedgwick, Eve. *Between Men: English Literature and Male Homosocial Desire.* New York: Columbia University Press, 1985.
Schweik, Susan. "The Voice of 'Reason.'" *Public Culture* 13.3 (2001): 485–505.
Serlin, David. *Replaceable You: Engineering the Body in Postwar America.* Chicago: University of Chicago Press, 2002.

Shah, Nayan. *Contagious Divides: Epidemics and Race in San Francisco's China-town*. Berkeley and Los Angeles: University of California Press, 2001.

Shakespeare, Tom. "The Social Model of Disability." *The Disability Studies Reader.* 2nd ed. Ed. Lennard Davis. New York: Routledge, 2006. 197–204.

Shapiro, Joseph. *No Pity: People with Disabilities Forging a New Civil Rights Movement*. New York: Random House, 1993.

Sharp, Lesley A. *Strange Harvest: Organ Transplants, Denatured Bodies, and the Transformed Self*. Berkeley: University of California Press. 2006.

Shilts, Randy. *And the Band Played On: Politics, People, and the AIDS Epidemic*. New York: St. Martin's, 1987.

Shklovsky, Victor. "Art as Technique." *Russian Formalist Criticism: Four Essays*. Ed. Lee. T. Lemon and Marion J. Reis. Lincoln: University of Nebraska Press, 1965. 3–24.

Siebers, Tobin, ed. *The Body Aesthetic: From Fine Art to Body Modification*. Ann Arbor: University of Michigan Press, 2003.

Siebers, Tobin. "Disability in Theory: From Social Constructionism to the New Realism of the Body." *American Literary History* 13.4 (2001): 736–51.

Siebers, Tobin. "Disability Theory." Unpublished manuscript.

Siebers, Tobin. "Hitler and the Tyranny of the Aesthetic." *Philosophy and Literature* 29.1 (2000): 96–110.

Siebers, Tobin. "Tender Organs, Narcissism, and Identity Politics." *Disability Studies: Enabling the Humanities*. Ed. Sharon L. Snyder, Brenda Jo Brueggemann, and Rosemarie Garland-Thomson. New York: Modern Language Association, 2002. 40–55.

Siebers, Tobin. "What Can Disability Learn from the Culture Wars?" *Cultural Critique* 55 (2003): 182–216.

Silko, Leslie Marmon. *Almanac of the Dead*. New York: Penguin, 1992.

Silko, Leslie Marmon. *Yellow Woman and a Beauty of the Spirit*. New York: Simon, 1996.

Simpson, Louis. Review of *Selected Poems*, by Gwendolyn Brooks. *New York Herald Tribune Book Week*, October 27, 1963, 27.

Sound and Fury. Dir. Josh Aronson. New York: Aronson Film Associates, and Public Policy Publications, 2000.

Snyder, Sharon, and David T. Mitchell. *Cultural Locations of Disability*. Chicago: University of Chicago Press, 2006.

Stanford, Ann Folwell. "'Human Debris': Border Politics, Body Parts, and the Reclamation of the Americas in Leslie Marmon Silko's *Almanac of the Dead*." *Literature and Medicine* 16.1 (1997): 23–42.

Starr, Paul. *The Social Transformation of American Medicine: The Rise of a Sovereign Profession and the Making of a Vast Industry*. New York: Basic Books, 1982.

Stephanson, Anders. *Kennan and the Art of Foreign Policy*. Cambridge: Harvard University Press, 1989.

Stiglitz, Joseph. *Globalization and Its Discontents*. New York: Norton, 2003.

Szalay, Michael. *New Deal Modernism: American Literature and the Invention of the Welfare State*. Durham, NC: Duke University Press, 2000.

Thomson, Rosemarie Garland. "Dares to Stares: Disabled Women Performance

Artists and the Dynamics of Staring." *Bodies in Commotion: Disability and Performance*. Ed. Carrie Sandahl and Philip Auslander. Ann Arbor: University of Michigan Press, 2005. 30–41.

Thomson, Rosemarie Garland. *Extraordinary Bodies: Figuring Physical Disability in American Culture and Literature*. New York: Columbia University Press, 1997.

Thomson, Rosemarie Garland. "Staring Back: Self-Representations of Disabled Performance Artists." *American Quarterly* 52.2 (2000): 334–43.

Titmuss, Richard. *The Gift Relationship: From Human Blood to Social Policy*. New York: Pantheon, 1971.

Treichler, Paula. "AIDS, Homophobia, and Biomedical Discourse: An Epidemic of Signification." *AIDS: Cultural Analysis, Cultural Activism*. Ed. Douglas Crimp. Cambridge: MIT Press, 1991. 31–70.

Tremain, Shelley, ed. *Foucault and the Government of Disability*. Ann Arbor: University of Michigan Press, 2005.

Valli, Clayton. "The Nature of a Line in ASL Poetry." *SLR '87: Papers from the Fourth International Symposium on Sign Language Research*. Ed. W. H. Edmondson and F. Karlsson. Hamburg: Signum Press, 1990. 171–81.

Valli, Clayton. "Snowflake." *Poetry in Motion: Clayton Valli*. Sign Media, 1989.

Wade, Cheryl Marie. "My Hands." *Vital Signs: Crip Culture Talks Back*. Ed. David Mitchell and Sharon Snyder. Marquette, MI: Brace Yourself Productions, 1996.

Wailoo, Keith. *Dying in the City of the Blues: Sickle Cell Anemia and the Politics of Race and Health*. Chapel Hill: University of North Carolina Press, 2001.

Wailoo, Keith. "Inventing the Heterozygote: Molecular Biology, Racial Identity, and the Narratives of Sickle-Cell Disease, Tay-Sachs, and Cystic Fibrosis." *Race, Nature, and the Politics of Difference*. Ed. Donald Moore, Jake Kosek, and Anand Pandian. Durham, NC: Duke University Press, 2003. 235–53.

Wald, Gayle. *Crossing the Line: Racial Passing in Twentieth-Century U.S. Literature and Culture*. Durham, NC: Duke University Press, 2000.

Walk on the Wild Side. Dir. Edward Dymtryk. Los Angeles: Columbia Pictures, 1962.

Wasserman, David, Jerome Bickenbach, and Robert Wachbroit, eds. *Quality of Life and Human Difference: Genetic Testing, Health Care, and Disability*. New York: Cambridge University Press, 2005.

Watney, Simon. *Policing Desire: Pornography, AIDS, and the Media*. London: Methuen, 1987.

Watten, Barrett. "Missing 'X': Formal Meaning in Crane and Eigner." *Total Syntax*. Carbondale: Southern Illinois University Press, 1985.

Weiss, Jeffrey. "Boxing Flick Flops in Medical Circles." *Dallas Morning News*, February 19, 2005. http://www.dallasnews.com/cgi_bin/gold_print.cgi, consulted 9/11/2005.

White, Susan. "*Vertigo* and Problems of Knowledge in Feminist Film Theory." *Alfred Hitchcock: Centenary Essays*. Ed. Richard Allen and S. Ishi Gonzales. London: British Film Institute, 1999. 279–98.

Whitman, Walt. "Song of Myself." *Leaves of Grass and Other Writings*. Ed. Michael Moon. New York: Norton, 2002.

Williams, Linda. "When the Woman Looks." *Film Theory and Criticism*. Ed. Gerald Mast, Marshall Cohen, and Leo Braudy. New York: Oxford University. Press, 1992. 561–77.

Wilson, Daniel J. "Crippled Manhood: Infantile Paralysis and the Construction of Masculinity." *Medical Humanities Review,* Fall 1999, 9–28.

Wilson, Rob, and Wimal Dissanayake, eds. *Global/Local: Cultural Production and the Transnational Imaginary*. Durham, NC: Duke University Press, 1996.

Williams, Patricia J. "Habeas Corpus." *The Nation,* April 11, 2005. http://www.thenation.com/docprint.mhtml?i=20050411&5=williams, consulted 9/10/2005.

Williamson, Aaron. *Hearing Things. Animated,* Spring 1999, 17–18.

Williamson, Aaron. Lecture, University of California, San Diego, March 3, 2000.

Williamson, Aaron. Review of "Joseph Grigely." Anthony d'Offay Gallery, London, March 16–April 20, 1996. *Art Monthly,* October 1999. 196.

Wittgenstein, Ludwig. *Lectures and Conversations on Aesthetics, Psychology and Religious Belief.* Ed. Cyril Barrett. Berkeley and Los Angeles: University of California Press, 1967.

Wittgenstein, Ludwig. *Philosophical Investigations*. Trans. G. E. M. Anscombe. New York: Macmillan, 1966.

Wolff, Richard. "World Bank/Class Blindness." *World Bank Literature*. Ed. Amitav Kumar. University of Minnesota Press, 2003. 172–83.

Wollen, Peter. "Blue." *Paris Manhattan: Writings on Art.* London: Verso, 2004.

Woodhull, Winnie. "Sexual Politics, Global Economies: Djibril Diop Mambety's *La Petite Vendeuse de Soleil*." Unpublished manuscript.

Wrigley, Owen. *The Politics of Deafness.* Washington, DC: Gallaudet University Press, 1996.

Yamashita, Karen Tei. *Tropic of Orange*. Minneapolis: Coffee House Press, 1997.

Žižek, Slavoj. "The Hitchcockian Blot." *Alfred Hitchcock: Centenary Essays*. Ed. Richard Allen and S. Ishii-Gonzales. London: British Film Institute, 1999. 123–39.

Žižek, Slavoj. *Organs without Bodies: On Deleuze and Consequences*. New York: Routledge, 2004.

Index

ableist rhetoric, disability aesthetics and, xi, 1–8, 177–79
abortion, bioethics and, 29–32
Absalom, Absalom (Faulkner), xiii, 42, 46–49
acquired immunodeficiency syndrome (AIDS): African epidemic of, 189–93; blindness due to, xiv–xv, 145–46, 157–65, 245n8; cultural framing of, 26–32, 177–80; global statistics on, 170–75; hemophilia and, xii–xiii, 36–57; identity politics and research implications of, 234n9; Jarman's images of, 157–65; recent advances in management of, 56–57, 236n20; visual images of, 145–46, 244n3
activist politics: disability aesthetics and, 2–8; global aspects of disability and, 192–75, 247n17; socioeconomics and, 117–20; theater and, 191–93
ACT UP, 160
ADA. *See* Americans with Disabilities Act
Adams, Bobby Neel, 186
Adams, John, 45–46
aesthetics: cultural theory and, 142–46; definitions of, 3; visibility theory and, 17–25
Afghanistan, disability and warfare in, 186–89
Africa: AIDS epidemic in, 189–93; film images of disability in, 179–84
Agamben, Giorgio, 215

agency: disability theory and role of, 16; in organ transfer narratives, 204–6
AIDS. *See* acquired immunodeficiency syndrome
air the trees (Eigner), 125–28
Algren, Nelson, 75–76
Allen, Donald, 123, 242n6
Allen, Robert, 44
Almanac of the Dead, xv, 199, 201, 215–20, 250n166
alterity, disability studies and, 33–34
Amenabar, Alejandro, 11
American Sign Language (ASL): children of deaf parents and, 112–13; Deaf President Now protest concerning, 239n1; early teaching films for, 82; Flying Words Project and, 83–87, 99; identity politics and, 28–29; poetics and, xiii–xiv, 100–115; textuality and, 94–99
Americans with Disabilities Act (ADA), 8, 116–17, 133; disability definitions in, 32, 173, 175–76; Eastwood lawsuit and, 15, 233n15; economic impact of, 169–75; globalization and, 193–96
Annie Dearest, 21–22
Antin, David, 27
Anti-Privatization Forum, 191
anti-Semitism: cultural theory of blood and, 43; in film noir, 238n22
Apartment, The, 71–72
Appadurai, Arjun, 173–75